macy's

The Store. The Star. The Story.

Robert M. Grippo

SQUAREONE
PUBLISHERS

COVER DESIGNER: Jeannie Tudor
IN-HOUSE EDITOR: Joanne Abrams
TYPESETTER: Jeannie Tudor
BACK COVER AUTHOR PHOTO: Christopher Hoskins

Square One Publishers
115 Herricks Road
Garden City Park, NY 11040
(516) 535-2010
(877) 900-BOOK
www.squareonepublishers.com

Library of Congress Cataloging-in-Publication Data

Grippo, Robert M.
  Macy's : the store, the star, the story / Robert M. Grippo.
    p. cm.
  Includes index.
  ISBN 978-0-7570-0309-7 (pbk.) — ISBN 978-0-7570-0212-0 (hardcover)
  1. Macy's (Firm) 2. Department stores—United States. 3. Macy, Rowland
Hussey, 1822-1877. I. Title.
  HF5465.U64M334 2009
  381'.1410973—dc22   2008041870

Printed in the United States of America

10 9 8 7 6 5 4 3 2 1

Contents

To my mom, Catherine A. Grippo,
who put me in front of our old Magnavox television
on Thanksgiving morning and introduced me
to the magic of Macy's.

Acknowledgments

This book was made possible by a large number of talented people, some of whom helped create the great emporium known as Macy's, and many of whom generously gave their time so that I could tell this wonderful story.

First and foremost, I would like to thank Rowland H. Macy, who opened a small fancy dry goods shop in 1858 and, with hard work and imagination, transformed it into a full-fledged department store. Without him, neither the store nor the star that is the Macy's of today would be possible. I also thank Margaret S. Getchell and Abiel T. LaForge, who worked alongside R.H. Macy to create a business that struck such a resounding chord with the public that a hundred and fifty years later, the name "Macy's" is known around the world. Phyllis Jones, the great-great-granddaughter of Margaret S. Getchell, graciously shared the diaries of both Ms. Getchell and her husband and colleague, A.T. LaForge, with me. These journals provide a rare glimpse into Macy's early years, and I thank Ms. Jones for allowing me to read them.

Several libraries and other organizations were helpful in unearthing long-lost images and little-known facts about the life of Rowland H. Macy before his success in New York retailing. I thank the staff of the Boston Public Library in Boston, Massachusetts; the late George H. Laing of the Haverhill Public Library in Haverhill, Massachusetts; Teddie Meronek of the Superior Public Library in Superior, Wisconsin; Marie Henke and Elizabeth Oldham of the Nantucket Historical Association in Nantucket, Massachusetts; and Daisy Hendrickson of the Recorder's Office in Yuba County, California.

I would like to express my gratitude to the many people who continued building the Macy's enterprise long after R.H. Macy's death, and shared their stories of the firm with me. First, I thank CEO Terry J. Lundgren—the "new Mr. Macy"—who has provided inspired leadership of the company since 2003, and was kind enough to discuss his role in Macy's history with me. Rachelle Stern, a senior attorney who is something of the resident Macy's historian, encouraged me to write the history of this fascinating store. Her love of the Macy's story was one of the sparks that got this project started and kept it going. Geri Cuile spent hours working to make this the best book about Macy's, and opened doors to many interviews with the company's executives of yesterday and today, including Robert Appleby, Rosemary Bravo,

Joseph B. Cicio, Frank Doroff, Edward S. Finkelstein, Alan Gold, Ed Goldberg, Hank Greenberg, Janet Grove, Robin Hall, Mark S. Handler, Joe Harris, Elina Kazan, Ron Klein, Gerald Dun Levy, Julie Mares, Art Matura, G.G. Michelson, Ted Ronick, Peter Sachse, Phil Schlein, Howard Slavin, Holly Thomas, and the late John Wendell Straus. I especially want to acknowledge George Voyer, who helped to clarify Macy's story during the middle of the twentieth century, and provided an insider's view of the amazing events that enabled Macy's to grow into an enduring modern icon. Thanks are also due to Diana Roio and Lorraine Krol, who ensured that the meetings with the busy Macy's executives went on as planned. This book would have never been as interesting or as accurate without the stories of these exceptional people.

I offer a special thank-you to Robin Hall, Senior Vice President of the Macy's Parade and Entertainment Group, who had faith in this project from day one and gave us total cooperation, including invaluable access to the Macy's archives. Because of his efforts and those of Bob E. Rutan, Macy's official historian, as well as Scott Byers, who manages the archives, I was able to use wonderful images to evoke Macy's through the decades. Scott cheerfully responded to numerous requests for photos, and even put some rather old and rare papers in my publisher's hands. Because of him, this book is a treat for the eye and allows the reader to fully appreciate the beauty of Macy's many parades, shows, and displays. In this regard, mention must be made of Martine Reardon, Executive Vice President of Corporate Marketing, who has much of the responsibility for Macy's annual events. Martine has both my gratitude and my respect for her ability to continually deliver on Macy's promise to be the biggest star on Broadway. Thanks are also due to Bill Smith, parade historian, and Bill Schermerhorn, the parade's long-time creative director, who contributed priceless information and insights to this narrative.

A number of past and present Macy's executives generously supplied photos for use in Chapter 7 of this book. I thank Joe Cicio, Edward S. Finkelstein, Robin Hall, Terry J. Lundgren, Jean McFaddin, Allen Questrom, and Myron E. Ullman, III, for supplying photos of themselves, and I offer a special thank-you to Juanita C. Seegal for providing a photo of her late husband, Herbert L. Seegal.

For approximately eighty years, the story of Macy's was inextricably linked to that of the Straus family. In recounting the history of the Strauses, I have been lucky to enjoy the guidance and support of Joan Adler, Executive Director of the Straus Historical Society, Inc. Joan generously supplied everything from detailed information about the family to rare photos of both the Strauses and the cut-glass treasures that they long produced and sold at Macy's. Joan even proofread the finished chapters, using her keen eye to spot errors that had eluded other readers. I will long remember the many hours spent with Joan as we exchanged information on the Strauses, and will forever be grateful for her enthusiastic encouragement and help.

Ethel Sheifer, the daughter of Macy's legendary taster William Titon, shared with me priceless stories about her father's experiences in the store on Herald Square, including tales of Macy's many innovations in the area of fancy groceries. I will always be grateful for these insights into Macy's past.

Words cannot express my thanks for the creative team at Square One Publishers. Rudy Shur, my publisher, believed in the project from the start and guided its completion as deftly as a captain steers a ship towards home. Joanne Abrams, my editor, not only fact-checked and edited the copy, but spent hours choosing the very best graphics for each chapter. Jeannie Tudor, Square One's talented art director, expertly combined text and graphics so that the book would be as beautiful and stylish as Macy's itself. For this and more, I extend my gratitude.

I offer deep and sincere thanks to my mother, Catherine A. Grippo. My mother inspired my love of Macy's many years ago, and has provided both practical help and unwavering support throughout the writing of this book.

Finally, I am aware that literally dozens of individuals—some of whom I don't know by name—have contributed to this book in various ways. Please accept my gratitude for your help in creating this epic American tale.

Introduction

Yes, part of the magic of Macy's is its Thanksgiving Day Parades, its showcase window displays, and its flower shows. And, of course, there is the amazing Herald Square emporium itself—the world's largest department store. But behind all the glitz and glamour of this American icon is a unique history that reflects the best of this country's entrepreneurial spirit. It is a story of resolve, skill, savvy, and vision. In many respects, it is the story of an American dream passed on from one generation to the next. It begins with a determined Nantucket boy who, after spending several years on a whaling ship, decides to try his hand in the world of business. Although the young man does not meet with immediate success, he learns through his mistakes and continues to persevere. Along the way, he meets other talented and determined people, and together—over decades marked by devastating wars as well as joyous peacetimes, by economic booms and financial downturns—they create a legend that is now known the world over.

This book was written to tell the untold story behind the remarkable department store called Macy's. The idea for this book took root years ago, when my father told me that, as a boy, he and his older brother would count the days from the beginning of November to their annual Christmas visit to Macy's Santa. At that time, my experience of Macy's was mostly limited to watching the yearly Thanksgiving Day Parade on television as my mom prepared our Thanksgiving feast. Now, as I think back to those happy hours spent viewing the magnificent floats, the larger-than-life balloons, the costumed dancers, and the colorful bands, I understand that the phrase "the magic of Macy's" is much more than a slogan. For me, Macy's *was* magic!

Over the years, as my interest in Macy's continued, I began investigating the history of Macy's, and what I found fascinated me. The story of this company is more than that of a successful business. It is also the story of wonderful individuals, each of whom contributed to Macy's in a unique way. And it is the story of a great country and the challenges it has faced in the last hundred and fifty years.

Chapter 1 looks at the early years of Rowland Hussey Macy, the founder of R.H. Macy & Co. Born

2

Macy's—The Store. The Star. The Story.

on the island of Nantucket, Massachusetts in 1822, Macy spent four years on a whaling ship before he decided to enter the world of retailing. But in 1844, when Macy established a humble needle-and-thread store in the city of Boston, he had a long and rocky road ahead of him. This chapter details the often difficult journey that would lead to the establishment of his last and most famous business—a store in Manhattan, New York.

Opened on Sixth Avenue, Rowland Macy's store, a small dry goods shop, immediately met with success and started growing by leaps and bounds. Like any entrepreneur, the young man from Massachusetts needed help to run his expanding business. Chapter 2 tells the extraordinary story of the talented people who worked with R.H. Macy during the store's first thirty years, and also looks at the unique principles of business that made Macy's different from other Manhattan emporiums.

Rowland H. Macy died in 1877, leaving the store in the hands of his partners. Yet soon, they too were gone. Who would take the helm of Macy's and steer it on a successful course? Chapter 3 begins the fascinating tale of Lazarus, Isidor, and Nathan Straus— three German immigrants who would not only change the shape of American retailing history, but also have a lasting effect on the great metropolis that they called home.

The little store on Sixth Avenue continued to grow over the years, with annexes being added to the original building. But by the turn of the century, the Strauses knew that larger, more modern quarters were needed if they were to continue to survive in New York's competitive environment. Chapter 4 looks at the 1902 construction of Macy's Herald Square store—a building so grand in its appearance and advanced in its technology that it would play a major role in moving the retailing center of New York uptown. This chapter also discusses the consumer services that made Macy's so successful, and examines the Strauses' unique benefit programs for their employees. Finally, it discloses how the sink-

ing of the *Titanic* had an unexpected effect on the house of Macy's, forever changing its fate.

Spanning the years from 1913 to 1939, Chapter 5 focuses on Jesse, Percy, and Herbert Straus—the brilliant merchant princes who updated and expanded Macy's, eventually turning it into the world's largest store. This chapter also looks at how both Macy's owners and its employees took an active part in critical home-front efforts during the Great War, and how the company not only survived the Great Depression, but actually took steps to help fellow New Yorkers during the nation's economic crisis. And for everyone who loves the Macy's Thanksgiving Day Parade, Chapter 5 discusses the fascinating birth of an event that was to become not only a Macy's trademark, but also a beloved American tradition.

Between 1940 and 1969, the nation experienced war and peace, an economic boom, and unprecedented expansion into the suburbs. Chapter 6 describes how Macy's responded to these events, constantly evolving to better serve its customers during changing times. Included in this chapter are discussions of Macy's move into suburban communities, the "war" between Macy's and Gimbels, the evolution of the flower show, and the creation of *Miracle on 34th Street*—an enchanting film that not only introduced Macy's to the nation, but forever linked Macy's to the magic of Christmas.

In the late 1960s and early '70s, economic stagnation contributed to urban decay, and Manhattan went through hard times. As the city became an unattractive place to live and shop, Macy's sales suffered along with those of many inner-city businesses, and the store became worn through neglect. Chapter 7 tells the amazing story of how one man not only restored the original beauty of Macy's Herald Square, but modernized it with fashionable boutiques and the sophisticated Cellar, turning a faded icon into a resounding success. It also describes how the Thanksgiving Day Parade was reinvigorated, and the Fourth of July fireworks and spring flower show— events that had been cancelled years earlier—were brought back, bigger and better than ever. Finally, it discusses the mergers and acquisitions that eventually transformed *Macy's* into *Macy's, Inc.,* a retailing giant with hundreds of stores nationwide.

Anyone familiar with the Macy's story knows that it must be told not just in words, but also in dazzling images. No words could adequately describe the stately architectural features of the Herald Square store, the spectacular Fourth of July fireworks shows, the magnificent displays that grace the annual flower show, or the whimsical balloons of the Thanksgiving Day parade. For this reason, every chapter of the book is filled with drawings and photos that bring the story of Macy's to life. As you turn its pages, you'll be able to visit Macy's original Sixth Avenue store, sell War Bonds with Macy's "Bondadiers," see colorful fireworks burst over New York Harbor, and watch your favorite floats as they make their way down Broadway. To put each event into proper historical context, fascinating "Footer Facts" are found along the bottom of many pages, letting you know—through words and pictures—about the cultural and political events, the fashion fads, and the pop-culture trends that have had their impact on the great store called Macy's.

While other retailers have come and gone over the last century and a half, Macy's has not only survived but also become part of the fabric of America. Although it encompasses over eight hundred stores, the truth is that Macy's is far more than the sum of its stores. With a legendary flagship emporium in the heart of Manhattan—with parades, fireworks, flower shows, and many special events—Macy's is a truly American phenomenon that touches people across the country. Whether you visit Macy's on Herald Square or watch a broadcast of its annual Thanksgiving Day pageant, you can't help but feel the magic. If this book adds to the magic of your Macy's experience and to your appreciation of Macy's place in American history, I will feel that it has succeeded, and for that, I thank you.

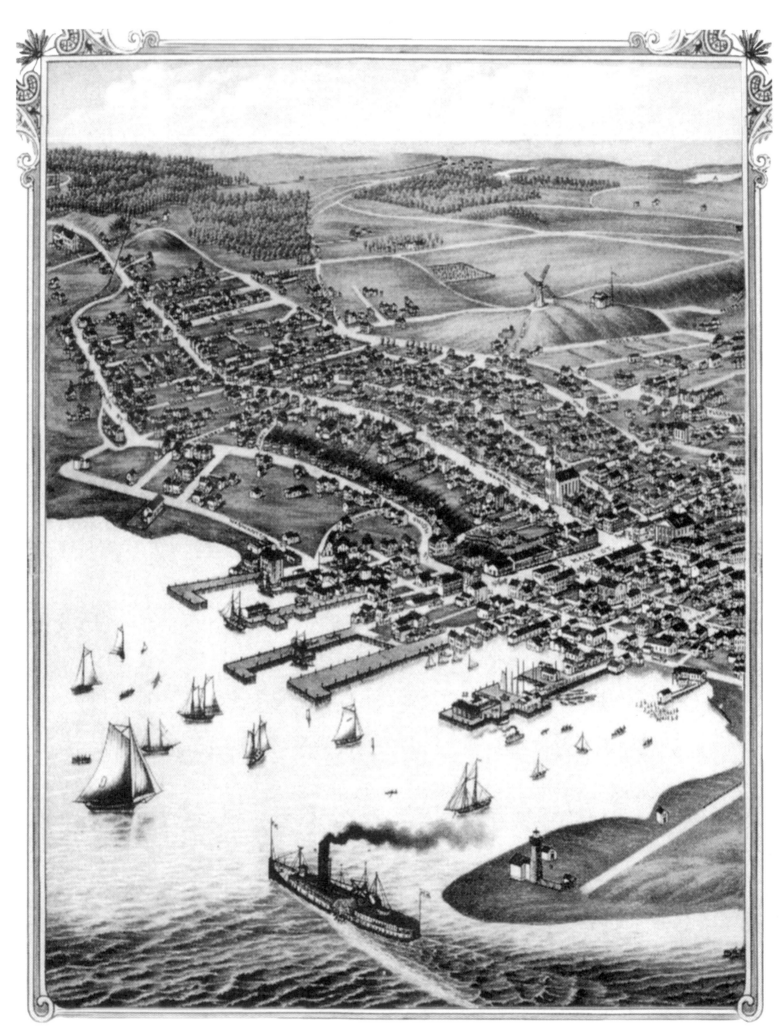

A bird's eye view of the bustling town of Nantucket looking southward in the late 1800s.

1.
The Epic Begins

Located thirty miles off the coast of Massachusetts, the island of Nantucket is a tiny piece of land that has played a surprisingly large part in American history. While this picturesque island has become associated with elegance and charm, its scenic ports and historic homes are actually the product of generations of industrious people. The European settlement of the island began in 1641, when the English deeded the island to merchant Thomas Mayhew and his son. Then in 1659, nine additional settlers purchased nineteen twentieths of the island from Mayhew. Among these settlers was Thomas Macy.

THE MACYS

The families that founded Nantucket had intended to farm and raise livestock on the island. When the land was too poor to sup-

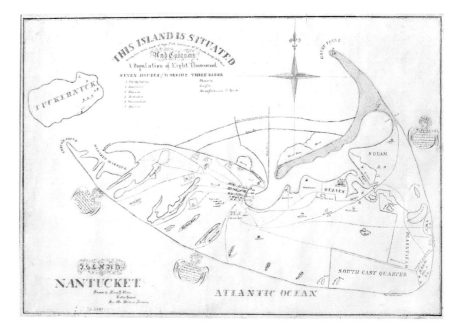

A map of Nantucket, ca. 1829, drawn by Lucy S. Macy at the Coffin School—the same school attended by Rowland H. Macy.

port those ventures, the settlers turned their attention to the sea. Despite the constant buffeting of storms and many wrecks caused by the ever-shifting sands surrounding the island, the Nantucketers built sturdy ships, fished the local waters, and mastered seaman's trades.

The community of Nantucket can trace its origins back to the original European settlers— Thomas Mayhew, Tristram Coffin, Richard Swain, Thomas Bernard, Peter Coffin, Christopher Hussey, Stephen Greenleaf, John Swain, William Pile, and Thomas Macy. These names are legendary in the history of the island.

At the start of the eighteenth century, Quaker missionaries visited Nantucket on their way to the mainland. Mary Coffin Starbuck—one of the most influential people on the island—converted to the faith, and the Society of Friends spread rapidly, with half of Nantucket's population eventually becoming Quakers.

It was during the eighteenth century that the people of Nantucket embraced Quakerism. At the same time, they ventured even farther from the island as they searched for whales. By 1810 it was said that many young women on Nantucket would refuse to marry a man who had not killed a whale, and it was also said that more than a quarter of all women on the island had been widowed by the sea. For nearly a century—from the mid-1700s to the late 1830s—Nantucket was the whaling capital of the world, with as many as 150 ships making port there during the industry's heyday.

A street map of Nantucket in 1834. The star indicates the location of John Macy's bookstore at 2 Fair Street. The shop served both the residents of the town and the crews of ships staying in the harbor.

Thomas Macy, one of Nantucket's first settlers, had a long line of descendants whose names recur often in the island's records. John Macy and his wife, Eliza, were members of the seventh generation of the family, and were fourth-generation Quakers. Married in 1809, John and Eliza already had three children when on August 30, 1822, they welcomed a new son into their family, Rowland Hussey Macy.

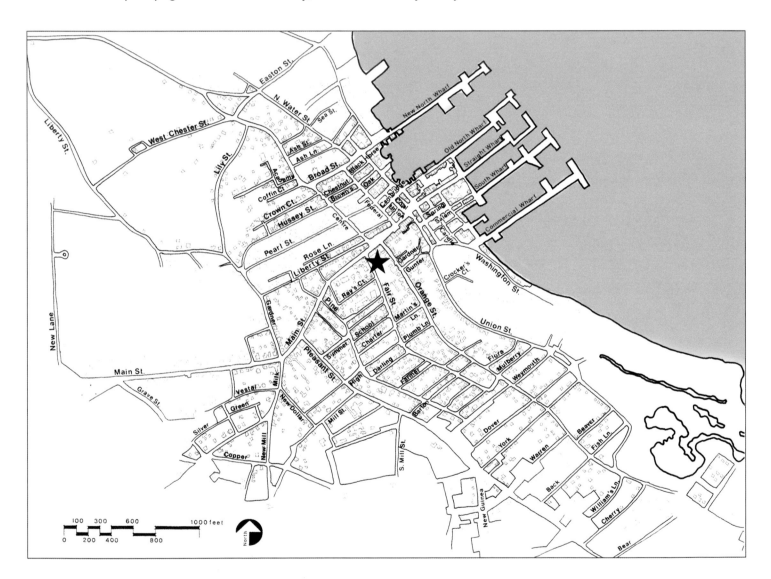

When Rowland H. Macy was born, the fifth President of the United States, James Monroe, was in office. Serving from 1817 to 1825, Monroe is best remembered for the Monroe Doctrine, which declared that European powers would no longer be permitted to colonize or interfere with the affairs of the newly independent Americas.

Nantucket's whaling industry began when a whale was sighted in the harbor during the 1700s. By the turn of the nineteenth century, the industry had exploded, and there were more millionaires living on the island than anywhere else in the world.

As a child in a large Quaker household, young Rowland was undoubtedly taught the importance of family, as well as the Quaker philosophies of simple living and strict honesty in business. When the time came for schooling, Rowland was enrolled in the Coffin Lancastrian School. Named for Sir Isaac Coffin, the school was a private institution that accepted only direct descendants of Tristam Coffin, an original Nantucket settler who had made a career in the British Navy. Like most of the island's inhabitants, Rowland qualified, and it was at the Coffin School that he learned to read and do his sums.

But Rowland Macy's world was not limited to school. His father was the proprietor of Nantucket's book and magazine shop, located at No. 2 Fair Street. Young Rowland probably spent many hours helping in his father's store, where he could read his fill of books and periodicals, and observe the everyday activities involved in running a shop. Many book and magazine sellers of the era were also printers, and it is likely that the boy watched as his father printed handbills to promote his wares. It may be that this early exposure to his father's business led to Rowland's later interest and exceptional skill in advertising his own retail establishments. But in his youth, Rowland shared Nantucket's love of the sea, and it was down to the sea that he went when he reached a suitable age.

THE GOOD SHIP *EMILY MORGAN*

Although many products came from the harvesting of whales, the one most necessary for Americans was oil, for whale oil began lighting the lamps of the colonies even before they won independence. Generations of Nantucket men bravely signed aboard ships that left the harbor for trips that would last not for days, but years. For the most part, the vessels returned home—sometimes with a hold of oil-filled barrels, and sometimes with depleted crews, partial loads, and sad stories. But if they returned, even a crewman's share of the profits could be substantial. Most sailors simply bought supplies at the local traders, supported their families, and signed up for a new voyage. But others used their wages to begin a new life.

Because of the immense wealth created by the whaling industry, Nantucket's captains built great mansions along Orange Street, close to the sea. Rowland must have passed these splendid homes every day, and undoubtedly his youth was filled with exciting stories of the sea. It would have been expected that he would try his luck at whaling.

For some reason—perhaps the disapproval of his worried parents or the favorable reputation of a particular ship's master—Rowland Macy did not

An ad in the *Nantucket Inquirer* for the *Emily Morgan*, a whaling ship berthed in New Bedford, Massachusetts.

President Andrew Jackson served from 1829 to 1837. Called "Old Hickory" for his toughness, Jackson helped shape the organization that was the basis of the modern Democratic party.

Originally, the residents of Nantucket arranged their homes so that the remaining land could be used for agriculture and sheep grazing. After the whaling industry began, the residential area was moved to the Great Harbor. First known as Sherborne, the town was officially named Nantucket in 1795.

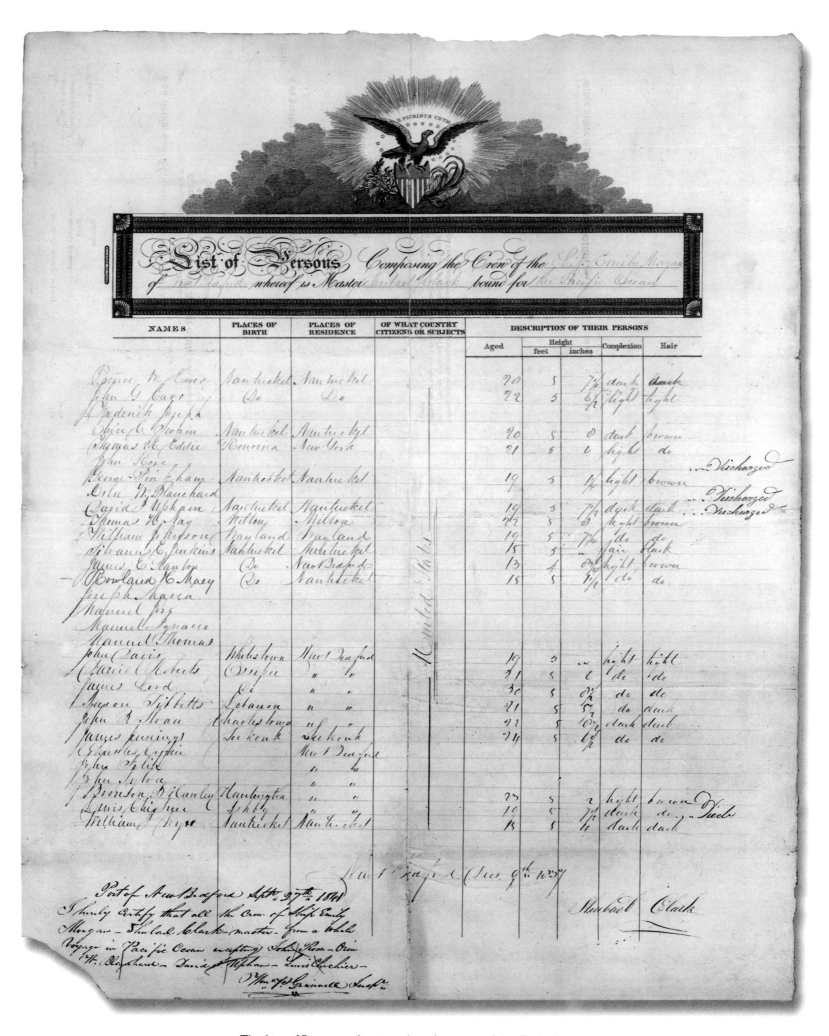

The List of Persons who signed on for crew of the *Emily Morgan*.
Rowland H. Macy's name has been printed in blue for easier identification.

The *Emily Morgan*, a three-masted whaling ship.

seek work on a ship berthed in Nantucket harbor. Instead, he traveled to New Bedford, Massachusetts with the intention of signing aboard a whaling ship. A notice in the *Nantucket Inquirer* may have caught young Rowland's eye. The notice gave word of the "Ship Emily Morgan, Capt. Shubael Clark to sail from New Bedford about 26th of November." Before the *Emily Morgan* sailed, Rowland H. Macy's name was added to the "List of Persons Compassing the Crew." He was fifteen years of age, only five feet one inch in height, and less than 130 pounds in weight, but Rowland was bound south to round Cape Hope and head for the Pacific Ocean.

It was Rowland's good fortune that Captain Shubael Clark was an experienced and successful seaman. Moreover, many of his ship's crew hailed from Nantucket, including George Pinkham, David J. Upham, and Silvanus E. Jenkins, Rowland's fifteen-year-old cousin. It is likely that Rowland was related to others among the crew, and that his baptism at sea would be witnessed by many friends and relatives.

Although Rowland Macy decided against making his living at sea, he never regretted the four years spent aboard the *Emily Morgan*. For the rest of his life, he proudly told people that he had gone to sea at only fifteen, and took every opportunity to regale them with stories of his whaling days.

As a means of passing the time during long sailing voyages, whalers often produced *scrimshaw*—elaborate carvings and engravings made on whale teeth or bones. The artwork could take the form of pictures, designs, or lettering, and was often highlighted with inks or other pigments.

At the start of the 1830s, fashionable women's clothing featured distinctive "leg of mutton"—or *gigot de mouton*—sleeves above cone-shaped skirts. By 1833, the tops of the sleeves had billowed to huge proportions, but they were to slim down by the end of the decade.

Although life aboard a whaling ship was both dangerous and difficult, the industry drew thousands of men. Some men craved the adventure and all hoped for financial rewards, for even the lowliest seaman received his share of the profits.

A whaling voyage was by no means a pleasure cruise. Life on the *Emily Morgan* would be hard, and it would build strength of body and mind. It would make a boy into a man. The *Emily Morgan* set sail on December 11, 1837, and did not return to the United States for four years. The only surviving portion of the *Emily Morgan's* log relates to 1838. It includes a letter signed by Joseph Ray, American Consul in Pernambuco (today, a state of Brazil), concerning David Upham, who left the crew by mutual consent. It also mentions an earthquake at sea, although it downplays this event. But mostly, the log recounts the day-to-day workings of a whaler.

The *Emily Morgan's* hunt for whales proved successful, and she returned to New Bedford on September 26, 1841 with a hold containing 108 barrels of whale oil, 2,879 barrels of sperm oil, 1,000 pounds of whale bone, and a cask of ambergris. The total cargo was probably worth over $85,000. Every member of the crew was rewarded, including common sailors such as Rowland H. Macy, who received a share amounting to between $500 and $550 for his nearly four years of work. That was a more-than-respectable sum in 1841. Rowland H. Macy was no longer an inexperienced youth with no resources of his own. He was a skilled seaman of nineteen who had money in his pocket. Yet during his long years at sea, Rowland had decided that, unlike many of his crewmates, he would not return to whaling. He was hungry for a different kind of adventure.

BOSTON

The return trip from New Bedford to Nantucket must have seemed much shorter to a man who had sailed both the Atlantic and the Pacific Oceans. Eager to see his parents, brothers, and sisters, Rowland planned to spend the 1841 Christmas holiday with his family. He especially enjoyed conversations with his brother Robert, who was two years his senior. Robert had decided to leave Nantucket to settle in Boston and work for the F.A. Jones Co., a leading dry goods firm. While selling ribbons and yard goods did not sound particularly exciting, the prospect of seeing Boston certainly did. Robert believed that Boston offered greater opportunity than Nantucket, and Rowland agreed. Early in 1842, the Macy brothers traveled together to Boston, the "Athens of America," to seek their fortunes.

Rowland H. Macy did not look for work at the dry goods firm that employed his brother, but quickly found a position as an apprentice printer. Perhaps due to the years he had spent in his father's bookshop, Rowland had an interest in the printing trade. He certainly knew of the successful career of Benjamin Franklin, whose mother, Abiah Folger, hailed from Nantucket. Rowland worked hard, and the busy print shop provided him with an opportunity to work on advertisements of all kinds, and learn what was effective and what was not. Even though Rowland's apprenticeship lasted

By the mid-nineteenth century, Boston had become one of the nation's wealthiest trading ports, as well as one of its largest manufacturing centers.

The term *yard goods* usually refers to textiles and related items. In the days before ready-to-wear garments, people relied on their local yard goods store for fabric, thread, ribbons, buttons, and various "notions," such as needles and pins—everything needed to make clothing at home.

but two years and he never became a master printer, the lessons he learned in Boston would be put to good use. By the age of twenty-one, Rowland was ready to try his skill at an entirely new venture.

Robert Macy, who was doing well in the dry goods trade at F.A. Jones, arranged a meeting between Rowland and George W. Houghton, a successful small dry goods merchant who was a client of Robert's firm. Rowland, Robert, and Houghton pooled their money, securing the merchandise and credit needed for Robert to stock a small specialty needle-and-thread store that Rowland would manage. In 1844, Rowland Macy began his career as a merchant in a shop located at 78 1/2 Hanover Street, Boston. From the start, Rowland tried to expand his line of merchandise to transform the needle-and-thread store into a dry goods establishment. There is no record of whether his initiative pleased or displeased his brother or their partner, George Houghton, but we do know that the business did not prosper. In one page of Rowland's surviving Hanover Street account book, he expresses his frustration, writing in a bold hand, "Worked two years for nothing, Damn it."

If business success remained elusive, Rowland Macy's private life blossomed. George Houghton convinced his brother Sam to come from Fairlee, Vermont and open a store in Boston. Shortly thereafter, sister Louisa Houghton arrived to visit her brothers, and met George's good friend, Rowland. The meeting led to a courtship, and marriage followed on August 24, 1844, six days before Rowland's twenty-second birthday.

In the seven years since setting sail on the *Emily Morgan*, Rowland had tried his hand at three different trades—whaling, printing, and the mercantile business—and finally settled on the last. He now ran a small store and was a married man, but the note of despair in his account book was not without reason. Although the circumstances of the failure are unknown, the Hanover Street store was forced to close.

Almost immediately after losing the needle-and-thread store, Rowland Macy opened another dry goods establishment on Boston's Washington Street. Although the young entrepreneur attempted to build the business through advertising—and there is reason to believe that he also began to secure merchandise through cash auctions rather than more conventional sources—the Washington Street store also failed. This time, Rowland had another mouth to feed, for in June 1847, Louisa had given birth to their first child, Rowland H. Macy, Jr. While the birth was a happy event, the loss of the store was not, and

Although the Hanover Street store ultimately failed, in later years, Macy talked about all that he had learned from the experience of running the store—how and when to buy merchandise, how to handle customers, and more.

An ad for Rowland H. Macy's dry goods establishment on Boston's Washington Street.

James Knox Polk began his presidency in 1845, a year after Rowland Macy launched his retailing career in a Boston needle-and-thread store. Although Polk lead the successful Mexican-American War and established a treasury system that lasted until 1913, he did not seek re-election when his term ended in 1849.

In the 1800s, women went to great lengths to shade and protect their fair complexions. Although bonnets provided some shade, the truly fashionable lady carried a *parasol*—a small, light umbrella used as protection from the sun. Eventually, this article became a status symbol.

Gold fever was fed by a number of publications of the time, including Henry I. Simpson's "The Emigrant's Guide to the Gold Mines, or Adventures with the Gold Diggers of California." Later called an "outright fraud," this 1848 booklet—written by a man who had never been to California—told how the author had unearthed a fortune in gold dust digging only with a pocketknife.

Rowland was forced to accept temporary employment in Sam Houghton's successful dry goods store on Tremont Street, as well as to give up his own residence and move in with Sam's family. But Rowland's dream for success was not to be satisfied in his brother-in-law's shop, and in 1848, Rowland's thoughts wandered westward, towards the California gold rush.

CALIFORNIA OR BUST

On January 24, 1848, while working at Sutter's Mill, a sawmill owned by John Sutter, James Marshall discovered traces of gold on the banks of California's American River. Even before the find was confirmed by President Polk, adventurous men from across the globe caught gold fever and traveled to California. The fever spread like wildfire and by the end of 1849, the population of California would soar to over 100,000. Among the first Americans to arrive were deserting crewmen from whaling ships. In fact, the rush to gold seriously injured the whaling industry, and well as other businesses. "Forty-niners" had to cross dangerous routes whether traveling by land or by sea. But such concerns did not deter Rowland Hussey Macy or his brother Charles. Both believed that California was where their fortunes would be made.

The first task Rowland faced was to convince Louisa of the wisdom of the venture. Young Louisa Macy realized that the endeavor was dangerous and would cause an extended separation, but agreed to let her husband try his luck. She had faith in Rowland and believed that he had the stamina necessary to survive the trip, which he had decided to make by sea.

On March 16, 1849, Rowland and Charles boarded the brig *Dr. Hitchcock* on the first leg of their long journey. Arriving at the Isthmus of Panama, they made their way by land across the rain forest to the Pacific Ocean. There, they boarded a steamer, the *Sylph,* for the last leg of their journey to San Francisco. They arrived on July 28, 1849, ready to seek their fortune.

No one knows exactly what Rowland and Charles did in their first year in California, but by the summer of 1850, Rowland had apparently changed his mind about sifting for gold. Macy had discovered that there was money to be made in supplying the needs of miners, and in August 1850, advertisements announced the advent of Macy & Co., a dry goods establishment Rowland had founded with partners Charles B. Mitchell and Edward B. Anthony. Levi Strauss, a San Francisco businessman, had enjoyed success in supplying prospectors with the goods they required. But while Rowland and his partners may have shared Strauss's insight, they did not enjoy comparable sales. The Macy & Co. partnership was dissolved on September 23, 1850—only about sixty days after the opening of the store—and Rowland decided to return to Louisa, using the profits he'd made on a quick sale of land. Brother Charles, who refused to abandon his dream of gold rush wealth, remained in California, where he died in 1856.

German-born Levi Strauss opened his San Francisco business in 1853. An importer of dry goods, he supplied the stores that served the Forty-niners. Not until the 1870s did Strauss produce the rugged, rivet-reinforced "waist overalls" that later would be known as *blue jeans* or *Levi's*.

The California Gold rush took a high toll on Nantucket's whaling industry, with many men deserting their vessels mid-voyage to seek their fortune out West. So great was the migration that in 1849, two Nantucket men produced a booklet entitled *A Correct List of Persons Belonging to Nantucket, Now in California*.

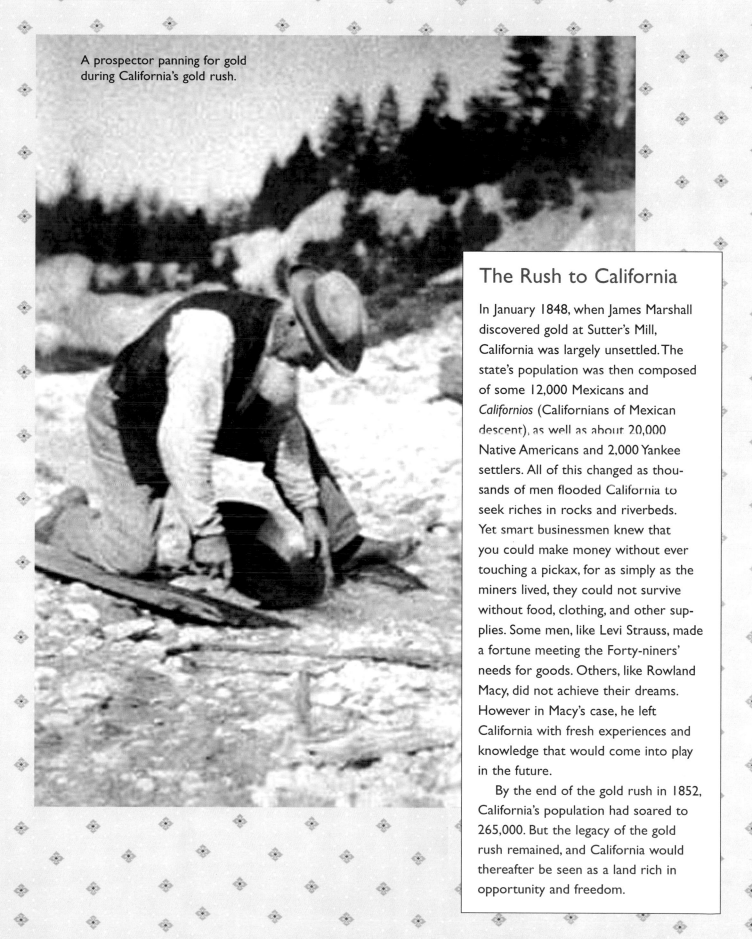

A prospector panning for gold during California's gold rush.

The Rush to California

In January 1848, when James Marshall discovered gold at Sutter's Mill, California was largely unsettled. The state's population was then composed of some 12,000 Mexicans and *Californios* (Californians of Mexican descent), as well as about 20,000 Native Americans and 2,000 Yankee settlers. All of this changed as thousands of men flooded California to seek riches in rocks and riverbeds. Yet smart businessmen knew that you could make money without ever touching a pickax, for as simply as the miners lived, they could not survive without food, clothing, and other supplies. Some men, like Levi Strauss, made a fortune meeting the Forty-niners' needs for goods. Others, like Rowland Macy, did not achieve their dreams. However in Macy's case, he left California with fresh experiences and knowledge that would come into play in the future.

By the end of the gold rush in 1852, California's population had soared to 265,000. But the legacy of the gold rush remained, and California would thereafter be seen as a land rich in opportunity and freedom.

ON TO HAVERHILL

When Rowland returned to Boston in the spring of 1851, his only funds were the money remaining from the California land sale. Again, family connections proved helpful. Rowland's brother Robert had opened his own dry goods establishment on School Street in Boston, and the business was successful enough to permit him to establish a second store in Haverhill, Massachusetts. Rowland's rather disappointing history in retailing did not deter either of the Macy brothers, and on April 1, 1851, under Rowland's management, Macy's Haverhill Cheap Store opened on Merrimack Street "for the purpose of transacting business in Fancy and Domestic dry goods." The Cheap Store was stocked with an assortment of dry goods, including cotton, gingham, and muslin cloth, as well as laces, ribbons, gloves, hosiery, and thread. Rowland was given authority to set store policy, and at a time when most stores routinely sold on credit, his April 3 advertisement in the Haverhill *Gazette* announced, "We buy exclusively for cash!!! We sell exclusively for cash. We have but one price. . . . No deviation except for imperfection." This last concept was revolutionary as well, because in most shops, customers were expected to haggle over prices, and the consumer who was adept at the bargaining process would pay a lower price than one who was less clever or determined.

It was at Haverhill that Rowland first displayed a flair for fresh and exciting advertising. "New Goods will be received from Boston and New York every week," exclaimed one advertisement. Another promised, "At this store may be found at all times the Best Stock of Fancy Dry Goods." His April 1851 ads featured a rooster holding a ribbon in his beak emblazoned with the words "The Original." No one knows why Rowland adopted a rooster as a symbol. Perhaps it was a printer's stock item that caught Rowland's fancy, or perhaps it meant that the Haverhill Cheap Store was something to crow about. Rowland's advertisements boldly announced the store's policies, particularly his insistence on cash transactions, which kept prices reasonable by avoiding the costs incurred when a customer failed to pay his bill. Dry goods stores operated on narrow margins in the best of times, and there was no room for uncollected accounts. Moreover, to keep the shoppers' attention, Rowland changed his ad copy each week to reflect newly acquired merchandise. This was very different from the practices of most merchants of the time, who had the same ads printed week after week. Rowland also bought more advertising space than was customary, publishing half-column and full-column ads, and often inserting several ads in a single issue of the *Gazette*.

Rowland's advertisements may have caught the eye of customers, but his rivals in the dry goods field were unimpressed. A few competitors used their own ads to assert that Rowland had no intention of staying in Haverhill, and was merely looking for a stake before moving on. The theory was reasonable given Rowland's history, and by the end of November 1851, the store was in

A Haverhill *Gazette* ad that spells out the benefits of Macy's one-price policy: "By adopting one price and never deviating, a child can trade with us as cheap as the shrewdest buyer in the country."

In 1850, as Rowland Macy struggled to make a success of his Haverhill Cheap Store, Millard Fillmore ascended to the presidency after the death of Zachary Taylor. One of Fillmore's first acts was to sign the Compromise of 1850, which temporarily resolved the nation's territorial and slave controversies, postponing the secession crisis and the Civil War.

Haverhill is one of the oldest historic communities in the State of Massachusetts. By the time Rowland Macy moved there in 1851, the city had already evolved into a major industrial center through the establishment of sawmills, gristmills, boat yards, and shoe manufacturers.

A full-page ad for Rowland H. Macy's Haverhill Cheap Store.

Like all dry goods stores, Rowland Macy's Haverhill Cheap Store contained bolts of all types of material, from cambrics and ginghams, to silks and velvets. Some of these fabrics had to be washed before they were made into clothes so that the finished garments would not shrink in size after the first laundering.

Macy's Cheap Store sold a variety of "Embroideries"—embroidered items such as collars, edgings, and sleeves. For those women who were handy with a needle, the store also stocked all types of needles and threads.

An ad for Macy's second Haverhill store. Although the sign read "Macy's Wholesale & Retail Dry Goods House,"
the emporium—the largest in Haverhill at one time—was popularly known as the New Granite Store.

During the 1850s, beneath her gown, a woman wore a loose undergarment called a chemise, topped with a corset. The corset was designed to give shape to the hips and waist and to support and lift the bust area. Often, it was trimmed with embroidery and lace.

Hoops became popular in the mid-1850s. The hoop underskirt—a garment stiffened with thin steel wire, whalebone, or other materials—extended the skirt of the dress into a fashionable bell-like silhouette. This dramatic shape made a woman's corseted waist appear narrow and reed-like.

trouble. Seemingly against all reason, the store closed for the four weeks preceding Christmas. One account claims it was padlocked because creditors had not been paid for the stock. Whatever the reason for the closing, Rowland was finally able to open his business for a "Peremptory Sale of the whole stock at cost and less than cost for twenty days commencing Christmas Day." The Christmas sale fended off creditors, and Rowland kept the store operating. The ads told customers, "We have been enabled by this sale to carry out our calculations and now find ourselves in a position to go into the market with the money as usual." Not only was solvency assured, but Rowland promised that "when the spring trade opens we shall have the earliest styles at the lowest cash prices."

The troubled beginning of the Haverhill enterprise made it necessary for Rowland to respond to his competitors' accusations, and respond he did. "It having been suggested by some that our store was only temporary we would call *particular attention* to this: that we now have proceeded to lay out our business for a period of ten years and if fair trading and low prices will sustain us, we have no fear for the results." Rowland Macy hoped that the Haverhill Cheap Store would be able to buy and sell entirely for cash, but as a new venture, it relied on credit. In view of Rowland's lack of past financial success, only Robert's success in Boston could be used to secure the requisite credit for the Haverhill store.

The Christmas sale appeased creditors, and by the spring of 1852, the Cheap Store appeared to be heading for brighter days under the leadership of "Rowland H. Macy, Agent." Robert B. Macy's name no longer appeared in store advertisements, and Rowland's ads reflected his increasing confidence. His announcements suggested that his store had an uncommonly large selection of goods, and his rooster offered an eye-catching and distinctive reminder. He stated that it was his intention "to be in the New York and Boston markets constantly, through the season, and every facility which I have will be improved to the utmost in taking every advantage of the market to buy my goods at the very lowest mark and give my customers good bargains during the whole season." Rowland also promised to provide the best customer service with "good and efficient clerks."

It was during Rowland's management of the Haverhill store that he initiated his policy of quoting prices in odd cents, including halfpennies. Several theories have been suggested to explain this innovation. Perhaps the practice was intended to keep clerks on their toes by having them make change for customer transactions. Or perhaps Rowland realized that customers generally noticed only the first numeral of a price that appeared in a printed ad. Understand, too, that United States currency included halfpennies until 1857, and that these coins were in circulation as late as the Civil War. The results were prices quoted at

No one knows exactly why Rowland Macy quoted prices in odd cents, and even halfpennies, in his Haverhill store. But since halfpennies were used in the United States until the Civil War, a price such as $14\frac{1}{2}$ cents may not have been unusual at the time.

In the 1800s and far into the 1900s, everyone carried a handkerchief. In his Havervill Cheap Store, Macy offered linen and silk handkerchiefs for Ladies, Gents, and Boys. The plain hankies were utilitarian, but the fancy ones—which were trimmed with lace, embroidered, or ornamented with the owner's initials—were worn or carried as an accessory.

When Rowland Macy owned his Havervill Cheap Store, soap-making was one of America's fastest-growing industries, and soap had changed from a luxury item to an everyday necessity. Thus, Macy offered his customers both Honey Soap and Fancy Soaps.

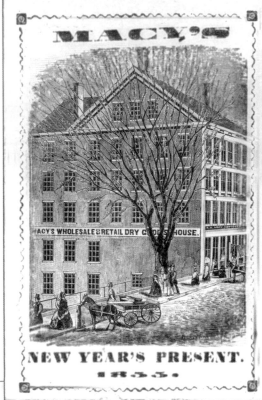

MACY'S
MACY'S WHOLESALE & RETAIL DRY GOODS HOUSE.
NEW YEAR'S PRESENT. 1855.

18

Macy's—The Store. The Star. The Story.

6   ANTICIPATIONS FOR THE FUTURE.

Having built up my business in Haverhill by doing it strictly on the *One Price* system, and *exclusively for cash*—buying for *cash* and *selling cheap*—I intend to lead on; and altho' I take to myself the credit of battering down and exploding the old system in this town, yet there is room for many improvements, and they will be adopted by me from time to time, as required; and nothing will be left undone in the future to keep my store where it is *now*, at the head of the Dry Goods business in Haverhill.   R. H. MACY.

MACY'S   7
CATALOGUE.

Silks, &c.

In Black Silks I always have a large assortment, from the cheapest to the most expensive.
All widths, qualities and prices.
Foulard Silks,
Changeable Silks,
Plaid and Fancy Silks,
Plaid Raw Silks,
Glacie and Lining Silks,
India Silks, Satins, &c.

Velvets.

A good assortment of Lyons Velvets, for Mantillas, Cloaks, &c.
Uncut Velvets for Bonnets,
Figured Velvets, for Dresses and Children.

10   MACY'S ORIGINAL
Housekeeping Goods.

As the best English and French manufacturers of these goods are in the habit of closing their consignments in job lots and at at auction, I can shew you French and English Toilet Quilts, Imported Blankets, Toilet Covers, Russia Crashes, Linen Towels, Diapers, Napkins, Doylies, Damask Covers, bleached and unbleached Linen Covers, bro. and bleach. Linen Damasks, bro. and bleach. Linens and Linen Lawns, at much less than the usual prices.

I always have a good stock of these goods, all qualities, and picking them way I do, I can always shew bargains.

24   MACY'S
Catalogue Continued.

Ladies' and Childs' Woolen Hoods,
Boys' and Girls' Woolen Sacks,
Ladies' and Childs' Under Vests,
A great variety of splendid Dress Fans,
Carpet Bags,
Fancy Baskets,
Twine Baskets,
All kinds Woolen Yarns,
Jacket Yarns,
Woolen Under Sleeves,
Boys' Suspenders,
Men's Suspenders,
Tidys,
Boys' Belts,
Woolen Leggings,
Dress Caps,
Breakfast Caps;
Sarsanet Cambric, &c., &c.

R. H. MACY.

Pages from the Macy's 1855 catalogue for his Haverhill, Massachusetts store. Note that this early catalogue featured listings of merchandise only, and included no illustrations of Macy's goods.

THE ORIGINAL

"14 $^1/_2$ cts per yard." Whatever the original justification, Rowland's pricing practices had gratifying results. Bargain-hunting shoppers traveled to the Cheap Store expecting to find the lowest prices in eastern Massachusetts.

By October 1852, Rowland was in the happy position of requiring more space. In November, he relocated to a multi-story building on 6874 Merrimack Street. The "New Granite Store," as it came to be known, was rented from Caleb D. Hunking, the landlord who also owned the house in which Rowland and his family lived. When Rowland joined the Freemason's Merrimack Lodge in Haverhill on November 8, 1852, he also developed a social relationship with Hunking, who was one of Haverhill's leading citizens. Life in Haverhill was good and in May 1853, Rowland and Louisa rejoiced at the birth of a daughter, Florence Macy.

Unfortunately, the improvement in Rowland's finances proved to be relatively short-lived. Towards the end of 1854, Rowland decided to offer new merchandise for sale at Christmas, and stocked his store with a number of "notions," toys, and other goods that he had never sold before. But Haverhill's economic conditions were not good, and Christmas sales were far poorer than expected. Rowland was worried, and for good reason: Despite his constant assertions that he bought and sold for cash only, he had actually purchased a good deal of stock on credit, assuming that he would be able to pay his debts in the new year. By late 1854, several stores in the area had failed and credit had tightened for those that remained. By 1855, the wolf was at Rowland's door, and in an effort to avoid bankruptcy, he decided to sell off all his stock at a spectacular sale. On July 30, 1855, Rowland announced the sale of the New Granite Store to his employee, E.F. Cushman. All the store's goods would be sold at their wholesale prices or less as Rowland attempted to convert his inventory into cash, settle all of his debts, and avoid another failure.

After reading Macy's announcement concerning the sale of his store, some of the store's creditors, led by Eben D. Jordan (co-founder of Jordan Marsh), brought suit for $25,000 against both Macy and Cushman. The charges alleged that Macy had fraudulently claimed that Cushman owned the store in order to shield himself from paying debts or suffering another blemish on his business record. Although there were creditors who claimed that Macy's actions were criminal, the suit proceeded in civil court and the store was placed in bankruptcy.

The judgment weighed heavily on Rowland, but he did not give up. Starting over in Haverhill or Boston would be nearly impossible, but Rowland Macy had learned a valuable lesson about managing creditor relationships, and wanted to continue in business. To provide for his family's immediate needs, he hired on as a goods broker for John Gilley at 18 Congress Street in Boston. Then Caleb Hunking, Rowland's former landlord, offered to advance Rowland funds for a new enterprise. But instead of staying in New England, Rowland had a different idea.

Once he reached adulthood, Rowland Macy worked for other people only when it was necessary to make ends meet. Macy was a born entrepreneur, and never stayed in another man's employ for very long.

Christmas has long been an important season for retailers, and Rowland H. Macy knew that he had to have toys, "notions," and other goods available for his customers. In the winter of 1854, though, Macy overstocked his store, leaving himself in poor financial condition when Christmas sales proved to be disappointing.

GO WEST, YOUNG MAN—AGAIN

The Wisconsin Territory was created in April 20, 1836, and included the present-day states of Wisconsin, Minnesota, and Iowa, as well as sections of North and South Dakota. The territory—pared down to its current size—didn't become a state until May 29, 1848, a decade before Rowland H. Macy decided to seek his fortune there.

In the 1850s, Americans were continuing to move westward, and the Midwest was becoming increasingly settled. The phenomenal growth was a source of wonder in the East, and to ambitious men, growth meant opportunity. Between 1840 and 1850, the population of Wisconsin had more than doubled, soaring from 140,000 to 305,400. Rowland thought that this state would be just the place to finally make his fortune. Once again, he left his family behind and headed west. Macy family lore recounts that despite the Haverhill debacle, Rowland had somehow managed to amass $3,000, enough to sustain his wife and children while he was away and give him a small stake. It seems likely that friend Caleb Hunking also loaned Rowland some money.

Rowland made his way west by train and boat. By August 1857, he had taken a hotel room at the "Superior House" in Superior, Wisconsin, and once again entered into partnership with his brother-in-law Sam Houghton. Their office at 345 Second Street was listed as "R.H. Macy Money to Let," while the office at 346 Second Street, which shared the same advertisements, did business as "S.S. Houghton—Real Estate Agent." Success in business often depends on luck, and Rowland's continued to be bad. The failure of the Ohio Life Insurance and Trust Company in August 1857 caused panic across the nation, and with land prices plummeting, Rowland headed back to Massachusetts in 1858.

Considering the short amount of time Rowland spent in Wisconsin and the national crisis that soon developed, it is surprising that his pockets were not empty when he again reached Massachusetts. But before the effects of the 1857 panic were felt, the entrepreneur had handled a number of land transactions, and he is thought to have returned home with as much as $8,000 in cash. Moreover, according to a story offered by the Macy family, Caleb Hunking refused Rowland's offer of repayment, thereby permitting Rowland to embark on another venture.

Rowland had traveled to New York on buying trips for the Haverhill store, and both he and Hunking felt that the growing metropolis was the perfect place to employ the innovative policies he had developed in Haverhill. Other accounts state that Hunking advanced Rowland additional sums, with the accepted figure being $3,000. What is certain is that the stars were finally aligned, and that 1858 would bring Rowland more than just another beginning.

METROPOLIS ON THE HUDSON

In the 1850s, no American city offered as much opportunity as New York. It was by far the largest city in America with a port that served as the country's primary gateway for commerce. Since the completion of the Erie Canal in

Built as a fort in 1811 and called West Battery, this New York structure was renamed Castle Garden in 1824, when it became an entertainment venue. Then in 1855, the fort was converted to an immigrant processing facility, which it remained until Ellis Island opened in 1892. Although at the time it was called the Emigrant Landing Depot, many New Yorkers still referred to it as Castle Garden.

The Panic of 1857 was a sudden downturn of the economy that ended a period of national prosperity and speculation. Although the panic was brief, more than five thousand American businesses failed within a year, and the effects did not dissipate until the Civil War.

1825, New York City had become the essential transfer point for goods and immigrants headed west. During the 1850s, it had gained a railroad connection to the Great Lakes. It also was responsible for building the world's fastest clipper ships. Even more impressive was its virtual monopoly of the transatlantic cotton trade. New York not only provided the legal and brokerage services that made cotton the king in the South, but also garnered significant profits from this trade.

Vast crowds of immigrants filled the streets of New York, requiring products of all kinds for their new lives, while a new and growing middle class was already famous for its consumption of goods. After losing seventeen blocks to fire in 1835, New York demonstrated its strength by rebuilding. New York City had created the finest municipal water system in the nation, constructed sewers that reduced the danger of disease, established a police department that helped protect its people and their businesses, and even hosted the 1853 World's Fair. Horse-drawn street cars and omnibuses filled streets, competing with an unending flow of pedestrian traffic that announced to all that New York City was open for business.

Of course, New York had some serious problems, as well. Ever increasing numbers of slum dwellers caused constant worry, and the police, whose job it was to prevent trouble, had instead staged a riot of their own in 1857. Yet the business district on the island of Manhattan continued to expand, and officials confidently predicted that the population would soon be one million. Newspapers and magazines declared that Manhattan had surpassed Boston as the cultural center of the United States.

Rowland was determined to start again in New York, and he would not be working alone. Again, his brother Robert served as an advance scout by taking a position in a Manhattan wholesale house. Both of Macy's sisters also called New York City home, and Sam Houghton, Louisa's brother, would soon follow Rowland. In late spring of 1858, the Houghton and Macy families shared a home at 332 Sixth Avenue. Their residence was conveniently located near that of Rowland's sister Charlotte (Mrs. David M. Valentine) at 60 West Fourteenth Street. Sam had agreed to work for Rowland in any new venture, so the two began to search out the location for a Manhattan store.

Rowland and Sam quickly discovered that New York dry goods activity was centered near City Hall on streets that included Broome, Grand, and Bowery. Pioneers of the business included Brooks Brothers (1818), Arnold Constable (1825), and Lord & Taylor (1826), but by the 1850s, the unrivaled leadership of the dry goods industry lay in the capable hands of Alexander T. Stewart. In 1846, Stewart had opened a "Marble Palace" on Broadway and Chambers that could be considered the first department store in Manhattan, and perhaps the world. Stewart's success was such that the focus of all shopping was gradually shifting towards the west side of the island. As Rowland sought a place for his shop, he recognized that he could not yet compete in

The Great Fire of 1835 took place on December 16 and 17, destroying the New York Stock Exchange as well as most of the buildings on the southeast tip of Manhattan around Wall Street. Because the fire occurred in the middle of an economic boom, the razed buildings were quickly replaced with sturdier, more fireproof structures.

The World's Fair of 1853, also called the Exhibition of the Industry of All Nations, was held in New York in the wake of London's successful 1851 Great Exhibition. The fair is perhaps best known for the glass-and-iron exhibition building known as the New York Crystal Palace.

During the 1850s, sewing machines went into mass production after Isaac Singer built the first commercially successful model. Powered by a foot treadle rather than the hand crank used in earlier machines, Singer's invention—which gradually became more affordable—allowed clothes to be created more quickly, whether by a homemaker, a seamstress, or a factory worker.

New York City in the 1860s.

size and scope with Manhattan's established firms and could not afford to rent a store near their shops. But he also knew that Manhattan offered sufficient customers for everyone.

Rowland found a location for his store at 204 and 206 Sixth Avenue, just one door off Fourteenth Street. The store was perhaps twenty-five feet wide by a hundred feet deep—although one Macy employee interviewed in the 1930s remembered it as being no more than twenty five by fifty feet in size. The rent was humble, too, at about $135 per month. Yet it was to be the site of a retailing adventure that would change the world of business forever.

R.H. MACY'S ON SIXTH AVENUE AND FOURTEENTH STREET

The history of R.H. Macy's is one of obstacles continually overcome. Pre-Civil War naysayers believed Macy to be an adventurer—a Bostonian trying to establish a business in a location where numerous predecessors had failed. But Rowland had faith in his new location and believed that Manhattan's rapid growth would soon fill its northern precincts. He pointed out that Fourteenth Street was already quite heavily traveled and that the ubiquitous omnibus system could readily transport customers northward. Already, there were indications that other New Yorkers shared his opinion. In August, only two months before Rowland opened R.H. Macy's in New York City, the Archbishop of New York had set the cornerstone for a new Saint Patrick's Cathedral far to the north at Fiftieth Street and Fifth Avenue. Rowland also noticed that several restaurants had opened to serve the growing population near the Fourteenth Street corridor.

Once he had selected his location, Rowland needed credit to help stock his new store. He met with success when he called on Mr. J. Maidhof of Meeker & Maidhof, dealers in dress trimmings. In 1896, when Maidhof recounted his first meeting with Rowland, he said that he had sensed the entrepreneur's drive and ambition to succeed in the competitive city. He recalled how a "short, robust but pleasant looking gentleman came to my store introducing himself as R.H. Macy," and walked out with "a line of credit of Eight Hundred Dollars on four months time." Maidhof was so impressed that he introduced Rowland to other contacts. "I then took him over to see Edward Lambert & Co, a silk and ribbon house and they also gave him a line of credit." Visits to wholesalers such as G. Rosenblatt & Bro., Calhoun, Robbins, & Co. (which specialized in "Yankee Notions" like pins and needles, buttons, razors, brooms, books, and window glass), and other suppliers followed. Based on Maidhof's recommendation and Rowland's confident manner, they all provided credit lines. Maidhof's importance to Macy's success cannot be overstated, but exactly what he found so convinc-

Businessmen certainly noted Macy's drive and ambition, but he must have also possessed an element of charm, for even after a series of business failures, people seemed more than willing to lend Macy money and extend credit.

In August of 1858, the cornerstone of Saint Patrick's Cathedral—the largest Catholic cathedral in the United States—was laid on Fifth Avenue in midtown Manhattan. At the time, midtown was far north of the populated areas of New York City.

Macy's original New York City store at 204 and 206 Sixth Avenue. Before the store was enlarged in later years, it measured only about twenty-five feet wide and a hundred feet deep.

ing about Rowland's presentation can only be imagined more than one hundred and fifty years later.

Rowland H. Macy opened his Sixth Avenue establishment on October 28, 1858. The sign on the front of the store read "R H Macy, dealer in dry goods, carpets, oil cloths and mattings." Counters filled with merchandise ran down each side of the store and also along the center of the room, creating two narrow aisles. Gloves were sold at a circular counter found at the center rear of the store. Customers who strolled into Macy's on that first day found "Fancy Dry Goods," which—according to ads—included "French embroidered collars, Cambric Flouncings, Feathers, real and artificial flowers, and French Head dresses." Items were advertised as imported, yet able to be "sold cheap." Other women's items included corsets, lace medallions, ribbons, collar and sleeve sets, and hosiery. For the "gents," there were "woolen and cotton socks, woolen shirts and drawers which we offer at a low figure."

When stock arrived at Rowland Macy's new store, it was first dropped down a chute in the front sidewalk and taken to the marking room in the basement. After being priced, the items were brought up to the store and placed on display. Once the customer selected an item, it could be purchased at the cashier's desk located at the rear of the store. This area also housed the office of Rowland and a bookkeeper.

From its opening, Macy's featured the odd pricing technique that Rowland had developed in Haverhill. Almost all items were listed at one to three cents below the dollar, implying savings to the customer. Macy's advertisements, too, appealed to the shopper who sought bargains. Rowland's first *New York Times* ad appeared on November 27, 1858, barely a month after opening. "Ladies and Gentleman—we invite you to call and look us over; our stock is all new; bought cheap. Give us a call we will save you money." Macy even advised his customers of the convenience of public transportation: "Ladies and Gentlemen who live down town, also strangers visiting the City, can very quickly find our store by taking the 6th-av. cars corner of Broadway and Vesey-street, near the Astor House, or at Canal-street and Broadway. Ladies and Gents, this will cost you 5 cents." The ad closed with the sage advice, "The ride will give you strength to look us over and buy judiciously!!"

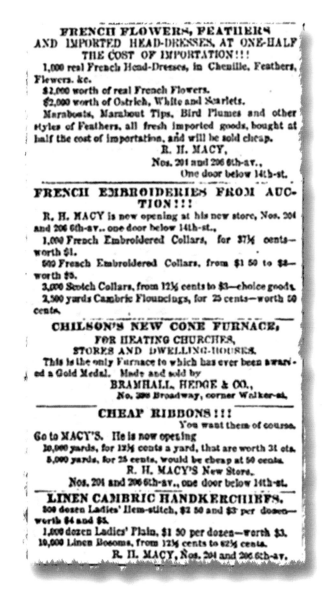

An early newspaper ad for Macy's Sixth Avenue dry goods store.

In the mid-1800s, New York City was one of the most crowded places on earth, and the inadequate transportation system made it difficult for residents and visitors to get from one place to another. Mass transportation was available in the form of the *omnibus*—essentially, a large stagecoach. In 1853, omnibuses carried 120,000 passengers per day in Manhattan.

The Lincoln-Douglas Debates of 1858 were held as Republican Abraham Lincoln and Democrat Stephen A. Douglas vied for an Illinois seat in the United States Senate. The series of seven debates was marked by eloquence on both sides, and previewed the issues that Lincoln would face in his 1860 presidential campaign.

26

Macy's—The Store. The Star. The Story.

AT R. H. MACY'S.
One door below 14th-st.
MACY KEEPS HOSIERY AND GLOVES.
MACY KEEPS ALL KINDS LINEN HANDKER-
CHIEFS.
MACY KEEPS EMBROIDERIES OF ALL KINDS.
MACY KEEPS A GOOD STOCK OF MOURNING
SETS.
MACY KEEPS A GOOD STOCK OF CAMBRIC
BANDS.
MACY KEEPS A GOOD STOCK OF VALENCI-
ENNES EDGINGS.
MACY KEEPS A GOOD STOCK OF BLACK LACE
EDGINGS.
MACY KEEPS LADIES' UNDER CLOTHING.
MACY KEEPS HOUSEKEEPING GOODS.
MACY KEEPS SHAKER FLANNELS.
MACY KEEPS BEST STYLES ALL-WOOL FLAN-
NELS.
MACY KEEPS CANTON FLANNELS.
MACY KEEPS BLEACHED AND BROWN MUSLINS.
MACY KEEPS TARLTON MUSLINS.
MACY KEEPS ANDERSON'S BOSOM LINENS.
MACY HAS LINEN NAPKINS, very cheap.
MACY HAS GENTLEMEN'S LINEN BOSOMS, 10
cents upwards.
MACY HAS GENTLEMEN'S NECK TIES, 25 cents up.
MACY HAS GENTLEMEN'S HALF HOSE, in every
quality.
MACY HAS GENTLEMEN'S UNDER SHIRTS AND
DRAWERS.
MACY HAS GENTLEMEN'S KID AND CLOTH
GLOVES.
MACY HAS GENTLEMEN'S WOOLEN GOODS.
MACY HAS WOOLEN BLANKETS.
MACY HAS HUCKABACK TOWELS, $1 50 a dozen.
MACY HAS PAPER CAMBRICS, in all colors.
MACY HAS HEADDRESSES, at 50 cents.
MACY HAS BONNET RIBBONS.
MACY HAS NECK RIBBONS.
MACY HAS SASH RIBBONS.
MACY HAS BLACK RIBBONS.
MACY HAS COLORED SATIN RIBBONS.
MACY HAS GOOD WHITE SATIN RIBBONS, 10c. a
yard.
MACY HAS NARROW BLACK VELVET RIBBONS.
MACY HAS WIDE BLACK VELVET RIBBONS.
MACY, in fact, keeps every width and quality of
BLACK VELVET RIBBONS.
MACY HAS CRIMSON VELVET RIBBON.
MACY has an endless variety of DRESS FRINGES,
TRIMMINGS, &c.
MACY HAS DROP BUTTONS.
MACY HAS DROP FRINGES.
MACY HAS FRENCH FLOWERS.
MACY HAS HAND-MADE RUCHES.
MACY HAS HOOP-SKIRTS, at 60c., 75c. and $1.
MACY HAS LADIES' CORSETS, 75 cents.
MACY keeps a full stock of LADIES' UNDER CLOTH-
ING of the very best quality. Ladies, please examine,
and you will never bother yourselves to make it, as we
sell it as low as can be afforded.
MACY HAS LADIES' CLOAKS AND RAGLANS,
From $2 50 to $7, all very cheap.
LADIES AND GENTLEMEN,
We invite you to call and look us over; our stock is all
new; bought cheap. Give us a call, we will save you
money.
Nos. 204 and 206 6th-av.
Ladies and gentlemen who live down-town, also strangers visiting the City, can very quickly find our store by
taking the 6th-av. cars corner of Broadway and Vesey-
street, near the Astor House, or at Canal-street and
Broadway.
Ladies and Gents, this will cost you five cents. Come
up and look at our large stock of new goods, as advertised above, if you do not purchase over twenty-five
cents worth; it will pay you well! We will sell you at
low figures, the ride will give you strength to look us
over and buy judiciously!!
Stores Nos. 204 and 206 6th-av., one door south of 14th-
st.
R. H. MACY.

The first day's sales totaled $11.06. But R.H. Macy's creative ads, coupled with word of mouth, obviously had great effect. On December 1, 1859, Macy's first year's sales total was $90,000, with existing store inventory valued at $34,000. Significantly, Macy reported that advertising costs amounted to $2,800, a figure that was approximately 3 percent of total sales. This may not seem impressive until you consider that the store's older, better-established competitors were spending only about 1 percent of total sales on ads. It's also important to realize that at the time, most newspaper ads appeared as what we now call "classifieds." Two- to four-line statements were printed in a single column of small type, with the first few words boldfaced. One ad followed another, column after column, with none of them standing out. Despite the constraints imposed on typeface and format by the newspapers, Rowland made his ads eye-catching. Sometimes he expanded the margins; sometimes he repeated the word "Macy's" over and over again at the head of the ad; sometimes he employed a zigzag layout. Moreover, while his copy might seem plain and conservative by today's standards, it was breezy and intimate for the time, and occasionally even displayed a subtle humor.

In its first year of business, R.H. Macy's overcame several setbacks. Less than three weeks after the store opened its doors, on November 8, 1858, a burglar used the second story of an adjacent building to gain access to the floor above Macy's. The enterprising thief cut a hole through the floor, dropped a rope ladder into the store, and stole $1,500 worth of satins, embroidered items, laces, and silks. The burglar left behind an important clue, an old coat of "a peculiar cut and the color was a remarkably dingy brown." Two police detectives were able to track down the owner of the coat, George Van Ness. Described in the press as a man of "stout muscles but slender morality," Van Ness was sent to prison. Although a search continued for both the stolen goods and any possible accomplices, it proved fruitless.

On October 20, 1859, a second incident was potentially far more dangerous. A defective gaslight in the store set a fire that was quickly doused, but caused damage estimated at nearly $1,500. Rowland recouped the loss through insurance and quickly announced a fire sale on damaged stock, but he knew that the inci-

Charles Dickens' second historical novel, *A Tale of Two Cities,* was published in weekly installments that began in April 1859 and ended in November of the same year. Depicting the plight of the French proletariat under the oppression of the French aristocracy, Dickens' masterpiece was to become one of the best-selling books of all times.

dent could have resulted in the complete loss of his growing establishment.

Despite obstacles and losses, Macy survived his first year in operation in New York. He had learned to write aggressive advertising with a creative flair, and had established a formal pricing policy that would characterize his retail future. His *New York Times* ad of June 14, 1859—"R H Macy's, One Price, Cash Retail House"—set a policy that would become world famous. Macy's entertained no bargaining and accepted payment in cash only.

Rowland Macy had traveled a long road from the day he first set out to make his fortune as a young lad of fifteen. Despite numerous failures, his New England roots had provided him with the pluck needed to move ahead towards success. And for all its difficulties, New York City provided the perfect environment for Rowland's talents by offering hundreds of thousands of consumers with cash in hand.

By the close of the 1850s, Rowland had brought together many of the elements needed to win his first true success as an entrepreneur. His ideas were fresh and bold, and the time was right for his unique style of retailing. A new decade was about to unfold, and Macy's Manhattan store would continue to grow, fueled not only by the talents of its founder, but also by those of several important people whom Rowland Macy had yet to meet.

Macy's attention-getting ads, including one for the fire sale that followed the store's gaslight accident of October 20, 1859. Note how—despite the limitations placed on typeface and format—Macy caught the reader's eye through repetition, the use of upper-case letters, and a clever arrangement of copy.

Rowland H. Macy.

2.
A Store Grows in Manhattan

In 1860, Manhattan had a population of over 800,000; it was not only the nation's largest city, but also its fastest growing metropolis. New York's population had quadrupled since 1830, its port had become a major player in world trade, and its shopping districts had expanded so rapidly that it deserved the title City of Commerce. Led by Mayor Fernando Wood, a wily politician dedicated both to free trade and the amassing of personal wealth by any means available, the city confidently faced the future even as the American Union entered its greatest period of crisis. The city that Mayor Wood led boasted America's widest variety of industry, acted as a gateway for half of the nation's imports, and served as the investment center for business enterprise.

As the threat of disunion continued to grow, Rowland Macy focused on his growing business. During Rowland's daily walk to his Sixth Avenue shop, he saw a thriving community of working people make their way through the crowded streets of a vibrant city. He knew that fully half of those who passed him had been born in faraway places and that they were not all his customers, yet he believed that they, like himself, were part of a great city of opportunity. Each passerby might someday purchase the goods that he would gladly provide. Macy knew that during his first two years in New York, his efforts had brought success, and he was certain his drive and ambition had at last found the right place to flourish. The hard lessons he had learned through a succession of failed ventures were only memories; New York was the city where he would succeed.

The bustling streets of New York City in the 1860s.

In 1861, shortly after R.H. Macy began to assemble his talented staff, Abraham Lincoln became the sixteenth President of the United States. Lincoln is best known for his inspirational leadership during the American Civil War and for issuing the Emancipation Proclamation of 1863, which committed the Union to ending slavery.

During Lincoln's term in the White House, First Lady Mary Todd Lincoln made frequent shopping trips to New York City, prompting criticism of her extravagance. In one four-month period, she is said to have purchased four hundred pairs of gloves.

Macy's New York

New York City was the industrial, commercial, and cultural center of the United States in 1860. Although it occupied little more than a third of Manhattan Island, New York was America's most populous city, its most active port, and the center of publishing, art, and theater. Manhattan was the place where Jenny Lind first sang for Americans (1850), home to the Crystal Palace and the Latting Observatory (1853), and the place where a great Central Park had been built for public enjoyment (1857). The banks of the city controlled the financial destiny of the nation; more than 4,300 manufacturing establishments were situated there, and over 60 percent of America's total imports and exports flowed across its docks. Yet as dominant as the city already was, its position as leader of the nation would be enhanced during the years of Civil War and Reconstruction.

From the time that the Seventh Regiment marched out from Manhattan to "save" Washington in April 1861, there never was any doubt of the metropolis's loyalty to the Union's cause. Even Mayor Wood belatedly came to support the war effort, and no city or state contributed more blood and money to ultimate victory. Fully a third of northern casualties at the Battle of Bull Run (July 1861) came from the Empire State as the city rallied 'round the flag. By the end of the war, New York men had fought in over 2,147 engagements, with over 50,000 of them dying to save the Union.

Jenny Lind, the "Swedish Nightingale."

Even as the flower of city manhood went off to battle, the business of the city expanded to fulfill wartime contracts. Many may know that the famous USS *Monitor* was built along the East River in 1861, but city businesses also provided a steady stream of uniforms, shoes, saddles, and other goods for Union armies. The loans and bonds that financed the armies had their origin on Wall Street under the care of brokers like Jay Gould. And not even war could prevent the creation of new city-based corporations, which made the largest (Steinway pianos) to the smallest products (Faber pencils). Although Union battle results were dismal in 1862, dedicated New York shoppers made possible the successful opening of a new A.T. Stewart department store on Broadway and Ninth Street in 1862, an "Iron Palace" that outpaced Stewart's original "Marble Palace" further downtown.

Given the magnitude of New York's contributions to Union victory, it is unfortunate that many people remember only the tragedy of the Draft Riots that scarred the metropolis in July of

Early Central Park.

1863. Conscription imposed on the working classes of the city was the primary cause, but lower-class workers also directed their anger against blacks. Mobs ruled the city for three days and many stores, Brooks Brothers among them, were looted. Some of the riots took place only blocks from R.H. Macy's. The Colored Orphan Asylum was burnt to the ground, and over one hundred lives were lost before Union soldiers restored order. There had been major tumults before 1863, with both the police and ethnic gangs rioting in 1857, but no incident tainted the city as much as the violence after the Union victory at Gettysburg. The Draft Riots reminded the nation just how violent and lawless its greatest city could be.

The Draft Riots of 1863.

Despite that great exception, patriotism and selfless cooperation were far more the rule for New York during the course of America's most bloody conflict. The city's contribution to winning the war was unrivaled, and Manhattan would also be the setting for its sad closing chapter. On April 25, 1865, the body of Abraham Lincoln came to New York on its way home to Illinois. Grieving city residents lined the streets as the funeral procession wound its slow path to City Hall, where over 125,000 paid their last respects to Lincoln as he lay in state. The Seventh Regiment, first to go to war in 1861, provided an honor guard for the president who had promised New Yorkers that he would never consent to secession.

During the terrible years of Reconstruction, New York reverted to doing what it did best—making money and financing expansion of the national economy. In 1866, the city had fifty-eight chartered national banking institutions. Although there were disruptions to its prosperity, the general story of Manhattan was one of unparalleled success. Immigration through Castle Garden provided a source of cheap labor, prosperity kept shoppers on the "Ladies Mile" of stores, and new businesses were constantly opening. In 1870, for example, Tiffany's moved uptown to Union Square and a toy store run by Frederick August Otto Schwarz opened on Broadway. The city had a population of 942,000 people, and they produced twice as much as they had only a decade earlier. Manhattan was on its way to becoming a world-class metropolis, and R.H. Macy & Co.—already a favorite with New Yorkers—was on its way to becoming a legend.

New York City Mayor Fernando Wood.

Rowland Macy had developed distinctive ideas about advertising, pricing, and retailing strategy, and he viewed his growing profits as a testament to his business acumen. But as a business strategist, he also recognized that even the most astute and hard-working entrepreneur has to recruit other talented people—skilled individuals who share his vision. Even as the national crisis deepened, Rowland found the workers who would help transform Macy's fancy dry goods store into America's department store. The names Margaret S. Getchell, Abiel T. LaForge, and Robert Macy Valentine may not be well-known, but—along with the better-known Nathan and Isidor Straus—they would join with Rowland to build not just a larger store, but a New York institution.

MARGARET S. GETCHELL

Like R.H. Macy himself, Margaret Getchell was formed by the hard and unyielding demands of life on Nantucket. Given the provincial nature of the island, it should be no surprise that the two actually were distant cousins. But while a man could easily leave the island to test and discover his talents in the outside world, such a daring course of action was not always available to young women. Nevertheless, in 1861, at the age of eighteen, Margaret became a schoolteacher in Richmond, Virginia, hoping to share her mathematics skills with her students. Unfortunately, her dream of teaching was cut short by two events. The first was increasing hostilities in the South, resulting in the closure of schools in Richmond. The second involved problems caused by an early injury that had robbed Margaret of sight in her right eye. Forced to leave Virginia, and realizing that continued teaching would put too much of a strain on her good eye, she began seeking a new career path. Beautiful, confident, and mature beyond her years, Margaret decided that cousin Rowland's new store in Manhattan presented just the opportunity she needed.

In 1862, a seemingly self-assured Margaret Getchell walked into R.H. Macy's dry goods store and asked to meet with Rowland Macy. Regardless of her poise and composure, she was a very young woman and was visiting the great metropolis for the very first time. Although Rowland was busy, he made time to speak to her, and soon learned that she was his distant cousin. Margaret explained that she was a former schoolteacher who wanted to build a new life, and felt that retail work would suit her. Her understanding of math, she believed, would be useful at Macy's. Exactly what course the interview took is uncertain, but Rowland liked her manner very much and felt obligated to help someone from Nantucket whose very presence proved her courage. He decided to offer her a job as cashier, a position of some importance because Macy's was a strictly cash store. Cash flow and accurate money accounting represented the lifeblood of Macy's business; they

In 1860, as the nation faced the threat of civil war, an ardent young patriot named Elmer Ellsworth headed for New York, where he organized fire department volunteers into what was called the New York Fire Zouaves. Members of the infantry regiment wore "uniforms" that included baggy red pants, sashes over blue bolero jackets, and fezzes. Women first began wearing the distinctive Zouave jackets as a show of patriotism, but the jackets soon became a wardrobe staple. When Ellsworth became virtually the first casualty of the war on May 24, 1861, the demand for Zouave attire only increased.

As a means of showing their patriotism, women embraced the bolero-style Zouave jacket throughout the Civil War. The original Zouave units were Algerian and Moroccan volunteers in the French Foreign Legion, but an American Zouave unit—the New York Fire Zouaves—was formed by patriot Elmer Ellsworth, who adopted the distinctive garb of the earlier soldiers.

For many decades, silk was the standard cloth for fine ladies' dresses, and most women had at least one "good" silk dress. Silk held dyes well, making a range of colors possible.

required recording ability, skill with numbers, and most important, honesty. It is a mark of Rowland's insight that he immediately saw all these qualities and more in Miss Getchell.

Margaret clearly wanted the offered position, but she surprised Rowland by recounting the story of her partial blindness. She told her cousin that she had recently had the injured eye removed and a glass eye installed in its place. She wanted Mr. Macy to know the truth about her handicap before hiring her. As impressed as Rowland had been by Margaret's demeanor, he was even more pleased by the young woman's forthrightness, and informed her that he had not noticed anything unusual about her appearance. Praising Margaret's honesty and determination, he congratulated her. She had the job.

Margaret immediately showed Rowland that she not only was a fast learner, but also had a natural flair for retailing. She approached her new job as a challenge, learning everything she could and constantly offering ways to improve business. Clearly, she had Rowland's ear. In the early 1860s, Rowland decided to add the military inspired Zouave jackets to the store's stock, along with capes, sacks, nightdresses, infant's cloaks, and dresses. Shortly thereafter, he expanded his line of goods again to include drugs and toiletry items such as soaps. Then the hat and trimmings department was enlarged. According to anecdotal accounts, Margaret was one of the forces behind these and many other improvements that helped Macy's grow during its infancy. In fact, years later, a Macy's employee was heard to say that Margaret was "the brains of the establishment and had made R.H. Macy's."

Margaret S. Getchell, the first American woman to hold an executive position in retailing.

As the nation moved from war to peace, Rowland Macy increasingly based his business decisions on Margaret Getchell's judgment and offered her ever greater responsibilities. In 1866—only four years after she became a Macy's employee—Margaret was named store superintendent, the first woman to hold an executive position in retailing. At that time, the young lady from Massachusetts oversaw two hundred mostly female employees in one of the most successful businesses in New York City.

Andrew Johnson succeeded to the presidency in 1865, after the assassination of Abraham Lincoln, and remained in office until 1869. Charged with reconstruction of the defeated South, Johnson blocked efforts to guarantee full equality for blacks. In 1868, the Senate attempted to remove Johnson from office and failed by a single vote.

Buttons were employed both as decorative touches and as fasteners. Fabric-covered buttons were common, as were those made of shell, glass, bone, leather, metal, and ceramic. More expensive buttons, intended for fancier garments, often featured beautiful portraits and elaborate designs.

Rowland Macy's primary reason for importing the mechanical singing bird—an object too expensive to be purchased as a child's toy—was to create a sensation that would draw crowds. Phineas T. Barnum, a close friend of Rowland and founder of P.T. Barnum's American Museum in New York, often visited the store to admire the rare and beautiful object.

Several stories show Getchell's dedication and Yankee ingenuity. On one occasion, the store was exhibiting an imported mechanical singing bird that was constantly surrounded by admiring customers. All was well until the bird abruptly stopped working. It was Margaret who took on the task of repairing the popular object. Using a penknife, pliers, and screwdriver, the fearless woman took the bird entirely apart and reassembled it. Soon, to the delight of Macy's customers and the store's bottom line, the bird was again in motion.

Margaret had a talent for imaginatively arranging merchandise. She insisted that doll house displays in the window would improve holiday sales, and on one occasion trained two small kittens to lie in a crib dressed as babies. She then had a photo taken of the adorable scene, ordered copies, and sold the photos. The unique remembrance immediately became a huge seller. Of even more importance to the store was her insistence that shoppers would flock to make last-minute purchases on Christmas Eve. Accordingly, on December 24, 1868, Macy's defied convention and remained open as a service to its customers. The result was sales that exceeded $6,000—the best day in the history of the store.

R.H. Macy had taken a chance on the talents of a young woman he hardly knew, and she had proved her value to the enterprise. Margaret even took an apartment directly across the street from the store so that she could keep an eye on the establishment. As time passed and her relationship with Rowland grew, Margaret was frequently invited to dinner at the Macys' house according to the customs of the time. During the ritual of long evening dinners, Margaret offered her views on trends and fashions of the era, increasing Rowland's understanding of his customers' needs. When Rowland's family relocated to 74 West Twelfth Street, he asked Margaret to move in and become part of his family. Although she had started as a stranger, Margaret Getchell had become an essential member of the public and private life of R.H. Macy.

ROWLAND MACY, JR.

Rowland Macy found a new and valuable family member in Margaret, and their father-daughter relationship was perhaps the most satisfying of his life. The hard reality was that his own performance as a biological father was far from trouble free; indeed, it was filled with concern, emotional pain, and personal disappointment.

Rowland was an ambitious man who spent long periods of time away from his family as he searched for business success. He had little to do with the raising of his children. It can be argued that prolonged absences and myopic concentration on his business made Rowland a stranger to his chil-

Until the end of World War One, when wristwatches became popular, the properly attired gentleman always carried a pocket watch. Usually, the watch was attached to a chain and a *fob*—a medallion or other ornament. This enabled the wearer to secure the watch to his coat, lapel, or belt loop.

Fashionable skirts were made as wide as possible during the 1860s, and were supported with hoops or multiple petticoats made of a stiff fabric called crinoline. Along with wide-cut shoulders and a fitted bodice, this style accentuated the smallness of the waist without the use of corsets.

dren, and that their reaction was one of abandonment. Whatever the reason, in August of 1864, when Rowland and Louisa's first child—son Rowland Macy, Jr.—was about seventeen, he ran away from home. For several weeks, his frantic parents heard not a single word from Rowland, Jr. When news finally came, the Macys were stunned. Their son had taken the ferry to the Newark Union Army Recruiting Headquarters, and using the alias of Charles H. Mitchell—the name of one of his father's early partners—had joined the 106th New York Volunteers.

In the summer of 1864, the Union Army under Grant was inexorably moving across Virginia, and the casualty rates were astronomical. Patriotism was in the air, and so was disgust at the cost of war. Exactly what combination of emotions led Rowland, Jr. to Newark can never be known, but what is clear is that he found army life difficult. Only ten days after joining the service, he abandoned camp and instead of returning home, made his way to Washington, DC. Virtually in the shadow of the Capitol, two detectives apprehended him and brought him to Forrest Hall Prison in Georgetown. While his parents endured the worst mental anguish, their son was tried for desertion and convicted on August 29, 1864. His youth worked in his favor, however, and he was merely sentenced to forfeit pay and allowance, and make good all time lost. Meanwhile he would be kept in prison.

On December 19, 1864, Rowland, Jr. was "to be returned under guard to such a regiment for duty as the General Commanding may direct." In fact, he was to be reassigned to the 106th Regiment, and on March 3, 1865, he took his place in the ranks of I Company under the command of Abiel T. LaForge. Rowland's new commander, only about twenty-two years of age himself, saw some good in the scared young man and took him under his wing. Captain LaForge even wrote a letter to General L. Thomas, asking that Rowland's sentence be removed: "He has been a member of my company since March 3, 1865 and has always conducted himself with so much propriety in camp and exhibited such soldier like qualities in battle and on the campaign, that I feel convinced that your clemency could not be extended to a person more worthy of it." Fortunately, young Rowland's record was cleared.

At some point before the end of the war, Rowland and Louisa learned of their wayward son's escapades, and the elder Macy crossed the Hudson and found his child drilling with I Company. During the visit he also met Abiel LaForge, and may even have been responsible for that officer's championship of his son. It seems clear that some quid pro quo was involved, for after the meeting, Abiel corresponded with R.H. Macy on numerous occasions, and even bought clothing for Private Macy. But despite all efforts on his behalf, Rowland, Jr. continued to disappoint his father, and perhaps even the young officer who took up his cause. By the 1870s, Rowland, Jr. had a drinking problem, seemed unable to keep a job, and was frequently in debt.

Records show that Rowland Macy, Jr. was not drafted into the Union Army, but was a substitute soldier—an individual who, for the sum of three hundred dollars, voluntarily replaced a conscript who wished to avoid military service.

Top hats, typically made of silk, were favored by men throughout the nineteenth century and the early part of the twentieth century. In the 1860s, Abraham Lincoln popularized the stovepipe hat—a version of the top hat that was tall and straight from top to bottom, rather than narrowing in the middle.

On November 14, 1864, General William Sherman began his famous March to the Sea. Beginning in Atlanta, Georgia and ending in Savannah, Sherman's troops lived off the land and destroyed much of the South's resources. In December, Sherman wrote to President Lincoln: "I beg to present you, as a Christmas gift, the city of Savannah."

36

Macy's—The Store. The Star. The Story.

The elder Macy's feelings about his son were captured in the will that he left in 1877: "I cannot entrust him with the care or management of any property. . . . I am compelled to acknowledge the failure of every effort made by me and others to that end." At the same time, though, Macy developed a true fondness for young Abiel who—promoted to major for "gallant and meritorious service"—seemed to have all the drive and ambition that his son lacked. Blood relationships were vital to Nantucket people, but Rowland Macy had come to believe that performance and morals were truer reflections of character. He would induct the very competent Margaret into his family, and when the newly demobilized Abiel came to him in 1865, he was fully prepared to help the man who had aided his floundering son. Perhaps he already perceived Abiel as a surrogate son, one whose achievements might overcome the pain of young Rowland's follies.

Rowland H. Macy's will left his considerable estate to his wife, Louisa, and his daughter, Florence. Only a small annuity was provided for Macy's son, Rowland, Jr.

ABIEL T. LA FORGE

Once his military service ended with an honorable discharge, Major Abiel LaForge headed for New York City to make his fortune. He arrived in Manhattan on September 3, 1865, rented a room, and planned his future. The Macy connection was his only tie to the city, and the discharged officer was soon invited to spend a Sunday with the Macy family. Abiel became a favorite guest of the Macys, and his diary entries include remembrances of many pleasant evenings listening to music played upon the family piano. Rowland and Louisa enjoyed the company of the young man, and Rowland willingly advised him about career plans. It seems significant that as early as September 29, 1865, Abiel recorded an important meeting with Mr. Macy:

> He and I lit a cigar and went back to the store where we could be alone and have a good talk, as Mr. Macy termed it. I told him briefly what I came to town for he then said that my best plan would be to get in some wholesale store if such was possible, he did not comment on the difficulties of getting a situation when you could not bring the recommendation of experience in the business with you, I had already learned that. (I did not go to see Mr. Macy until the 12th of this month because I was afraid he would consider that I had come with a claim on his gratitude.) The next day he took me around to A.T. Stewarts the most wealthy merchant of N.Y., to J. Glafflans, the largest dry goods dealer in the U.S., and to Mr. Jaffreys, a very large wholesale house employing about seventy clerks in the one store, besides having agents in Europe and the East Indies.

It is clear that Rowland was willing to help the man who had attempted to assist his son. Indeed, he even offered Abiel a position at Macy's but

Ulysses S. Grant took office in 1869, the same year that Abiel LaForge accepted a position with R.H. Macy & Co. Known best as the Union general who led the North to victory during the Civil War, Grant has long been considered a weak and ineffective president. Nevertheless, he made revolutionary efforts in the areas of black rights and Native American policy.

The spoon bonnet was a fashionable form of feminine headwear during the 1860s. The upturned, highly ornamented brim did little to protect a woman's delicate complexion, but was a wonderful means of framing her face.

advised the young man that the better opportunity for long-term success would be found in a wholesale house. LaForge was grateful both for Rowland's introductions and his job offer, but he did not want to accept a job at Macy's, feeling it would be only belated payment for his kindness to Rowland, Jr. Instead, Abiel found employment with the new dry goods firm of Mills & Gibb at a starting salary of $500 per year. He was immediately successful, but continued to seek advice from the man he considered a mentor. Moreover, during an evening at the Macy's he had met Margaret Getchell, and a spark had ignited. On March 29, 1866, Abiel wrote in his diary, "I was again around at Mr. Macy's Tuesday evening. Miss Getchell his cashier was there also. Spent the evening very pleasantly, saw Miss G. on the car[riage] when she left for home." Rowland Macy may have had little faith in his wayward son, but affairs in his surrogate family were proceeding quite nicely.

Abiel was bright and hard-working, so Rowland periodically renewed his offer of employment. It was not until early in 1869, however, that Abiel left Mills & Gibb to accept a position at Macy's. In a letter to his sister, he enthusiastically wrote, "So here I am at Macy's, buyer of laces, embroideries, handkerchiefs and trimmings. My branch of the store will sell about $200,000 a year." Clearly he was on the road to success, and success made him bold. His relationship with Margaret had continued to blossom, and he could now act. On April 26, 1869, Abiel wrote to his sister, "Allow me to announce with all due modesty, my approaching marriage with a young lady who is now very prettily employed (not two paces from me) in working a beautiful pair of slippers." He bragged with the hopefulness of first love that "The lady is I think one of the best women that ever lived. . . . Miss Margaret S. Getchell, that's the name in full." The two were married on June 8, 1869 and no one was happier than Rowland H. Macy.

Abiel T. LaForge, Macy's first junior partner and husband of Margaret Getchell.

In 1870, New York basked in the sunlight of an extraordinary decade. Despite the traumas of war and Reconstruction, the city's population had soared to almost 950,000 souls, while both the products it manufactured and its property had doubled in value. New York's port remained the most prof-

Boots were the most common men's footwear during the Civil War period. Sturdy and long-wearing, they were essential for horsemen, working men, and anyone who spent time outdoors. Although most boots were dyed black, work boots sometimes remained a natural tan color.

Most fabrics of the period were solid in color, but stripes, plaids, dots, and prints were also fashionable. Elaborate prints were reserved for the gowns of the wealthy, as yards of fabric were required to match the patterns at the seams.

itable in America as fully 71 percent of national trade passed through its docks. No city offered a better business climate, and the shoppers of Manhattan had already made clear their preference for Macy's emporium.

Unforeseen events had brought Margaret Getchell and Abiel LaForge to Rowland Macy's store, but chance had created an exceptional retailing team. In the 1870s, Rowland treated Abiel not only as a trusted friend and employee, but also as the son that Rowland, Jr. had failed to become. On many occasions, the two men traveled on buying trips abroad, played billiards together, and shared good cigars while Margaret managed daily operations. Not surprisingly, Rowland showed his faith in Abiel by making him the first junior partner in the firm—a decision all the more impressive because Abiel, throughout his career at Macy's, was plagued by tuberculosis. That insidious disease sometimes confined him to bed for days at a time. Nevertheless, the expanded management team continued to make Macy's a major player on Manhattan's retail scene, and profits continued to rise.

A Card.

ONE THOUSAND DOLLARS REWARD. The reports which have been in circulation recently in regard to my having failed in business, or of my intentions to fail, are unqualifiedly false, and without any foundation whatever. I will pay ONE THOUSAND DOLLARS REWARD for evidence which will convict any responsible party or parties who originated the reports. R. H. MACY, 14th-st. and 6th-av. —*Advertisement.*

French and English Perfumery in great variety. DITMAN & CO., Astor House Pharmacy.— *Advertisement.*

HAZARD & CASWELL'S cod liver oil is the best. —*Advertisement.*

R.H. Macy was well aware of the importance of a good reputation, so when someone circulated a false rumor that his store was failing, he quickly published a denial of the story and even offered a reward for the name of the person who had made the claim.

ROBERT MACY VALENTINE

R.H. Macy was bitterly disappointed that his son did not share in the building of his business. Yet he contemplated the future with some confidence, since chance and his own acumen had created an effective alternative to strict succession. But there was yet a third element that Rowland added to his store's management structure during these eventful years. Even as the store's reputation grew, its busy leader gradually recognized that his nephew, Robert Macy Valentine, had much to contribute to the business.

Robert had been born in 1850, and received his education in Providence, Rhode Island and New York City. In 1868, he entered commercial life—not in his uncle's store, but in the wilderness of what was then called the Idaho Territory. Valentine remained working there for four years, a continent removed from friends and family. Then in 1872, Rowland's sister Charlotte asked her brother to take Robert into the retail dry goods trade. Rowland, perhaps remembering the dividends he had reaped from meeting Margaret, agreed to take a chance on the young man, and Robert traveled east to begin training. He must have been an apt pupil, because in 1875, Rowland made him the second junior partner of R.H. Macy's. Not surprisingly, Valentine's arrival at the business was seen as a challenge to Abiel, and Rowland was suspected of fostering an in-house rivalry.

The staff soon discovered that Robert had a management style very different from that of Abiel. Abiel was well-liked, treated everyone with kindness and respect, and at Christmastime was known to take Macy's employees out to dinner to express his appreciation for jobs well done. Robert was

In the 1870s, the crinoline petticoat was replaced with the bustle. Formed of stiff frills of horsehair cloth or small wire frames, and worn under the skirt, the bustle made dresses flatter at the front and fuller at the back, providing a silhouette that was very different from the bell-like shape that had preceded it.

No longer constrained by the economies of the Civil War era, 1870s women's fashions often featured puffs, ruchings and ruffles, ribbons, fringes, elaborate drapery, and flounces. Different fabrics and colors were sometimes combined in an elaborate and unexpected manner.

The Macy's Star is Born

Everyone familiar with Macy's is also acquainted with the red star, which has long been the company's trademark. Although the exact origin of this logo is lost in time, we do know that the star was adopted by the founder of the company, Rowland H. Macy. The earliest mention of it appears to have been in an 1861 ad, which refers to "the Star of Empire . . . the Star of Fashion." Soon the symbol itself—formed by asterisks or other typesetting characters, and often featuring the company's name at its center—began appearing in newspaper ads for the growing emporium.

Why did Rowland Macy choose the star to represent his store? Certainly, Rowland viewed his store as a leader in the field. But it is also thought that Macy's founder, proud of his seafaring background, selected the symbol as a reference to the nautical star that has long been popular with sailors worldwide.

WESTWARD! HO!!

"*Westward the Star of Empire takes its way!*"
So does the Star of Fashion and the Graces;
Judging, at least, by the vast crowds, each day,
Rushing to MACY'S.

Broadway no longer tempts with costly glare,
With fancy shop fronts, and still fancier prices;
Cheapness—if good and tasteful for the fair—
Is what entices.

Therefore, we find SIXTH-AVENUE to grow,
Daily, in favor with all sects and classes,
And not a Broadway palace, people know;
MACY'S surpasses.

Look at his GLOVES! while other folks elsewhere
Charge for their gloves a price almost fictitious,
For SIXTY-THREE CENTS MACY robes the fair
In kids delicious!

See what a rich assortment, too, he brings
Of LINENS, FLOWERS, EMBROIDERIES and LACES,
RIBBONS, HEAD-DRESSES, and a thousand things
For pretty faces!

Hither flock mothers with their pets, and beaux
Come with the objects of their hearts' devotions,
To see the sterling wonders MACY shows
In YANKEE NOTIONS.

Bedecked by him the very plainest lass
Is Venus—in her beau's imagination,
And youngsters, too—in mamma's eyes—surpass
All in creation!

"Westward the Star of Fashion takes its way!"
That it should poise o'er MACY'S is not funny;
'Tis that he SELLS GOODS EQUAL to BROADWAY;
FOR MUCH LESS MONEY!

R. H. MACY,
Nos. 204 and 206 6th-av.,
Two doors from 14th-st.

First star ad, early 1872.

Holiday star ad, December 1872.

A star as it appeared in the late 1800s on the Macy's façade.

40

Macy's—*The Store. The Star. The Story.*

less friendly, and in the words of one employee, "he trusted no one." Later, when Robert ascended to the post of senior partner, he imposed a system of fines on his employees to keep them punctual and accurate. There was a fine for arriving late for work, a fine for returning late from lunch, and a fine for making errors on the job. To Robert's credit, he was as quick to penalize himself for one of these transgressions as he was to fine a Macy's clerk or cashier.

Robert Valentine put in long hours, arriving early in the morning and often not leaving until eight in the evening. On the door to his office was a sign that read: "Confine your conversation strictly to business, and be brief and to the point." While at work, Robert lived by this rule, although there were times when Robert let down his guard. On one occasion, for instance, Robert arranged for a horse-drawn sleigh to carry his workers over a newly fallen blanket of snow, while he and his wife followed behind in a smaller sleigh. But we are moving ahead of our story, for yet another element of Macy history dates from the 1870s, and in time it became the most important of all the events in the decade.

THE STRAUSES

A young Nathan Straus.

It seems fitting that the immigrant experience was responsible for this last great change in the Macy hierarchy. No American city is so identified with immigration as New York, and newcomers to America had long been welcomed at the store on Sixth Avenue. Immigrants took advantage of Macy's cheaper prices, and many of them found employment in the stockroom and, ultimately, on the shopping floor. Macy obviously recognized talent when he saw it and was always ready to offer encouragement and opportunity. But not even he could imagine the revolutionary changes in store when a young salesman visited Macy's in March 1874, and asked that his family's wares be carried on the growing list of Macy's merchandise. Nathan Straus represented a new wave of immigration to America, and his family would in time change the world of Manhattan retailing.

Nathan's father, Lazarus Straus, had emigrated from Germany to the State of Georgia in 1852, seeking peace and order after the failed Revolution of 1848 in the German states. Two years later, he was joined by his wife, Sara; daughter, Hermina; and three sons, Isidor, Nathan, and Oscar. Initially, Lazarus sold dry goods from a pushcart, but it wasn't long before he bought a dry goods store and then entered the cotton trade. The family prospered until the Civil War brought financial ruin. Only then did the Strauses relocate to New York City, where they established L. Straus & Sons, a china and glassware firm. Although business was good, the family was always looking for ways to improve it further, and it was this ambition that brought Nathan into R.H. Macy's office.

During the day, 1870s dresses had high necklines that were rounded, squared, or V-shaped. At night, low necklines and very short, off-the-shoulder sleeves were fashionable. A velvet ribbon was sometimes worn high around a woman's bared neck, with the ends of the ribbon trailing behind.

On January 3, 1875, New York politician William Marcy Tweed—popularly known as Boss Tweed—escaped from debtor's prison and fled to Cuba. Tweed had been convicted of stealing over $100 million from New York City taxpayers through political corruption. Recaptured in 1876, he died in jail two years later.

LOCAL MISCELLANY.

R. H. MACY & CO.'S OPENING.

A RICH ASSORTMENT OF CHINA, GLASS, AND PARIAN WARES—SOMETHING NEW IN BRONZES—NOVELTIES IN TOILET SETS, PORCELAIN, &C.

The "opening" of R. H. Macy & Co., whose extensive establishment is situated at the corner of Sixth avenue and Fourteenth street, is took place yesterday. Their display of goods is always particularly interesting, but on this occasion, one department has been so extended that its hitherto abundant attractions were greatly enhanced. This is the department devoted to china ware. It has been increased to about three times its original size, and is subdivided into four branches, which include respectively china, majolica, glass, and Parian wares. Before however, inspecting, these beautiful articles of taste and luxury, the visitor would do well to go through the departments devoted to, other wares. By putting himself or herself in communication with Miss Bowyer, the General Superintendent, all the courtesies and polite attentions of the establishment will render a complete inspection of the stock a matter of little difficulty. In the several portions of the building will be found every article which either luxury or necessity could suggest. There are, outside the china, glass-ware, &c., fifteen well-arranged and amply-stocked departments, which are of course properly subdivided. On the main floor, level with the street, is contained everything which might come within the description of dry goods. This portion of the building is tastefully frescoed, and is notably well-arranged in all its details. Here will be found everything commonly sold in dry goods stores, besides many wares of a more special character. The handsome bronzes which were exhibited yesterday formed a marked feature in the opening. They are of great beauty of design, and the design is satisfactorily supplemented by ability of execution. Some of these bronzes are exquisitely delicate in detail, while not a few are quite novel patterns. There are two companion figures which will doubtless strike the most casual visitor. They are intended to represent "The Sower" and "The Reaper," the one in the act of scattering the seed on the earth, and the other standing erect and sharpening his scythe. Books of great variety, and covering a very wide field of literature, perfumes, and innumerable distilled essences, articles of *bijouterie*, with a score of etceteras, will be found in this department. On the floor above is displayed everything in the nature of house-furnishing goods. A cottage or a palace might be furnished out of this extensive mart.

A September 24, 1874 ad highlighting the Strauses' china department.

But, as has been stated, the principal attraction of the opening was the department devoted to china, glass-ware, and the like. You reach this department by descending a broad walnut staircase from the main building, and entering it, you find the most extensive stock of the kind which the City can boast. The new room which has been added to this department is about three times as large as that in which the business was formerly carried on, while both are well lighted, excellently finished, and, above all, abundantly stocked. When going through this portion of Macy & Co.'s extensive establishment, it would be advisable for the visitor to seek the good offices of Mr. Nathan Strauss, who has special charge of this department, and who will readily facilitate an inspection of the beautiful wares which it contains. Mr. Strauss has just returned from Europe with extensive purchases, having traveled through France, Germany, Austria, and Italy in quest of the finest specimens. The department, as stated, is subdivided into four branches, in which china, majolica, glass, and Parian wares are exhibited. The china ware is arranged in cases at the sides of the room, and is also displayed to good advantage on centre-tables running lengthwise. Among the most beautiful sets exhibited is a delicate pink, containing 300 pieces valued at $999. There is another very beautiful blue set, while there are several very handsome sets in Japanese ware, some again of neat French gray, and others exquisitely painted with clusters of fruit and bordered with different colors. Toilet sets are here in new and beautiful shades, and in great variety of design, and porcelain of wonderful beauty is also exhibited. The extent and variety of the exhibition are at once apparent, as it ranges from the most delicate Sevres to the homely but more useful pipkin. The majolica ware is unusually extensive, consisting of many designs in beautiful coloring. Particularly noticeable in this branch of the department are some very handsome cheese dishes and vases for conservatories. The glass-ware is also of great variety, both in respect to design and coloring. Epergnes for fruit and flowers, finger-bowls in various hues, and shallower than those manufactured here, are abundantly exhibited. Among the Venetian ware there is one particularly attractive article. It consists of a long, slender pitcher, with a dark snake-handle twining round it, the pitcher being connected with the base by a transparent dolphin, perfectly carved. It is of blended rainbow hues in a combination said to be inimitable in this country. It is alleged, at all events, that several houses have unsuccessfully tried to reproduce this glass. Here again is a filmy, transparent, sapphire-tinted glass, hemispherical in form, and joined to its delicate base by a dark, glittering, coiled serpent. Another beautiful piece is a small clock, supported by a female figure, perfectly molded, which when held to the light seems to catch the most delicate shades of the topaz, ruby, emerald, and sapphire. The Parian ware is also very beautiful, there being especially some large busts which commanded wide attention yesterday. It is interesting to know that these busts may be made from photographs, and are frequently executed to order abroad. These are some of the attractions which Macy & Co. exhibited at their Fall opening. It remains only to add that they do not favor a prohibitive tariff, but aim rather at popular prices.

A Fourteenth Street view, looking west (1873).

The corner of Sixth Avenue and Fourteenth Street (1883).

Nathan was only twenty-six years old when, with a wrapped package under his arm, he met Rowland Macy. The parcel contained two china plates— dishes that represented the goods which Straus wanted Macy's to stock. At first Rowland laughed at the idea, but Nathan was insistent and his family's reputation was good. Moreover, the young man from Georgia did not ask for very much beyond the opportunity to sell. After some negotiating, Nathan made his sale and Rowland agreed to lease the Straus family a 25-by-100-foot space in the basement of the building. Within a year, the venture had turned into a huge financial success. Even more unexpectedly, Lazarus and sons Nathan and Isidor became close friends with Rowland and Louisa Macy. According to Margaret Getchell's diary, the two families had Thanksgiving dinner together, celebrated the Fourth of July together, and even spent the summer at Rowland's country home. Despite the closed and bigoted spirit of the times, a family of New Englanders from Nantucket and German Jews from Bavaria had become friends. The union of the Macy and Straus clans was satisfying to all concerned.

By 1877, less than two decades after the establishment of R.H. Macy & Co., the business that had begun on a shoestring and bright hope was flourishing. Rowland had astutely assembled a group of exceptionally gifted partners, all of whom had contributed to the store's success. Margaret Getchell and Abiel LaForge were a dynamic retailing duo and led an enthusiastic and dedicated staff. Robert Valentine had channeled his own energy, drive, and discipline into building his uncle's business. New and profitable lines of merchandise had expanded the originally limited offerings of the store, and the addition of the Straus lines of china, glassware, and silver—the family offered the largest selection of china in the nation—had enhanced annual profits. Nobody realized that cruel events would soon shatter this union of talents.

A person of boundless energy, Nathan Straus found it difficult to spend his days in an office. Instead, he became L. Straus & Sons' energetic salesman. Visiting store after store, Nathan opened china and glassware concessions.

An October 25, 1874 ad featuring gloves made by Macy and LaForge.

Macy's main aisle.

A view from the Fourteenth Street staircase.

The silk department.

The original Macy's Sixth Avenue store was a small space—about twenty-five by a hundred feet—and as the business grew over time, this space was added to on a storefront-by-storefront basis as leases became available on neighboring properties. In 1869 alone, an extension doubled the size of the original store, and by the time of Rowland Macy's death in 1877, the emporium was composed of eleven buildings. This was not a massive, box-shaped department store, like those we know today, but an L-shaped series of structures that were adjacent to one another, but not always linked together by pass-throughs. Customers who wished to browse through several different departments would sometimes have to stroll out onto the sidewalk and re-enter another building to find the merchandise they sought. When pass-throughs were created, shoppers often had to step up or down as they moved from department to department. Because the various structures had not been built to form a single establishment, the floors were of slightly different heights.

To a degree, the growth of the original Macy's store reflected the evolution of the clothing industry itself. In the nation's early years, nearly all clothing was made at home by the family, with the remaining garments being produced by seamstresses and tailors. Thus, R.H. Macy's original inventory mostly consisted of the materials needed to make clothes—fabric, thread, needles, and patterns, for instance—as well as small finished items such as gloves, collars, and fancy cuffs. Undergarments, such as corsets and socks, could also be purchased ready-made during these early years. Over time, as larger finished goods such as dresses became available, they were added to Macy's stock, and the number of departments grew.

The Civil War had a profound effect on the ready-made clothing industry. At first, all military uniforms were made in workers' homes under government contract. But as the war progressed, factories were built to more efficiently meet the demands of the troops. This mass production of uniforms necessitated the development of standard sizes, which after the war were used to produce the first commercial sizing for men. Ready-made women's garments became available more slowly.

His Establishment, Unlike Any in the Country

Of course, Macy's sold far more than dry goods and clothing. By the 1870s, Rowland had drawn together an extensive assortment of quality merchandise that included confectionary, toiletry items, curtains, bed linens, toys, jewelry, books, stationery, paintings, sewing machines, soda water, lamps, clocks, statuettes, flatware, china, glassware—the list seems endless. In the first decade of the store's existence, the toy department alone expanded so much that R.H. Macy's became *the* toy store of Manhattan.

Rowland constantly reached out to the people of New York and surrounding areas by placing ads in popular newspapers, including *The New York Times, New York Herald, New York Tribune,* and *Brooklyn Daily Eagle.* His announcements advised readers of the many types of items available, made special mention of merchandise that had recently arrived, and pointed out that all of Macy's wares were available at "popular prices."

In the nineteenth century, most of the shoppers who frequented Macy's were women. These customers were not the poorest people in the city, for the poorest had little money with which to purchase items, but they were not the richest either, as women of the upper classes generally sent their servants to buy what was needed. So the crowds that flooded Rowland Macy's store, eagerly examining his growing line of goods, were composed of the growing middle class and the upper-middle class. Nevertheless, Macy's was open to all, and the inventive displays visible through its large plate-glass windows showed tempting wares to all passersby, rich and poor. So when members of the working class were able to save enough money (for Macy's was then a cash-only business), they would visit the store to make a purchase—perhaps a lace collar and cuffs for a very special occasion.

The growth and success of Rowland Macy's store was due in no small part to New York's swelling population. With the first great wave of immigrants arriving in 1845, and no end in sight—and with astounding economic growth as well—Rowland's city was teaming with people who needed, wanted, and were able to afford a variety of goods. For tens of thousands of people, Macy's, with its high-quality wares and low prices, was the place to shop.

The glove department.

A holiday doll exhibition.

Fine art and china.

OBITUARY.

ROWLAND H. MACY, MERCHANT.

The cable announces the death of Rowland H. Macy in Paris, on Thursday. He was the controlling member of the firm of R. H. Macy & Co., which for a number of years has done a popular trade in fancy dry goods at the corner of Sixth-avenue and Fourteenth-street. His energy and enterprise in business and the strict attention which he gave to every detail of it, gained for him a host of stanch friends. Laborious work during his best years brought him, at the age of 56, to a sick bed, suffering from Bright's disease of the kidneys, of which he died. He was advised by physicians and friends to take a trip to Europe, and he finally consented. About seven or eight weeks ago he left the City, accompanied by his wife and children, and since his arrival on the other side he resided mainly in Paris. His friends in this City know very little of his early history. He was a native of New-England, and was a sailor—a man-of-war's man some say—in his youthful days. He abandoned the sea and went into the dry goods business in Boston, and showed such foresight and discrimination that he made rapid advancement in that trade. After a while he embarked in business for himself, but in 1856 he, like many others, was forced to succumb to the pressure of an impending financial panic. In 1857 he came to this City and went into business in a small way on the very corner where the great store which bears his name is now situated. The first store he opened was only 17 by 40 feet in extent, and his stock was correspondingly small. A number of other dealers had been unfortunate in their ventures on that corner, and it was predicted by down-town merchants and others that Mr. Macy would meet with a similar fate. Coming from Boston as a stranger, he was looked upon as an adventurer, and he could command no credit. He braved all this opposition, however, and good luck attended him. With tact and pluck he first established his credit, and it was not long before he became known as a prudent, energetic, and painstaking merchant. He bought and sold on as extended a scale as his ready cash would allow, and he soon had the gratification of knowing, from the increase in his business, that the sentiments of those who predicted his speedy downfall had undergone some change. Wholesale merchants urged him to buy their commodities, and offered him credit without stint, but he refused to depart from the cash system which he adopted early in his career. When Mr. Macy went into business here, 20 years ago, he employed two or three assistants. When he died there were at least 400 persons working in his store. From £5 a day his receipts had grown into thousands. In fact, from comparatively nothing he became one of the best known and most successful merchants of the day. It is estimated that he leaves a fortune of $1,500,000. Persons in authority at his late place of business state that two years ago Mr. Macy entered into an agreement with R. M. Valentine and A. T. La Forge, his partners, whereby they should take immediate control of all his affairs in the event of death suddenly overtaking him; hence, his death will cause no material change in the management of the firm. He is especially regretted by all of the attachés of the house, who extol him as a fair-minded man, who dealt out even-handed justice to all. Nothing can be said about the disposition of the remains, except that they will certainly be brought here for interment.

OBITUARY NOTES.

Samuel McLaughlin, the noted "horse" man, and formerly driver for the late Mr. Vanderbilt, died at his home near Newburg, on Thursday night after a short illness. His disease was enlargement of the liver.

Edward S. Sayres, aged 77 years, died at his residence in Philadelphia on Thursday. Mr Sayres was for many years consul for Denmark, Sweden, and Brazil at the port of Philadelphia, and at the time of his death was Vice-Consul for Portugal.

TRAGEDY STRIKES R.H. MACY'S

Rowland H. Macy was recognized by one and all as "The Captain"—the man who was responsible for keeping the retail ship on course. Unfortunately, his health had begun to decline in 1870, and continued to worsen throughout the '70s. Early in 1877, Rowland's doctors advised him to take a vacation to restore his health. Rowland agreed and left for Europe, where one of his stops was to be Baden-Baden, Germany—an area known for its therapeutic hot mineral springs. But Rowland's recuperation was not to be. On March 29, 1877, with his wife by his side, Rowland Hussey Macy died in Paris at the age of fifty-four.

The sudden death of "Captain" Macy changed little in the management of the store he had built. Abiel LaForge and Robert Macy Valentine would carry on as co-partners, and papers were quickly drawn up and signed to formalize their business relationship. The new team agreed that for a period of time, the name of R.H. Macy's, well-known for nineteen years in New York City, would be retained. In time, though, the institution they led would become LaForge and Valentine's. But death respects no corporate plans and the Macy's name endures to this day.

Since his military service in the Civil War, Abiel T. LaForge had suffered bouts of tuberculosis of varying intensity. At times he was bedridden; at times he seemed to make a full recovery. As a health precaution, in 1876, Abiel and Margaret had begun making yearly trips to Palatka, Florida after the Christmas season so that Abiel could avoid the rigors of a New York winter. When the happy couple left New York by train for their annual vacation on January 28, 1878, they had no inkling that Abiel was ill. While en route, Abiel suffered the first of a series of hemorrhages and on February 11, 1878, he passed away. A grief-stricken Margaret wrote in her diary, "My loss is so great that I cannot bring myself to write the details of it." She and her five children, however, would not suffer financial hardship. Before Abiel and Margaret had left for Florida, Robert Valentine had told Abiel that in 1877, the store had grossed $1,873,205, with sales exceeding those of any previous year. On May 11, 1879, Margaret sold Abiel's share of the business to Robert for the sum of $82,500.

Macy's was now in the hands of Robert M. Valentine, and he was ready to take charge. Robert was not happy with all of the business decisions that had been made by his Uncle Rowland, and he planned major changes in the store's operation. He was not pleased

In 1877, the year that Rowland H. Macy died during a trip abroad, Rutherford B. Hayes took the oath of the presidency after a bitterly disputed election. Hayes worked hard to heal the wounds left by the Civil War, but generally failed at civil service reform. Having announced in advance that he would serve only one term, Hayes retired from office in 1881.

that L. Straus & Sons' china and glassware department was "going ahead so fast"; it was not an integral part of a dry goods emporium, and he did not like the atmosphere. Indeed, Robert was overheard saying that he would not renew the Strauses' contract to lease space in the store. But again death intervened, and Robert M. Valentine never acted on this decision. On February 15, 1879—a year after the death of partner Abiel LaForge—Robert died. He was only twenty-eight years of age.

The death of Robert M. Valentine placed Macy's in the hands of Charles B. Webster, a distant cousin of Rowland H. Macy and Robert M. Valentine. Webster's employment in the store had begun in 1876 when, for the weekly salary of ten dollars, he became a floorwalker, supervising sales personnel and helping with customer problems. Webster was family, and family counted for much in the Macy firmament, so after the death of Abiel T. LaForge in 1878, Webster—who by then had been promoted to a buyer—was made a partner in the firm. When less than a year later he became sole owner of Macy & Co., he did not have the experience needed to run the quickly growing business, and he knew it.

WEBSTER AND WHEELER TAKE THE REINS

On February 16, 1879—the day after Robert Valentine's death—Charles Webster gathered the store's employees together. "I will run this business or die in the attempt," said Macy's new owner. Yet Webster recognized that he needed assistance, and the man to whom Webster turned for help was Jerome B. Wheeler.

Jerome Wheeler was not only the brother-in-law of Robert M. Valentine, but was also noteworthy for his experience both in the military and in business. During the Civil War, he had enlisted as a private in the Sixth Regiment of the New York Cavalry and was rapidly promoted. Wheeler participated in nearly every battle of the Army of the Potomac, and in General Philip H. Sheridan's Shenandoah Valley Campaign, as well. After the war ended, Wheeler traveled to New York City, where he accepted a position at the firm of Holt and Company, a well-known commission merchant. There, too, Wheeler experienced great success, and after a time was admitted into the firm as a partner. Eventually, Wheeler retired from Holt and Company, and at the invitation of Charles Webster, he joined R.H. Macy's.

Charles Webster and Jerome Wheeler had somewhat different styles of management. Webster's employees described him as "a very dignified man," who every morning would walk silently through the store, making a mental note of anything that was amiss. He would then relay his observations to the superintendent of the store, who was expected to correct the situation. He

Accompanying Rowland and Louisa Macy on their final trip was Nathan Straus. The Strauses often visited Baden-Baden for "the cure," and may have suggested that Rowland stay there during his convalescence.

Although Rowland Macy was innovative in regard to retailing practices, he had old-fashioned prejudices against inventions such as the electric light. Therefore, it wasn't until more than a year after Rowland's death that Macy & Co. installed its first arc light outside the Sixth Avenue store. While not entirely dependable, this fixture—one of the first arc lamps to be seen in Manhattan—proved to be a big attraction.

Throughout much of the nineteenth century, the frock coat—with its knee-length skirt, long sleeves, center vent, and lapels—was a must for the fashionable gentleman. The coat was popularized by Prince Albert, consort to Queen Victoria.

In 1879, Thomas Edison improved upon a fifty-year-old idea and created a reliable, long-lasting incandescent light. The first public demonstration of this light was held in December 1979, when Edison illuminated his Menlo Park, New Jersey laboratory complex. During the next several years, Edison created the electric industry.

R. H. MACY & CO.

GRAND CENTRAL FANCY AND DRY GOODS ESTABLISHMENT.

14th Street, 6th Avenue, & 13th Street, New-York City.

The above cut gives a partial view of our department of Ladies', Misses', and Children's Shoes and Slippers.

This branch of our business, which was started only a few years ago as an experiment, is now one of the principal features of our establishment. Its success was assured from the start, and the rapidly increasing business has compelled us each year to enlarge and increase its facilities until now it is the largest store of the kind in the United States. In addition to the stock shown, we keep a large reserve of all styles, shapes, and sizes, so that it is almost impossible for a customer to ask for anything in the shape of a lady's shoe that we cannot immediately furnish.

We keep only first quality goods, purchase directly from the manufacturers, and sell at the lowest margin of profit, and if our shoes do not prove as represented, the money will be cheerfully refunded.

C. B. WEBSTER, *Firm.*
J. B. WHEELER,   R. H. MACY & CO.

An 1883 ad describing Macy's shoe and slipper department.

once said to a long-time employee, "I do not say much, but I have very good eyes." Although Webster was slow to make up his mind, once he gave an order, he expected it to be followed to the letter. He was also known as a patient, modest man who was kind to those who worked for him, but he preferred to manage from a distance.

Jerome Wheeler, on the other hand, was an affable and approachable man who was very popular with the employees. Rather than handling problems through the store's superintendent, Wheeler dealt directly with his employees and forged personal and professional relationships with them. They, in turn, actively sought his direction, and at times even confided in him.

Despite Webster and Wheeler's different personalities and management styles, they endeavored to work as a team in the running of the store. To a degree, they followed Rowland Macy's recipe for success by buying and selling for cash only. But unlike the store's founder, they did not use a great deal of advertising, perhaps because they thought it was of limited value, or perhaps because they felt that they could not write the fresh and imaginative copy that had helped Macy's to flourish during its early years. Because of this failing, as well as factors yet to be discussed, the store became somewhat less profitable during the Webster and Wheeler years. Many observers of the time said that the fact that Macy's survived at all was due to the momentum generated by its founder.

Interestingly, during the decade or so of Webster and Wheeler's ownership, the china department leased to L. Straus & Sons was the store's *most* profitable area, producing almost 20 percent of all sales. One reason for this was the Strauses' method of maintaining inventory. Webster and Wheeler kept inventories low so that they would tie up a minimum of cash. The downside of this policy was that customers were sometimes unable to find the items they sought, and would often purchase the items from one of the store's competitors, such as A.T. Stewart. The Strauses, on the other hand, believed in keeping their department fully stocked so that customers would have a wealth of items from which to choose. This approach proved highly successful.

TROUBLE IN PARADISE

The business partnership of Charles B. Webster and Jerome B. Wheeler, which had begun with so much optimism in 1879, was to end in 1888. While no one knows the exact order of the events that caused Wheeler to leave Macy's in 1888, we do know about several incidents that drove a wedge between the two men.

One problem arose over the employment of Martha Toye, who was initially hired as a floorwalker, and was promoted to superintendent of the store

In 1876, Charles B. Webster's father, Josiah Webster, had asked friend and relative Rowland Macy if his son could work in R.H. Macy's for a year or so. Josiah wanted Charles to get broad selling experience in the large Manhattan emporium before joining Josiah in his Providence, Rhode Island store. Fate intervened, and Charles Webster was to remain at Macy's for his entire retailing career.

During the mid- and late-1880s, the bustle reached its greatest proportions, extending almost straight out from the back of the waist. Often, it was ornamented with a profusion of frills, swags, drapes, and ribbons.

James A. Garfield took office as President on March 4, 1881, and served for only a few months before being assassinated on July 2, 1881. Known as the last of the log cabin Presidents, Garfield attacked political corruption and attempted to win back the respect that the presidency had lost during Reconstruction.

50

Macy's—The Store. The Star. The Story.

MR. WHEELER'S FAREWELL.

TAKING LEAVE OF HIS OLD ASSISTANTS AT MACY'S.

Jerome B. Wheeler, who has just retired from the firm of R. H. Macy & Co. in order to give his personal attention to his interests in the West, last evening entertained at his residence, 47 East Fifty-seventh-street, the buyers and heads of department of that house. There was a party of 21, including Miss Abbie Golden, the head cashier; James Bell, W. J. Burdett, J. H. Thompson, Miss Belle V. Cushman, Miss L. A. Brady, E. H. Jewett, S. P. Fletcher, E. H. Jewett, W. Pitt, the Superintendent; P. K. Terry, J. J. Duffy, W. J. Jeffrey, William Onderdonk, D. C. Bowne, J. W. Hutchinson, Amos MacDonald, W. A. Applegate. Joseph Wilcox, and M. H. Chase. After dinner Little, the recitationist, and Perry brothers, the bell ringers, gave an entertainment.

In bidding farewell to his former associates, Mr. Wheeler described the circumstances of his entering the firm, and ascribed the increase of business as due in great part to the ability, integrity, and loyalty of his guests. He had endeavored to treat employes as men and women, and not as mere machines, and in doing this had not sacrificed either dignity or discipline. The regret he felt at severing his connection with Macy's employes would be softened by the knowledge that the two gentlemen who were to enter the firm—Messrs. Isidor and Nathan Straus—were possessed not only of business foresight but of kindly hearts. Their alliance with the old firm meant the assurance of continued prosperity and a brilliant future for the great commercial organization of which they formed a part.

Mr. Wheeler has investments in coal and silver mines in Colorado, and his mining camp at Aspen has developed into a flourishing town, with electric lights, two railroads, water works, and smelting works. Mr. Wheeler is a native of Troy, and in early life moved to Waterford, N. Y. At the beginning of the war he enlisted as a private in the Sixth Regiment of New-York Cavalry, and was rapidly promoted. He participated in nearly all the battles of the Army of the Potomac and in Gen. Sheridan's campaign in the Shenandoah Valley. He attained a place on the staff of Major-Gen. Devin, where he remained till the close of the war. He came to New-York in 1866, and soon after accepted a position with Holt & Co., commission merchants. To this firm he was afterward admitted as a partner, retiring from it in 1879 to enter the firm of R. H. Macy & Co.

The January 3, 1888 article announcing Jerome Wheeler's retirement.

in 1886. Webster, who was responsible for Miss Toye's promotion, liked her because she kept the store clean and was quick to correct any problems. His support of Miss Toye makes perfect sense when you consider Webster's hands-off management style, which required the store's superintendent to directly deal with any problems that Webster had observed. Unfortunately, Miss Toye often did so at the expense of the staff's morale. Described as a "tall majestic woman, with a coldly handsome face and stern manner," Toye was disliked and feared by most Macy's employees. In one instance, she fired a cash girl because an inspection of her clothing revealed that she was "not clean." In another incident, she badly treated a scrubwoman, causing Miss Miller, head of stock for the Strauses' china department, to quit. Eventually, Toye's cruel management style prompted the staff to draw up a petition demanding that she be removed from her position, while Nathan Straus began threatening to pull his business out of the store if Toye was not fired.

Despite the problems caused by Toye, Webster continued to protect her. This baffled some members of the staff while causing others to believe that Webster was attracted to the superintendent. Webster could not always be on the premises, though, and while he was away on a buying trip in Europe, Wheeler took the opportunity to fire Toye—presumably because she had refused to carry out an assignment. Webster, returning from his trip, was predictably upset, and asked Isidor Straus for his counsel. When Isidor advised him not to rehire Toye, Webster instead financed the woman's acquisition of a millinery shop. As it turned out, the store failed and Toye was eventually rehired by Macy's, where she continued to work until her retirement. But the earlier years of her career had most assuredly caused friction between Webster and Wheeler.

Further tensions arose over Jerome Wheeler's investments out West. At some point, Wheeler had traveled to Colorado, where, using his profits from Macy's, he began to invest in various ventures, including a mineral water bottling plant, a cattle ranch, and several banks. He even helped finance the railroad's expansion to Pikes Peak.

Although Charles Webster was not happy that his partner was pulling money out of R.H. Macy's to finance outside business ventures, Wheeler refused to dissolve his other investments. Certainly, these enterprises had the potential to interfere with the business of running the New York department store. At

The modern three-piece men's suit evolved from the nineteenth-century *sack suit* or *business suit.* Originally large and baggy, this garment became more fitted during the latter part of the 1800s. A banker might wear a sack suit to a picnic, but a less prosperous man—who probably didn't own a frock coat—would consider the sack suit his Sunday best.

In the latter part of the 1800s, dress reformers widely criticized women's use of tight lacing in pursuit of a tiny waist. Strangely, many reformers believed that the corset itself was necessary for health and beauty, and objected only when women laced the garment too tightly.

one point, Webster became gravely ill while traveling in Europe. Although Webster's wife had cabled the store to say that her husband might not recover, Wheeler was planning to immediately leave for Colorado, where his fortunes had begun to decline. A Macy's employee convinced Wheeler to stay and attend to business at home, but the rift between Wheeler and Webster continued to widen.

At the end of 1887, as Jerome Wheeler's western investments continued to deteriorate, he decided to sell his interest in the firm to Charles Webster and Webster's brother. It was decided, too, that a Macy's accountant by the name of Terry would join the partnership. This seemed like an excellent move for the company, as Terry had been a faithful and capable employee for many years. Perhaps just as important, he was well liked by the staff, being "patient and kind to everyone."

But Terry never became a partner. Soon after Wheeler made his decision to leave the company, Terry admitted to Wheeler that he had embezzled nearly $10,000 of the firm's money. Although Wheeler first hesitated to share this confidence with Webster, he realized that Webster had to know about Terry's actions. Webster was therefore informed, and Terry soon left the employ of Macy & Co. No one else was implicated in the embezzlement.

On January 3, 1888, an article appeared in *The New York Times* describing a dinner that marked the end of Jerome Wheeler's association with R.H. Macy's. But even as Wheeler left the stage, new players entered, for the previous day, the *New York Herald* had announced that Isidor and Nathan Straus were now partners in the firm of R.H. Macy & Co. The Strauses had bought a 45-percent interest in the store.

The first thirty years of R.H. Macy & Co. had been exciting and eventful, but also tumultuous. The store most certainly had flourished and made a name for itself in the bustling metropolis, but with the death of R.H. Macy and his initial team of hand-picked leaders, it had lost the creativity and strong management it needed to survive in a city characterized by tough competition and continual change. Would the Strauses be able to provide the direction that Macy's needed? In 1888, loyal Macy's customers and staff could only watch and wait.

Jerome Wheeler became aware of Colorado's Pikes Peak in 1883, when he brought his wife there to enjoy the mineral springs of Manitou. Impressed with the area, he not only backed the Colorado Midland Railroad but also built the Wheeler Block—a three-story building that included a bank and an opera house.

Bonnets of the 1880s were relatively small and worn high on the back of the head, away from the face. Typically, they were ornamented with ribbons, pleated velvets, vibrantly colored plumes, lace, and silk flowers.

Grover Cleveland took the office of the presidency in 1885 and served until 1889 in the first of two nonconsecutive terms. The first Democrat elected after the Civil War, Cleveland vigorously pursued a policy barring special favors to any economic group.

Shoppers crowd the street outside R.H. Macy & Co., 1890s.

3.
Enter the Strauses

It was 1888, and New York City was continuing to expand, change, and thrive. The upper classes had never been more prosperous, but there was also much opportunity for the city's growing number of working immigrants, who were eager to succeed in their new home. In 1883, the Brooklyn Bridge had been completed, tying together Manhattan and Brooklyn, and making inevitable the creation of the Greater City of New York. Every year, more people poured into the metropolis, and as New York merchants knew, everyone—from established Manhattan families to the newest Castle Garden arrivals—needed and demanded goods.

Against this backdrop, Isidor and Nathan Straus became partners in R.H. Macy & Co., one of New York's first and foremost department stores. Since 1874, the Strauses had run Macy's china and glass department, the most profitable division of the store. While the brothers had certainly demonstrated a unique talent for retailing, it was not known if they could successfully take the helm of a business that was already of considerable magnitude, but that for some time had been without truly inspired leadership. Fortunately for New York's growing population, the Strauses would not only usher in a new and exciting chapter of Macy's history, but also make changes that would forever transform the world of retailing.

The Brooklyn Bridge nearing completion in the 1880s.

The twenty-third President of the United States, Benjamin Harrison entered the White House in 1889 and served one term, leaving office in 1893. Known as the "centennial president" because his inauguration marked the hundred-year anniversary of George Washington's first term, Harrison is perhaps best known for signing the Sherman Antitrust Act, which was the first federal law designed to protect trade and commerce.

The City of Greater New York was officially created on January 1, 1898, when New York City annexed land from surrounding areas. The newly formed metropolis was comprised of five boroughs—Manhattan, the Bronx, Brooklyn, Queens, and Staten Island (Richmond County)—and included 3.4 million people.

The Straus Family

Lazarus and Sara Straus.

Lazarus Straus was born in Otterberg, Germany in 1809. In 1852, seeking a better life after the failed Revolution of 1848, Lazarus Straus emigrated to the United States, where he was eventually joined by the rest of his family—wife Sara; daughter Hermina; and sons Isidor, Nathan, and Oscar. The Strauses settled in a modest two-room house in Talbotton, Georgia. Thus began the amazing story of the family's success in America.

Lazarus Straus first sold dry goods from a pushcart, but was soon able to open a small dry goods store. To stock his store, Lazarus brought a great deal of merchandise from Philadelphia wholesalers and importers, but during the Civil War, all of that trade, as well as all communication with the North, was cut off. Over time, Lazarus Straus incurred debt with northern businesses.

In June 1863, eighteen-year-old Isidor Straus, the eldest of the sons, was sent to Europe, where he hoped to build blockade-running ships that would sell cotton in Europe. Although circumstances made this venture impossible, Isidor—young, but intelligent and fiercely determined to succeed—remained in Europe throughout the American conflict, earning $12,000 in gold by trading in bonds.

Lazarus Straus had long intended to move his family to Philadelphia after the Civil War. But when Isidor returned from Europe, he convinced his father to try his luck in New York City. Lazarus arrived in Manhattan in 1865. He had with him about $25,000, which was just a bit more than he needed to pay his debts. Almost immediately, Straus began calling on his creditors to ask what he owed. Virtually all the creditors had written off their debts by

Isidor and Nathan Straus.

In 1888, George Eastman offered the "Kodak" camera for sale. This easy-to-use device, which featured a fixed-focus lens and single shutter speed, had a low price that appealed to the average consumer. Within a few years, Eastman had created a full line of cameras.

During the 1880s and 1890s, the bicycle—originally, a dangerous toy for daring young men—became an everyday mode of transportation for both men and women. The "safety bicycle," invented in 1885, featured equal-size wheels, a steerable front wheel, and a chain drive, making it possible for anyone to use and enjoy it.

then, but Lazarus insisted on paying them back with interest. The creditors were more than a bit astonished, and the Straus name became as good as gold.

After satisfying their debts, the Strauses had about $6,000 with which to found a new company. By using this cash as well as their excellent reputation, they launched L. Straus & Son, a china, glassware, and silver wholesaling business. The "Son" was Isidor. Nathan joined the firm later, becoming the business's enthusiastic outside salesman. At that point, the younger Straus opened a selling office for the firm in Chicago, traveled throughout the United States to seek additional markets, and scoured Europe for new wares. Nathan was full of energy and was a wellspring of ideas, both good and bad. Older brother Isidor patiently sorted through Nathan's many plans and schemes, and made the best ones work. Despite the brothers' different personalities—or, perhaps, because of them—the partnership was to prove unbeatable.

L. Straus & Sons prospered from the start, grossing about $60,000 the first year and eventually becoming one of the most extensive glassware and china import houses in the United States. At first, the Strauses sold their wares to the newly emerging department stores. They then operated leased china and glass departments not only in Macy's, but also in Wanamaker's of Philadelphia, Pennsylvania, and Woodward & Lorthrop in Washington, DC. The Straus name became well known and highly respected throughout the United States and in many areas of Europe, as well.

Lazarus, Isidor, and Nathan Straus leased a space in R.H. Macy & Co. for thirteen years before becoming partners in the firm in 1888. At that time, the Strauses' department was the most profitable in the store, generating a whopping 20 percent of Macy's sales. And this dynamic family was just getting started.

Ida and Isidor Straus's wedding photo.

Lina and Nathan Straus's wedding photo.

During the late 1880s, most dresses had a high collar, a tight-fitting bodice, long tight sleeves, a long v-shaped waist, a large shelf-like bustle, and an asymmetrically draped skirt with a street-length hem. Worn with a high-crowned hat, this fashion created a sense of exaggerated slimness and height.

In 1888, actress Sarah Bernhardt wore fashions from the Directoire period while starring in *Tosca*. This led to a new trend of shorter waists coupled with undraped, relatively simple skirts. One fashion editor applauded the Directoire style, saying that women were weary of arranging the draperies of the earlier fashion.

R. H. MACY & CO. | R. H. MACY & CO.

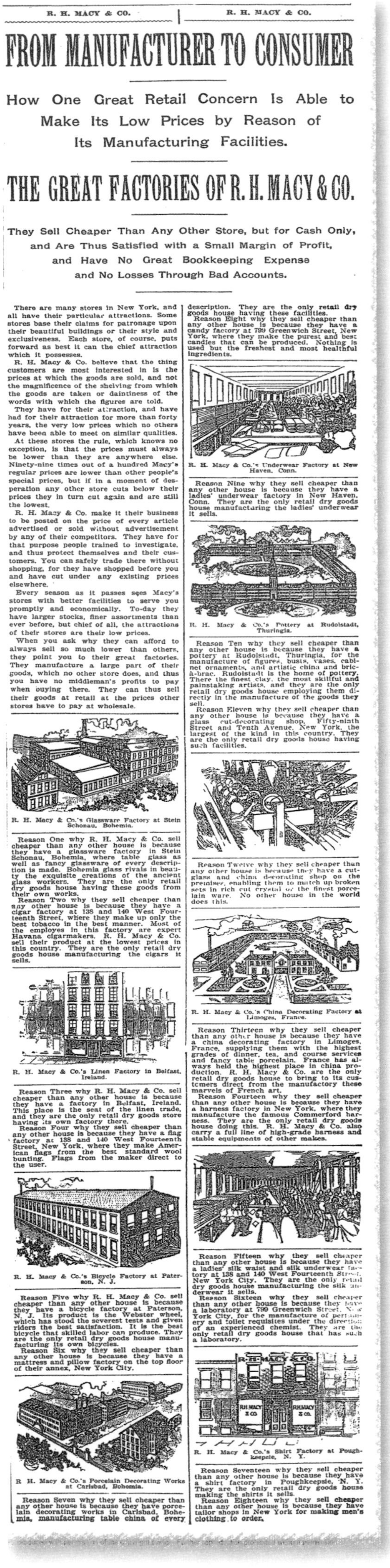

FROM MANUFACTURER TO CONSUMER

How One Great Retail Concern Is Able to Make Its Low Prices by Reason of Its Manufacturing Facilities.

THE GREAT FACTORIES OF R. H. MACY & CO.

They Sell Cheaper Than Any Other Store, but for Cash Only, and Are Thus Satisfied with a Small Margin of Profit, and Have No Great Bookkeeping Expense and No Losses Through Bad Accounts.

There are many stores in New York, and all have their particular attractions. Some stores base their claims for patronage upon their beautiful buildings or their style and exclusiveness. Each store, of course, puts forward as best it can the chief attraction which it possesses.

R. H. Macy & Co. believe that the thing customers are most interested in is the prices at which the goods are sold, and not the magnificence of the shelving from which the goods are taken or daintiness of the words with which the figures are told.

They have for their attraction, and have had for their attraction for more than forty years, the very low prices which no others have been able to meet on similar qualities.

At these stores the rule, which knows no exception, is that the prices must always be lower than they are anywhere else. Ninety-nine times out of a hundred Macy's regular prices are lower than other people's special prices, but if in a moment of desperation any other store cuts below their prices they in turn cut again and are still the lowest.

R. H. Macy & Co. make it their business to be posted on the price of every article advertised or sold without advertisement by any of their competitors. They have for that purpose people trained to investigate, and thus protect themselves and their customers. You can safely trade there without shopping, for they have shopped before you and have cut under any existing prices elsewhere.

Every season as it passes sees Macy's stores with better facilities to serve you promptly and economically. To-day they have larger stocks, finer assortments than ever before, but chief of all, the attractions of their stores are their low prices.

When you ask why they can afford to always sell so much lower than others, they point you to their great factories. They manufacture a large part of their goods, which no other store does, and thus you have no middleman's profits to pay when buying there. They can thus sell their goods at retail at the prices other stores have to pay at wholesale.

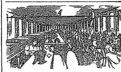

R. H. Macy & Co.'s Glassware Factory at Stein Schonau, Bohemia.

Reason One why R. H. Macy & Co. sell cheaper than any other house is because they have a glassware factory in Stein Schonau, Bohemia, where table glass as well as fancy glassware of every description is made. Bohemia glass rivals in beauty the exquisite creations of the ancient glass workers. They are the only retail dry goods house having these goods from their own works.

Reason Two why they sell cheaper than any other house is because they have a cigar factory at 138 and 140 West Fourteenth Street, where they make up only the best tobacco in the best manner. Most of the employes in this factory are expert Havana cigarmakers. R. H. Macy & Co. sell their product at the lowest prices in this country. They are the only retail dry goods house manufacturing the cigars it sells.

R. H. Macy & Co.'s Linen Factory in Belfast, Ireland.

Reason Three why R. H. Macy & Co. sell cheaper than any other house is because they have a factory in Belfast, Ireland. This place is the seat of the linen trade, and they are the only retail dry goods store having its own factory there.

Reason Four why they sell cheaper than any other house is because they have a flag factory at 138 and 140 West Fourteenth Street, New York, where they make American flags from the best standard wool bunting. Flags from the maker direct to the user.

R. H. Macy & Co.'s Bicycle Factory at Paterson, N. J.

Reason Five why R. H. Macy & Co. sell cheaper than any other house is because they have a bicycle factory at Paterson, N. J. Its product is the Webster wheel, which has stood the severest tests and given riders the best satisfaction. It is the best bicycle that skilled labor can produce. They are the only retail dry goods house manufacturing its own bicycles.

Reason Six why they sell cheaper than any other house is because they have a mattress and pillow factory on the top floor of their annex, New York City.

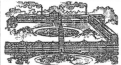

R H. Macy & Co.'s Porcelain Decorating Works at Carlsbad, Bohemia.

Reason Seven why they sell cheaper than any other house is because they have porcelain decorating works in Carlsbad, Bohemia, manufacturing table china of every description. They are the only retail dry goods house having these facilities.

Reason Eight why they sell cheaper than any other house is because they have a candy factory at 799 Greenwich Street, New York, where they make the purest and best candies that can be produced. Nothing is used but the freshest and most healthful ingredients.

R. H. Macy & Co.'s Underwear Factory at New Haven, Conn.

Reason Nine why they sell cheaper than any other house is because they have a ladies' underwear factory in New Haven, Conn. They are the only retail dry goods house manufacturing the ladies' underwear it sells.

R. H. Macy & Co.'s Pottery at Rudolstadt, Thuringia.

Reason Ten why they sell cheaper than any other house is because they have a pottery at Rudolstadt, Thuringia, for the manufacture of figures, busts, vases, cabinet ornaments, and artistic china and bric-à-brac. Rudolstadt is the home of pottery. There the finest clay, the most skillful and painstaking artists, and they are the only retail dry goods house employing them directly in the manufacture of the goods they sell.

Reason Eleven why they sell cheaper than any other house is because they have a glass cut-decorating shop, Fifty-ninth Street and Tenth Avenue, New York, the largest of the kind in this country. They are the only retail dry goods house having such facilities.

Reason Twelve why they sell cheaper than any other house is because they have a cut-glass and china decorating shop on the premises, enabling them to match up broken sets in rich cut crystal or the finest porcelain ware. No other house in the world does this.

R. H. Macy & Co.'s China Decorating Factory at Limoges, France.

Reason Thirteen why they sell cheaper than any other house is because they have a china decorating factory in Limoges, France, supplying them with the highest grades of dinner, tea, and course services and fancy table porcelain. France has always held the highest place in china production. R. H. Macy & Co. are the only retail dry goods house to bring to its customers direct from the manufactory these marvels of French art.

Reason Fourteen why they sell cheaper than any other house is because they have a harness factory in New York, where they manufacture the famous Commerford harness. They are the only retail dry goods house doing this. R. H. Macy & Co. also carry a full line of high-grade harness and stable equipments of other makes.

Reason Fifteen why they sell cheaper than any other house is because they have a ladies' silk waist and silk underwear factory at 138 and 140 West Fourteenth Street, New York City. They are the only retail dry goods house manufacturing the silk underwear it sells.

Reason Sixteen why they sell cheaper than any other house is because they have a laboratory at 790 Greenwich Street, New York City, for the manufacture of perfumery and toilet requisites under the direction of an experienced chemist. They are the only retail dry goods house that has such a laboratory.

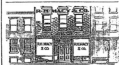

R. H. Macy & Co.'s Shirt Factory at Poughkeepsie, N. Y.

Reason Seventeen why they sell cheaper than any other house is because they have a shirt factory in Poughkeepsie, N. Y. They are the only retail dry goods house making the shirts it sells.

Reason Eighteen why they sell cheaper than any other house is because they have tailor shops in New York for making men's clothing to order.

THE STRAUSES TAKE MACY'S BY STORM

The Strauses were more than eager to join in the running of Macy's along with co-partner Charles B. Webster. Between 1879 and 1888, no one with strong merchandising experience had been at the helm of the large company, and while the store had not only stayed afloat but actually managed to grow, its progress had been neither rapid nor especially noteworthy. The Straus brothers announced that they would work towards restoring the traditions established by Rowland H. Macy. Isidor was the organization man, while Nathan was the promoter. The youngest brother, Oscar, chose not to work in the family business, opting instead for a life in public service—a decision wholeheartedly supported by Isidor and Nathan.

On January 14, 1888, less than two weeks after the *New York Herald* announced the new partnership, Isidor Straus wrote to his brother Oscar, "I am spending my time entirely uptown so as to familiarize [myself] with the working of everything, it is an exceedingly pleasant task as all the surroundings are happy in the extreme." On Charles Webster, he added, "Charley and myself constitute the firm, we seem by instinct determined that we all get a lot of fun and agreeable episodes out of each day's hours."

The Strauses began by creating a ten-year plan that would take the store to 1898 and beyond. Part of their strategy involved selling items that were specially manufactured under the Macy's brand. By eliminating the middleman, the Strauses knew that they could charge the lowest prices in town while still maintaining excellent quality. Immediately, they began leasing factories both in the United States and abroad, and commissioning the production of goods from existing manufacturers. By 1898, Macy's was able to boast that it had cigars, American flags, mattresses and pillows, shirts, candy, and harnesses produced in New York; bicycles manufactured in Patterson, New Jersey; glassware and porcelain made in Bohemia; ladies underwear made in New Haven, Connecticut; linen woven in Belfast, Ireland; and china produced in Limoges, France.

The Strauses also kept prices low by seeking out new overseas imports. Most astonishing to the modern consumer is that, in time, they would hire armies of comparison shoppers to constantly check on the competition. They considered it their responsibility—not that of their customers—to know the prices for which items were selling and offer them for less.

Oscar Wilde's *The Picture of Dorian Gray* caused quite a stir when it appeared in *Lippincott's Monthly Magazine* on June 20, 1890. Although the short novel was originally viewed as being "unclean" and "contaminating," it is now considered a modern classic.

The Art of the Strauses

When Nathan Straus walked into R.H. Macy & Co. in 1874, Rowland Macy could see that he was an ambitious and energetic young man. What he could not have guessed was that Nathan, along with father Lazarus and brother Isidor, would not only immeasurably add to the store's profits, but also enhance the company's reputation by presenting the public with some of the most beautiful, high-quality glassware and china available.

Very soon after the Strauses' department opened in the basement of Macy's, it became known as the city's most extensive display of china, pottery, Majolica, and glass. It also received high praise in New York's newspapers. A *New York Times* article published in 1887 stated, "There is probably no better place in the country to study the character,

An egg-shaped punch bowl.

the gracefulness of outline, the delicacy of blending shades and quiet and brilliant colorings in pottery and glassware than at R.H. Macy & Co." The *Times* writer praised all of the Strauses' wares, but called particular attention to the glass. "The line of cut and engraved glass tableware is deserving of more than a passing reference, as the cutting and engraving is done on the premises by the most skilled and celebrated artisans," said reporter Richard Spenlow.

For a period of several years, L. Straus & Sons had glass-cutting operations both in Macy's and at 14 Jay Street in New York City, and often won prizes for its designs. In 1893, six prestigious awards were conferred on the Strauses at the World's Columbian Exposition in Chicago. The certificate reads, in part: "The designs are original, very handsome, and most skillfully executed. The cutting is bold, the shape angles are well kept, the workmanship is perfect, and the polish excellent. . . . All this work calls forth the highest tributes to American skill and originality in concept."

L. Straus & Sons did not engrave its glass with the company's name, but instead affixed a paper label to each piece. Because paper labels can be lost over time, not all present owners of the Strauses' work are aware of its origin. But at the turn of the century, discerning shoppers knew that the finest and most fashionable glassware and china was produced by the Strauses, and was to be found at R.H. Macy & Co.

A tiered centerpiece with "Isabella" pattern.

R. H. Macy & Co.
Straus Cut Glass, 1880 – 1902
6th Avenue and 14th Street, NYC, NY

1892-93 Catalogue, back cover
Courtesy of Macy*s Department Store

R.H. Macy's 1892–1893 catalogue
advertising the Strauses' cut glass.

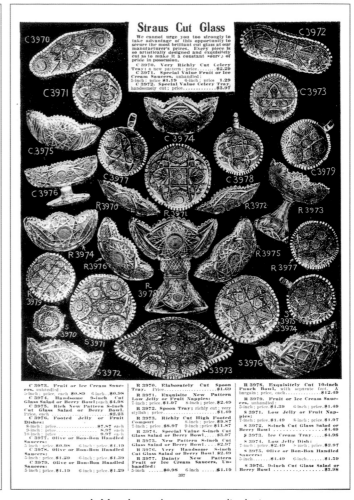

A Macy's catalogue page displaying
the Strauses' glass creations.

Under the Straus family's direction, the store's offerings were enlarged by the opening of new departments. Harnesses and saddlery were added in 1889; groceries, in 1893; liquor and wine, in 1895; and a furniture department, in 1896.

The Strauses also oversaw the continuing physical expansion of R.H. Macy's. In January of 1889, Isidor struck a deal to rent the "Meyers" store on Thirteenth Street at $3,500 per year for five years, and an option for another five years at the same price. The plan was to expand the two upper floors for more sales space and add three passenger elevators. Additional buildings were erected in 1892 and 1893, each time generating further interest in the rapidly growing house of Macy & Co.

In 1896, Macy's attracted attention yet again by erecting a new building on Fourteenth Street, directly across from the store's main structure. A six-story edifice with a front of eighty feet and a depth of over two hundred feet, this addition was reported in the September 13, 1896 *New York Times* as being "larger than most retail stores are in their entirety." The new building

In September 1895—more than ten years before Henry Ford put the Model T on American roads—Macy's attracted crowds of people with its exhibition of two "French horseless pleasure carriages." According to *The New York Times*, because of their lightness, the carriages were of doubtful utility in transporting goods. As pleasure vehicles, however, they seemed practical, safe, and rapid, maintaining a speed of sixteen to twenty miles an hour on good roads. This helped explain the "fancy price" of $1,200.

As the 1890s began, women's skirts widened and flared. At the same time, the bustle began to diminish in size, and finally disappeared. Leg of mutton sleeves—first popular in the 1830s—made a comeback, eventually swelling into great puffs that extended high above the shoulders.

Ellis Island began accepting immigrants to the United States on January 1, 1892, and processed nearly 12 million people before closing operations on November 12, 1954. Centuries before, the island had been part of a federal system of coastal fortifications that protected New York from the British.

was devoted to "masculine needs"—ready-made mens' clothing, bicycle sundries, neckware, hosiery, underwear, boots, shoes, and hats. The main store was already quite crowded, and Macy's advised men that this annex would not only make it easier for them to buy garments and other supplies, but also render it unnecessary to wait their turn at the counter with women. Catering both to the man who had to make purchases and to the gentleman who sought a retreat from the hustle and bustle of the city, Macy's even offered a large reading and smoking room complete with magazines, newspapers, and stationery.

The Strauses' early years of partnership were not without obstacles. In 1893, the nation was hit by the worst economic depression it had yet experienced. Many blamed the crisis on the Sherman Silver Purchase Act of 1890. The act, which was intended to boost the economy, required the US government to purchase additional silver each month with notes that could be redeemed with silver or gold. This plan backfired when investors turned in silver treasury notes for gold dollars, depleting the government's gold reserves. The Panic of 1893, which followed, resulted in a series of bank failures as well as the failure of several railroads. All in all, over 500 banks and 15,000 companies collapsed—many in the West—and at the peak of the panic, 17 to 19 percent of the nation's work force was unemployed. The panic also caused a series of debilitating strikes, including the Pullman Strike of July 1894, which shut down much of the nation's transportation system.

Letters exchanged between the Straus brothers tell us that Nathan and Isidor were deeply concerned about the economic situation, about the suffering population, and, of course, about their own business. On August 4 of 1893, Isidor informed Nathan, "Mills and factories are shutting down . . . that carries with it a tremendous suffering of laboring people that are out of employment." In that same letter, Isidor advised his brother to curtail production and shipments.

Interestingly, Isidor Straus was a friend of President Grover Cleveland, and may have been instrumental in starting the nation on the road to recovery. Charles Webster, the Strauses' co-partner, urged Isidor to travel to Washington, DC and meet with the President to discuss the financial crisis. Isidor finally agreed, and in the summer of 1893, he strongly advised Cleveland to repeal the Sherman Silver Purchase Act. The extent of Isidor's influence is not known, but in August, under significant pressure from the President, Congress rescinded the law.

A September 13, 1896 article announcing Macy's new annex for "masculine needs."

PLACE OF TRADE FOR MEN

NEW BUILDING TO BE OPENED BY R. H. MACY & CO.

Male Buyers Will No Longer Have to Struggle About the Main Store to Get Their Supplies—A Large Room Wherein They May Lounge, Read the Papers, and Write Letters—Rapid Growth of the House of Macy.

The expansion of retail trade in the district around Fourteenth Street has had its newest illustration in the erection of a new building by R. H. Macy & Co. on Fourteenth Street, directly opposite the firm's main structure. This old and famous house evidently does not apprehend that the centre of the shopping district will in many years be shifted from their corner, since the new building they will open to-morrow is larger than most retail stores are in their entirety, having a front on Fourteenth Street of 80 feet, and running through to Fifteenth Street, a depth of 206 feet, with six stories and a basement.

The house of Macy started thirty-eight years ago in a little corner store at Fourteenth Street and Sixth Avenue, with a force of one clerk, besides the proprietor, and its first day's sales amounted to $1.11. The house has grown until it covers an entire block on Sixth Avenue, stretching back 250 feet on Fourteenth Street, and also occupies a ten-story building, covering four lots, on Thirteenth Street, while some time ago the cigar and liquor departments were housed in a separate building on Fifteenth Street. Even these quarters have proved inadequate, and the inconvenience of heaping the main structure further skyward has led to the firm's recent move, the erection of the fine new building that will be open to the public to-morrow.

The new Macy store occupies the site of the old Scotch Presbyterian Church, on the north side of Fourteenth Street, and is six stories high, fire-proof, with walls of brick and iron, marble stairways, and hardwood floors. It is lighted throughout by electricity and heated by steam. The ceilings are lofty, and the salesrooms present a most airy and inviting appearance. With the exception of a floor set aside for furniture—a new department just added to Macy & Co.'s business—the building is devoted altogether to masculine needs, and it will no longer be necessary for men to await their turn at the counter with women in purchasing articles of men's wear.

The ground floor, from Fourteenth to Fifteenth Street, is devoted to men's ready-made clothing, with bicycle sundries, neckwear, hosiery, and underwear in front, and in the rear boots and shoes and hats. A new departure for the accommodation of the male patrons of the store is found on the second floor, where a room 50 feet by 30 feet is set apart as a reading room for men, supplied with the magazines and daily papers and conveniences for smoking. Writing tables and stationery are also among the furnishings of the room, which is planned to provide a pleasant and luxurious lounging place. The remainder of the floor contains the bicycle and sporting goods departments, and the third floor is devoted entirely to furniture.

The three upper stories have not yet been set apart to any purpose. They will be employed as stock rooms for the present, and probably in the future some of the departments in the main store that need enlarged space will be taken over there. The effect of the opening of this annex will at once be seen in the increased convenience of buyers in the main building, where the pressure will be much reduced by the removal of much of the custom to the more spacious quarters in the annex and the increased space thus placed at the disposal of the other departments.

It is well known that R. H. Macy & Co. sell only for cash. They also buy exclusively for cash, and thus, neither giving nor taking credit, are able to give their customers the benefit of all the saving that results from a strictly cash system. Another factor in making their prices low is the extent to which they manufacture their own goods. The house of Macy has its own porcelain works in Carlsbad, Bohemia; its own pottery in Rudolstadt, Thuringia; its own china factory in Limoges, France; its own glassware factory in Steinschonau, Bohemia; its own linen factory in Belfast, Ireland; its own handkerchief house in St. Gall, Switzerland; its own designers in Paris; its own ladies' underwear, silk waist, and skirt factories in New-York, Brooklyn, and New-Haven; its own glass cutting factory on the premises; its own chemical laboratory at 790 Greenwich Street; its own harness factory at 185 Sixth Avenue; its own cigar factory in Poughkeepsie, and its own bicycle factory in Paterson, N. J.

A March 26, 1889 article advising ladies about Macy's "seasonal novelties."

The Ladies' Mile

Although R.H. Macy & Co. was a well-known and successful store in the 1880s and '90s, it was by no means the only store in the area that offered high-quality clothing, household items, and other goods. In fact, the original Macy's was part of the "Ladies' Mile," a shopping center so named because most of the people who frequented it were women.

The Ladies' Mile extended from Eighth Street to Twenty-Third Street, along Sixth Avenue and Broadway. The seeds of the Mile were sown in 1846 with the opening of Manhattan's first department store, A.T. Stewart's. Within a decade or so, Stewart's was joined by R.H. Macy & Co., and eventually, the Mile also hosted retailing giants such as Arnold Constable, B. Atlman's, Best & Co., Siegel-Cooper, W. & J. Sloane, and Wanamaker's. But dozens of smaller stores also competed for the business of eager shoppers, who traveled to the area by foot, by carriage, or—after 1878—by the elevated train, or "el." For many of the women who flocked to the Mile, shopping was not just a necessity but also a diversion from everyday life. Through New York's stores and the varied merchandise they displayed, women caught a glimpse of the world beyond home and family, and even found employment. In fact, the majority of workers on the Ladies' Mile were female.

As shopping became more popular, savvy storekeepers added amenities—-restaurants, restrooms, coat checks, and even nurseries—to their emporiums. The stores grew in splendor as well, becoming virtual palaces of retailing. An 1893 handbook extolled the wonders of the Ladies' Mile:

> All America goes to New York for its shopping, when it can. . . . The brightness of Broadway, the vivacity of lower Fifth Avenue, the sparkle of 23rd Street, are made up of the splendid temptations of the shop windows, and the groups of charming people who linger about them spellbound. . . . What are the Paris boulevards, or even Regent Street, to this magnificent panorama of mercantile display?

South Manhattan's "panorama of mercantile display" continued to be a draw until the turn of the century, when retailing began to move uptown. But the buildings that housed fine merchants such as Macy's remain to this day, providing a link to the Gilded Age, when the finest objects sold in America lured New Yorkers to the Ladies' Mile.

CONTINUING A TRADITION— MACY'S CHRISTMAS STORE

Although the Strauses were determined to enlarge and improve R.H. Macy & Co., they well understood the importance of maintaining the much-beloved traditions that had long attracted shoppers. One of the most popular of these was the store's extravagant Christmas displays.

From the opening of the New York store, Christmas was an important season for Macy's, as it was for most other retailers. Rowland Macy always held his "Holiday Opening" at the start of December, and continued to advertise until the end of the season, when he announced his after-Christmas sales. Margaret Getchell has been credited with suggesting special late hours on Christmas Eve of 1868, so that shoppers could make last-minute purchases. The new hours were so successful that Macy's began staying open late—until half past nine—throughout the month of December. At the turn of the century, the Strauses extended the evening hours to ten o'clock.

Although early Macy's Christmas ads made mention of special holiday wares for every member of the family, they placed particular emphasis on dolls and other toys. The Strauses made sure to highlight the fact that Macy's

During his years as President of the United States, Grover Cleveland was one of the many distinguished people who visited the original Macy's store. Several times, he brought with him the Secretary of the Treasury, John G. Carlisle. Financier Russell Sage was another loyal Macy's customer.

Admiring crowds view Macy's dazzling holiday window displays.

A December 13, 1901 ad for the "glamour" and "brilliance" of Macy's Christmas Store.

was "a Christmas Store for the Young and the Old"—not just for kids. In addition to toys of all types, they advertised luxurious men's and women's slippers, as well as fine men's dress coats, dress suits, and a range of other gifts suitable for adults. They also offered Macy's as an antidote to weariness caused by "the drudgeries of life." A trip to Macy's Christmas Store, they promised, would lift the spirits of even the most jaded shopper.

Of course, the people of New York City traveled to Macy's for more than just shopping, for Macy's was also famous for its enchanting holiday windows. In the mid-1870s, Rowland Macy had caused a stir by replacing the holly-decorated Christmas merchandise usually displayed in his Fourteenth Street windows with an imaginatively arranged collection of dolls. Illumination with electric lights soon followed, and Macy's quickly became *the* store to stroll by during the Christmas season. The Strauses continued this tradition, ensuring that generations of New Yorkers would make Macy's a yearly holiday destination.

EMPLOYEE WELFARE PROGRAMS

Throughout much of their lives, Isidor and Nathan Straus were active philanthropists, and their concern for others was clearly reflected in their day-to-day conduct at Macy's. The Straus brothers were hard workers and demanded equal dedication from their staff, but they also showed true affection and caring for all those who worked at their ever-expanding business. Just as they would bundle themselves up in the midst of a snowstorm to make their way to the store, Isidor and Nathan would go to great trouble to visit an employee who was ill or to attend the funeral of a long-time worker of L. Straus & Sons. If one of the brothers noticed that a Macy's employee seemed troubled or unwell, he would enquire about the problem and then provide any assistance that was needed, whether it was additional money, a new suit of clothes, or the services of a physician. This sincere interest created a warm family feeling and esprit de corps that was long remarked upon by Macy's employees, who usually addressed the Strauses as "Mr. Isidor" and "Mr. Nathan."

But the Strauses did more than offer support to the occasional worker; they also created policies and programs that gave their employees practical help both on a daily basis and in times of greater need. Nathan and Isidor Straus became the first men in the United States to form a Mutual Aid Society at their place of business. Macy's workers who wished to participate would pay yearly dues based on a tiered formula. In return, as needed, each person received a certain amount of money towards medical services, which were provided by a physician associated with the store. Any deficit the society experienced was covered by R.H. Macy & Co.

Rowland Macy introduced the first in-store Santa Claus in 1862, and the Strauses continued this charming tradition of offering a "real" Santa who would greet young shoppers and talk to them about their Christmas wishes. This portrait, designed by American illustrator Thomas Nast in the mid-1800s, served as a model for jolly "St. Nick" at that time—and still does today.

On April 23, 1896, an early film projector called the Vitascope—invented by Thomas Armat and manufactured by Thomas Edison (shown at left)—was used to show motion pictures at Koster and Bial's Music Hall on Broadway and Thirty-Fourth Street. Years later, the music hall would be replaced with Macy's flagship store.

On December 25, 1896, American conductor and composer John Philip Sousa wrote his magnum opus, "Stars and Stripes Forever." An act of Congress eventually made this work the National March of the United States.

The Drive for Safe Milk

Although Nathan Straus worked to help the needy in many ways, his main cause was health. Nathan became aware of the widespread problem of unsanitary milk after the death of two of his children from raw milk infected by a tubercular cow. Soon, he was a passionate believer that pasteurization—the heating of milk to kill harmful microorganisms—should be enforced by the government as a means of eliminating milk-borne tuberculosis, typhoid fever, scarlet fever, and diphtheria among infants and children.

At his own cost, and after intense bacteriological investigation, Nathan built a plant that sterilized milk bottles and pasteurized milk. In 1892, he opened the first of many depots offering safe milk at low cost or, for those who could afford not even this, at no cost at all. By 1920, Straus had funded the establishment of almost three hundred milk stations in thirty-six United States cities, as well as locations abroad. Literally millions of bottles of pasteurized milk were being dispensed each year.

A milk depot at 348 East Thirty-Second Street.

At first, farmers and milk distributors loudly objected to the cost of pasteurization, while doctors and scientists complained of "new-fangled" ideas. But as infant mortality rates sharply dropped in the areas surrounding his milk depots, Nathan's views took hold. Prior to the establishment of the pasteurization plant and milk depots, 125 out of every 1,000 babies born in New York City died each year from milk-borne infection. After safe milk became available, the death rate dropped to 15.8 per 1,000. In the 1920s, Congress enacted sanitary milk regulations, and Nathan Straus turned over his milk depots to public agencies.

Although Nathan Straus privately funded his drive against "The White Peril," it should be noted that he was also actively involved in public service. Nathan was President of the New York City Board of Health, Commissioner of Parks in New York City, and United States delegate to the 1911 World International Congress for the Protection of Infants. On Nathan's seventy-fifth birthday in 1923, as congratulatory messages streamed in, Theodore Roosevelt sent his greetings, "There are no two men for whom I have a greater respect than Nathan Straus and his brother Oscar. . . . Both of them have been ready at all times to contribute not only money, but more important still, their untiring devotion and work to the service of their fellow citizens."

The East Third Street Pier depot—the first milk station in the United States.

The Mutual Aid Society soon gained popularity, and every year, the employees arranged different functions to add to the society's funds. In 1894, for example, 2,000 people attended a dance held at the Lenox Lyceum concert hall on Madison Avenue and Fifty-Ninth Street. The event, which was covered by the press, featured a promenade, reception, and dance. The society also hosted a yearly picnic, which included athletic contests.

In 1888, Macy's began to provide low-cost lunches for its employees. It had come to the Strauses' attention that two women in their employ were nearly starving themselves in order to provide care for their sick mother. Macy's response was to open a dining hall that offered soups, sandwiches, and pie to every employee at a nominal fee, and a full meal for five cents. The cash girls, parcel wrappers, and stock girls were given milk and coffee free of charge, while employees in higher positions paid one cent for each beverage.

The year 1888 also saw the beginning of a program that made regular provision to pay employees' doctor's bills and funeral expenses. Funds were also made available to employees who grew too old to continue working or became incapacitated.

The Strauses were even interested in providing their Macy's family with low-cost vacations. A house in Monroe, New York, surrounded by 350 acres of orchards, was made available to employees at the cost of six dollars per week. The price of transportation to and from the house was entirely covered by R.H. Macy & Co.

It should be noted that the Strauses' programs to help others went far beyond assistance to Macy's employees. During the rough depression winters of 1892 and 1893, Nathan operated a chain of centers that distributed food and coal to the needy, and also offered lodging with breakfast. Perhaps most noteworthy, though, is that at a time when the quality of milk was often so poor that it resulted in infant sickness and death, Nathan was instrumental in providing safe milk for children everywhere through the establishment of pasteurization plants and milk distribution centers.

During a difficult New York winter, Nathan Straus placed an unsigned advertisement in local papers, offering a free Thanksgiving turkey to anybody who couldn't afford one. Thousands of turkeys were given to thousands of people, none of whom knew that Nathan Straus had graciously provided their dinner.

WEBSTER STEPS ASIDE

Although the Straus brothers and partner Charles B. Webster clearly were on friendly terms, from the beginning of the partnership, the Strauses played a more active role in Macy's management. During Webster's long vacations abroad, he and Isidor kept in constant contact, with Isidor providing information about sales. But Isidor did not encourage Webster to hurry home and tend to business. Rather, he wrote, "Prolong your trip and enjoy yourself." Isidor and Nathan had energy, drive, and experience, and Webster gladly deferred to their business decisions.

Webster's interest in running Macy's continued to diminish with time. Interestingly, until his death in 1916, Webster kept an office in the store, and

The leg of mutton sleeve disappeared around 1896, and was replaced by sleeves that more closely followed the line of the arm. Skirts adopted a trumpet shape, fitting closely over the hips and flaring out just above the knees. Corsets elongated, giving women an S-curve silhouette.

Because of upper-class America's extravagant show of wealth during the late 1800s, this era is often referred to as the *Gilded Age*. The term was coined by Mark Twain and Charles Dudley Warner, who wrote a book of the same name in 1873.

every day, would join either Isidor or Nathan for lunch. But in 1896, eight years after the partnership had begun, Webster sold his interest in R.H. Macy's to the Straus brothers for the amount of $1,200,000.

At this time, the Strauses were facing a sizeable challenge in the form of Siegel-Cooper & Co., a department store that claimed to be "The Largest Store in the World." Ads for the store had begun to appear in January 1895, when retailer Henry Siegel announced that his company "would establish in New York City a mammoth department store modeled on the plan of its Chicago house." Many newspaper articles seemed geared specifically to criticize Macy's, which had become a maze of buildings spread out over Thirteenth Street and Fourteenth Street, with cramped aisles within. "Mammoth Building in Sixth Avenue Will Be No Tinder-Box Structure and There Will Be Plenty of Space for Customers," read one headline. The article further stated that Siegel-Cooper would be 85,500 square feet—more than double the size of R.H. Macy's.

When Siegel-Cooper & Co. opened on September 12, 1896, it was, in fact, a sight to behold. Situated on Sixth Avenue and West Eighteenth Street, the elaborate Beaux-Arts building—a block long and six stories high—was con-

A postcard of the Siegel-Cooper Department Store, an elaborate New York "shopping resort" opened in 1896.

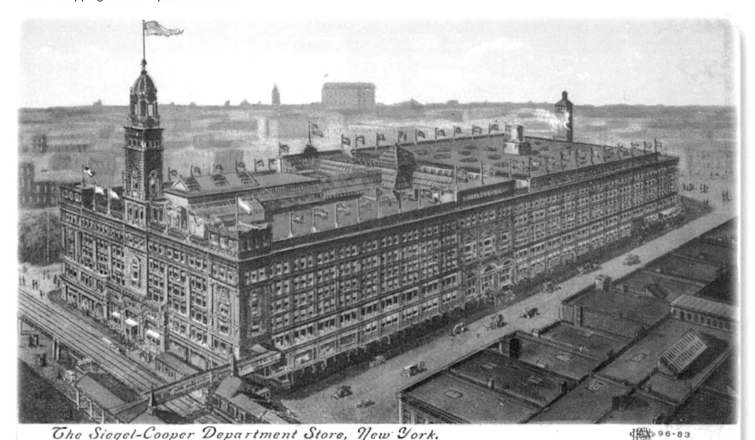

The Siegel-Cooper Department Store, New York.   96-83

In the late 1890s, men who were engaged in sports, sailing, and other casual activities could wear a *blazer*—a navy blue, brightly colored, or striped flannel coat cut like a sack coat. The blazer could be single- or double-breasted, and often featured patch pockets and brass shank buttons.

On March 24, 1900, Mayor Robert Anderson Van Wyck broke ground for the first subway in the City of Greater New York. Van Wyck was the first New York City mayor who served after the five boroughs were combined into one political entity.

structed on a scale never before seen in Manhattan. *The New York Times* called it a "shopping resort," and reported that it employed 2,000 people. Moreover, it had "commodious electric elevators," "broad marble staircases," a restaurant that would serve "healthful food," and a doctor's office with a physician always on hand in case of sudden illness.

Macy's had run out of room for expansion at its Sixth Avenue location, and modernization would have been difficult. Nevertheless, for the time being, the store would remain where it was and as it was, and Siegel-Cooper would have its day as the largest store in the world.

A NEW GENERATION OF STRAUSES

Around the time that Macy's was facing the Siegel-Cooper threat, Isidor Straus's three sons were coming of age and entering the business. Born in 1872, Jesse Isidor Straus graduated from Harvard in 1893, and accepted his first job at the Central Hanover Bank. Yet it was always known that Jesse would eventually work at Macy's. In 1893, the Strauses bought a half interest in the Brooklyn retail store Wechsler & Abraham. Renamed Abraham & Straus, the newly acquired store was a perfect training ground for Jesse. Then in 1896, Jesse moved to R.H. Macy & Co.

Percy, born in 1876, reportedly had hopes of pursuing a teaching career. But when he graduated from Harvard in 1897, he immediately began working for R.H. Macy's as well.

Jesse and Percy began learning the trade in Macy's receiving department, and then moved up the ladder of positions until each became a buyer. Jesse then worked in administration, promotion, and sales, while Percy learned about personnel management, maintenance, and delivery. As a reward for their hard work, Jesse and Percy each eventually received 5 percent of the store's net profits.

Herbert Straus, the youngest of the three, was born in 1881. He would begin working for Macy's in 1903 after his graduation from Harvard.

The leases on some of the Sixth Avenue property were set to expire in 1903, and land rentals in the area were rising steeply. Moreover, the store was in great need of repair. But even if R.H. Macy & Co. renovated the store and renewed leases, the business would be unable to compete with the likes of Siegel-Cooper. The Straus family—now bigger and stronger than ever before—had important decisions to make as the new century began.

After a stint at the Hanover Bank, Jesse Isidor Straus was eager to begin his career at Macy's. Father Isidor, though, insisted that Jesse start as a salesman at Abraham & Straus and work hard for each and every promotion.

The feminine ideal of the late nineteenth and early twentieth centuries was personified by the Gibson Girl. Created by illustrator Charles Dana Gibson, the Gibson Girl was tall and slender, yet with ample bosom and hips. Her youthful face was adorned with a soft pompadour hairstyle, puffed for a cloud effect.

When engaged in shooting and other rugged outdoor activities, the stylish turn-of-the-century man wore a *Norfolk jacket*. Usually made of a sturdy tweed, the single-breasted Norfolk featured boxed pleats over the chest and back, and had a full or half belt constructed of the same fabric.

4.
A New Beginning—
Herald Square

Williamsburg Bridge Approach, New York City.

At the turn of the century, New York City was growing and excelling in every way. The population of the metropolis was soaring, making New York the most populous city in the nation. Skyscrapers were going up—the tallest in the world. The Williamsburg Bridge was being built—the largest suspension bridge in the world. And a new subway system was under construction—the longest in the world.

The Straus family, owners of R.H. Macy & Co., wanted to benefit from the city's seemingly limitless opportunities for growth. But the Strauses had a problem. Over the years, Macy's had added annexes to the original store on Sixth Avenue and Fourteenth Street, but by 1901, there was no further room for expansion. Starting in the 1890s, a generation of superstores had begun sprouting up on Sixth Avenue, the largest being Siegel-Cooper, a visually stunning palazzo a full block in length. If Macy's was to compete with these newer, larger stores, the Strauses would have to move to more spacious quarters.

CONSTRUCTION BEGINS

On April 20, 1901 New York City newspapers proclaimed "Macy's Store to Be Transferred to Herald Square." The article further stated, "It became known yesterday that R.H. Macy & Co. have practically concluded negotiations for a long lease of all the property on the west side of Broadway, between Thirty-fourth and Thirty-fifth Streets. . . . On this site a mammoth store will be erected."

An early postcard of the Williamsburg Bridge, which provides a direct route from Williamsburg, Brooklyn to Manhattan's Lower East Side.

In 1900, New York City's transportation system was so inadequate that it could take hours to get from Harlem to Wall Street. To solve this problem, ground was broken for a Manhattan subway system that year. The subway's twenty-one miles of tunnels and fifty-eight miles of track would make New Yorkers more mobile than ever before.

In 1901, while the Strauses were planning a new Macy's, Theodore Roosevelt became President of the United States. Roosevelt, who remained in office until 1909, believed that the President should be "steward of the people" and act for the public good. With this in mind, he "busted" trusts, conserved national parkland, and steered the nation into active world politics.

◀ The original Thirty-Fourth Street entrance of Macy's Herald Square store.

Isidor Straus.

Nathan Straus.

Since some time in the 1890s, the Straus family's real estate agent, Leopold Weil, had been secretly negotiating with several different landowners to obtain the block of property needed for the intended "mammoth store." The largest parcel had been the site where Koster and Bial's Music Hall once stood and Thomas Edison had first projected his Vitascope motion picture. Since many smaller parcels and existing leases were involved, the property took some time to acquire. A small handful of especially enterprising tenants with unexpired leases entertained dreams of huge buyouts. Their hopes were dashed when Macy's issued this statement: "It has been definitely decided to permit those tenants with strange notions as to the value of their leases to remain in undisturbed possession until the expiration thereof. Very liberal offers were made to all who held unexpired leases . . . the two or three who did not see fit to accept may now conceal their chagrin as best they can." The Strauses were willing to wait for the property to become available.

On July 17, 1901, the newspapers at last announced: "Macy and Co. Buy Koster & Bial Site." The land totaled 180 feet on Broadway, 405 feet on Thirty-Fourth Street, and 380 feet on Thirty-Fifty Street. Only a small piece of property on the northwest corner of Thirty-Fourth Street and Broadway was not included, making a "notch" in the Strauses' new acquisition.

The contracting firm of George A. Fuller Co. was given the job of clearing the site of the old structures and erecting a new building, while architects De Lemos & Cordes—already known for the spectacular Siegel-Cooper department store—would design the new Macy's. Clearing of the site began on May 16, 1901 and the cornerstone for the building was laid on April 23, 1902, with three generations of Strauses in attendance. The store was scheduled to open in November 1902.

L. Straus & Sons, who were technically the owners of the property, wanted the new Macy's to have the best of everything. Jesse Isidor Straus, Isidor's eldest son, sailed to Europe to visit the large retail establishments in England and France, and see firsthand the machinery, devices, and methods used in business there. The Strauses would employ only what was judged to be "superior."

On May 17, 1901, the New York Stock Exchange crashed for the first time. One of the people responsible for this event was Edward Henry Harriman, who had tried to gain control of the Northern Pacific Railway by buying up shares. When the price of other railway stocks fell, investors panicked, causing the market to collapse.

At the turn of the century, Edwardian fashion was rooted in Victorian style. A corset molded a woman's shape, tilting the figure so that the low bosom shifted forward, and the posterior moved backwards. The tiny waist of Victorian times was still in vogue, as was a flowing skirt.

TWO BIG REAL ESTATE DEALS ON BROADWAY

Macy's Store to be Transferred to Herald Square.

Mammoth Building on Block from 34th to 35th Street—Adjoining Block Secured by Other Interests.

Two deals in real estate have just been effected involving two entire block fronts on Broadway, between Thirty-third and Thirty-fifth Streets, which promise to have more far-reaching effects than any similar transactions of recent years.

It became known yesterday that R. H. Macy & Co. have practically concluded negotiations for a long lease of all the property on the west side of Broadway, between Thirty-fourth and Thirty-fifth Streets, extending westerly to Koster & Bial's Music Hall, and that on this site a mammoth store will be erected.

Independent of this deal, but undoubtedly influenced in a large measure by it, Henry Morgenthau and Hugh J. Grant have bought from the estate of the late Thomas N. Lawrence, through Richard M. Montgomery, the entire block front on the west side of Broadway, between Thirty-third and Thirty-fourth Streets. This property extends 150 feet on Thirty-third Street and about 80 feet on Thirty-fourth Street, and has been held at about $2,000,000. Messrs. Morgenthau and Grant are President and Vice President, respectively, of the Central Realty Bond and Trust Company, but in this transaction they are acting as individuals and not as representatives of that corporation. None of the leases in the old buildings has over a year to run, but no improvement of the property is contemplated by its present purchasers, unless their expectations of a rapid advance in values and an active market for property in that neighborhood shall prove to be unjustified.

Nathan Straus, the head of the firm doing business under the name of R. H. Macy & Co., declined last evening to say anything regarding the prospective removal of their establishment from Fourteenth to Thirty-fourth Street. Mr. Straus sent his nephew to say to a NEW YORK TIMES reporter, who called at his house, that reports to the effect that the Macy concern is buying the property at Thirty-fourth and Thirty-fifth Streets are without foundation.

"Is it not a fact that Mr. Straus is negotiating for a long lease of the property?" was asked.

"Ah, that is another matter," replied Mr. Straus's nephew, who then went on to explain that the matter was not yet in such shape as to warrant any announcement from Mr. Straus.

The proposed store, according to present plans, will be ten stories in height, and on account of its great area will probably be one of the largest buildings in the world in point of floor space. The block between Thirty-fourth and Thirty-fifth Streets has a Broadway frontage of 211.3 feet, while the property included in the site extends 375 feet on Thirty-fourth Street and 267 feet on Thirty-fifth Street. The new building will be put up by the George A. Fuller Company.

A conservative estimate of the value of the land included in this site is $3,000,000, which means that the annual ground rental will not be less than $150,000. Several individuals and estates are interested in the property. The northwest corner of Broadway and Thirty-fourth Street is owned by the Pell estate. The records show that Susan J. Palmer owns the Thirty-fifth Street end of the block—the Hotel Aulic property—together with several parcels adjoining on that street. The inside lots on Broadway are held by the Aycrigg, Hegeman, and Grinnell estates, and these same owners also hold title to all of the street lots.

As is usual in securing control of a plot including so many small parcels, existing leases have been the cause of many delays in the negotiations. It is said that Haaren & Hencken received over $100,000 to relinquish their long lease on the Hotel Aulic, and other tenants of the stores on Broadway have received handsome bonuses.

Real estate men have heard no more interesting or significant news in many a day than that there is to be a department store at Herald Square—because of its bearing upon at least three different neighborhoods. The effect upon Herald Square itself seems to be obvious, and indeed talk was heard yesterday of negotiations for the Broadway Tabernacle property, at the northeast corner of Broadway and Thirty-fourth Street, while it was asserted on good authority that a syndicate had already acquired the buildings 139 to 145 West Thirty-fifth Street, just west of Broadway, recently occupied as the Tivoli and Pekin.

Heretofore Twenty-third Street has been regarded as the northerly limit of the retail dry goods district, and shrewd buyers of realty have evidently looked upon it as a permanent limit, judging by some of the prices that have been paid for small Sixth Avenue lots to the south of it. With a large store at Thirty-fourth Street, however, the possibilities of the section between Twenty-third and Thirty-third Streets will doubtless appear in a new light. Real estate men who discussed the subject yesterday were inclined to believe, moreover, that the removal of the Macy store from Fourteenth Street would not be without effect on that thoroughfare.

An April 20, 1901 article announcing the Strauses' lease of property for their new "mammoth store."

In 1901, when the Straus family arranged to lease property for the construction of their new Herald Square store, the value of the land was estimated at $3 million. While this may sound like a trivial amount in the twenty-first century, consider that in today's dollars, it would be roughly equal to $71 million.

In 1902, the *20th Century Limited*—an express passenger train that traveled between New York City and Chicago—had its first run. Known for both style and speed, the *20th Century* served such famous passengers as Theodore Roosevelt, actress Lillian Russell, and businessman "Diamond Jim" Brady.

72

Macy's—The Store. The Star. The Story.

A November 21, 1902 ad announcing the close of the Fourteenth Street store and the opening of "the New Macy Store."

R. H. Macy & Co.'s Attractions Are Their Low Prices.

Macy's

Both Sides 14th St.   from 13th to 15th, 6th Av.

To=morrow Will Be the Last Day at the Old Store.

Our Old Buildings	Our New Store
13th to 15th St. at Sixth Avenue. { Both Sides of 14th St.	Broadway at Sixth Avenue { 34th to 35th Street
Will Be Closed Permanently To=morrow Night.	**Will Be Opened in a Few Days**

Watch the Papers for Opening Announcement

Great Reductions To=morrow.

There are hundreds of lots of merchandise throughout the store that we do not care to move. They will be closed out to-morrow at great price-reductions. All other broken lines that develop during the day will be marked down—marked down low enough to in-sure their distribution before the day is over.

The Old Macy System at the New Macy Store:

We Give No Credit.
We Give No Discounts.
We Give No Commissions.

But We Sell Cheaper Than Other House

NO MAIL ORDERS CAN BE FILLED THIS WEEK.

In the early 1900s, women wore extreme-ly high fabric collars during the day. Often made of lace, these exaggerated collars were kept in place by silk covered wire. Although this fashion made the neck look long and slender, it contributed to a somewhat rigid appearance.

When Edward VII visited Bad Homburg in Hessen, Germany, he brought back the homburg—a stiff felt hat with a brim that has a sharply turned-up edge all around. The homburg immediately became popular as an accessory less formal than the top hat, but more formal than the bowler and fedora.

In the summer of 1902, Macy's began advertising special sales intended to reduce the amount of stock that would have to be moved from its old location to its new home. Already, elaborate plans were being made so that the merchandise could be transferred quickly and efficiently, without greatly disrupting business. As the summer ended and autumn leaves began to blanket the streets of the city, New Yorkers waited expectantly to see the new R.H. Macy & Co.

MACY'S MOVES UPTOWN

On Monday November 3, 1902, the Fourteenth Street Macy's was closed for the last time. Immediately, some 250 trucks and wagons loaded with merchandise began making the twenty-block journey from the old store to the new. Along the route, both Macy's employees and police were posted to ensure that the relocation of goods proceeded without a problem. The transfer was accomplished in just four days, and the new R.H. Macy & Co. had its grand opening on Saturday November 8, 1902.

During the days of the move to the Herald Square store, rubbish— wooden packing boxes, waste straw, and paper—was stacked up outside the new Macy's as high as the second story windows. Early each morning, New Yorkers lined up to get their share of the wood, which could be used as fuel in their homes.

De Lemos & Cordes' rendering of R.H. Macy's new Beaux-Arts-style store. At the time, this architectural firm was already famous for designing the Siegel-Cooper department store.

STORE OF R. H. MACY & CO., "HERALD" SQUARE, NEW YORK, N. Y.
De Lemos & Cordes, Architects.

Manhattan's Herald Square before the construction of the new Macy's store.

A rare photo of the 1902 construction of Macy's flagship store.

The Strauses had spared no expense on the Macy's building. By the time of the store's completion, building costs had totalled $4,980,000. Nine stories high, Macy's was designed in the Beaux-Arts style popular at the time and featured classical ornamentation, from statues and wreaths to elaborate moldings. Over two million pounds of ornamental bronze, iron, and other metals had been used to make the store as beautiful as it was massive. The elegant carving over the Thirty-Fourth Street entrance proclaimed "RH Macy & Co."

The interior of the store was as stunning as its exterior. Compared with the original Macy's, of course, the Herald Square store was wonderfully spacious, with over a million square feet of floor space. It was said that if all the wood planking used in the building were placed end to end, it would stretch from New York to seventy-five miles past Detroit, Michigan. Six graceful marble-and-iron stairways allowed shoppers to walk in style from one floor to another. Yet Macy's also provided a more modern means of navigating the store in the form of thirty-three hydraulic elevators and four wooden escalators, which had the capacity to move 40,000 people an hour.

Ample illumination permitted shoppers to fully examine the store's extensive wares. Eighty electric motors powered 15,000 incandescent lamps, as well as 1,400 enclosed arc lamps.

State-of-the-art systems had been installed to transport both merchandise and cash throughout the store. A full eighteen miles of pneumatic brass tubing carried money from the sales floor to the cashiers, and thirty conveyors moved parcels from one area of Macy's to another. When merchandise was to be delivered to customers' homes, conveyor belts carried the packages from the main wrapping floor to the delivery department. There, the items were sorted from a mechanical circular table and transferred to another belt, which sent the packages to waiting wagons.

> R. H. Macy & Co.'s Attractions are Their Low Prices
>
> # Macys
>
> B'way at 6th Ave.   34th to 35th St.
>
> NEW YORK CITY,
>
> ## Will Open
> ### Their New Store
> ### This Morning at 9 o'Clock,
>
> BROADWAY | 34th St.
> AT | to
> SIXTH AVE. | 35th St.
>
> ☛ *The Old Building at Fourteenth Street and 6th Avenue Is Closed.*
>
> The Old Macy System at the New Macy Store.
>
> **We Give No Credit.**
> **We Give No Discounts.**
> **We Give No Commissions.**
> **But We Sell Cheaper Than Any Other House.**
>
> **Special Notice: Department of Deposit.**
>
> To facilitate purchases by customers who do not like to have goods sent C. O. D. we will open a Department of Deposit. By placing money to your credit with this Department your purchases can be referred to it for payment. Interest will be allowed on balance at the rate of four per cent. per annum, to be computed every three months, with the distinct understanding that the account is only for the payment of purchases in the house and not for general banking purposes

A November 8, 1902 ad announcing that day's opening of the new Macy's store.

Ice skating first became fashionable in the mid-1800s, and by the turn of the century, children and adults alike enjoyed this winter sport. The skates of the time were metal blades that attached to the wearer's shoes by means of straps, screws, and clamps.

At the turn of the century, cigarette cases made a fashionable gift for the smoker who sought to protect his cigarettes from being crushed. An elegant case was made of silver or other precious metals, and embellished with etched designs of animals, fruit, or flowers, as well as the individual's monogram.

The Notch in Macy's Department Store

Anyone passing Macy's flagship Herald Square store would think that the entire structure, including the shorter section directly on the corner of Thirty-Fourth Street and Broadway, belongs to Macy's. After all, the sign on the corner proclaims "Macy's: The World's Largest Store." But this conclusion would be wrong, for the corner of Thirty-Fourth and Broadway has *never* been a part of Macy's department store.

When the Straus family's realtor, Leopold Weil, began negotiating for the Herald Square land, the corner property was owned by Alfred Duane Pell. While traveling overseas, Pell, in communication with Weil through letters and cablegrams, agreed to sell the land for $250,000. Then the newspapers got wind of the Straus deal, and in April 1901, all of New York knew that land was being purchased for the construction of a new Macy's. Shortly thereafter, Pell received a competing offer for $375,000. The second offer was made by an agent of Henry Siegel, one of the owners of the Siegel-Cooper & Co. department store. There are various theories as to why Siegel wanted the land. Perhaps the most compelling is that Siegel wanted to establish a new store on the old Macy's site to attract Macy's old customers, and planned to offer the Herald Square corner to the Strauses in return for the old Sixth Avenue lease. Whatever the motivation behind the offer, Pell sold to the highest bidder—Siegel's agent, Robert Smith. Smith then offered the plot to the Strauses at the price he had paid, but strangely, the Strauses chose not to purchase the property. Instead, they had their architects build around the holdout, creating a ground-floor arcade behind it and constructing a shortcut between Broadway and Thirty-Fourth Street.

The five-story building that now produces a "notch" in the Macy's store is a remnant of the nineteenth-century structure purchased by Robert Smith. A façade camouflages the fact that it is not part of Macy's, and around 1945, the store began advertising on the structure. But to this day, it remains a separate property.

R. H. Macy & Co.'s Attractions are Their Low Prices.

Macy's — B'way at 6th Ave. — 34th to 35th St.

Broadway at 6th Avenue, 34th to 35th Street.

R. H. Macy & Co.'s Attractions are Their Low Prices.

Macy's — B'way at 6th Ave. — 34th to 35th St.

Broadway at 6th Avenue, 34th to 35th Street.

R. H. Macy & Co.'s Attractions are Their Low Prices.

Macy's — B'way at 6th Av. — 34th to 35th St.

We Sell Goods Cheaper Than Any Other Store---But for Cash Only,

The New Store Is Ready.

Every Department Beneath the Roof Is a Complete Store.

Broadway at 6th Avenue---34th to 35th Street.

Features of the Store. — Floor Space.

Floor space ...... the primary need. Over twenty-four acres...... perhaps that standard of measurement is easiest for unmathematical minds to comprehend. Only those people whose profession is to juggle with big figures can properly take a mental grasp of the immensity of the store's floor area. You will probably more fully realize it when we tell you that if it were reduced to a shop 20 feet wide it would be nine miles long, or a length equal to the distance between the Battery and Harlem River at 141st Street. If the strips that cover the floors were placed end to end they would reach from New York to seventy-five miles beyond Detroit, Michigan.

— 4,000 employees.
— 2,000,000,000 pounds weight of building.
— 26,000,000 pounds structural steel and iron.
— 2,180,000 pounds ornamental bronze and iron.
— 5,340,000 common bricks.
— 2,305 separate columns.
— 18 miles of brass tubing and galvanized iron pipe in the pneumatic cash system.
— 46 miles of beams.
— 738 miles of flooring planks.
— 42 miles of electric wiring.
— 150,000 square feet of window area.
— 33 hydraulic elevators.
— 4 escalators, aggregate carrying capacity 40,000 persons an hour. They step for you, steadily, safely.
— 6 massive iron and marble stairways.
— 1,400 enclosed arc lamps.
— 15,000 incandescent lamps.
— 11 water tube boilers, capable of developing 5,500 horse power.
— 3,040 horse power engines and dynamos.
— 80 electric motors.
— 30 parcel conveyors.

Manufacturing for Ourselves

A single slender margin of profit between maker and retail buyer—such is the policy that provides greatest values. Macy's manufacturing interests are not approached by those of any other store in America. In every department the highest standard is scrupulously maintained. The following list indicates the diversity of the "feeders" we own from which this great business draws much of its matchless sinews of trade:

— A Glassware Factory in Bohemia
— A Cut Glass Factory on our Premises
— A Porcelain Decorating Shop at Carlsbad
— A China Decorating Shop at Limoges
— A China Decorating Shop on the Premises
— A Handkerchief Factory at Belfast
— A Shirt Factory at Poughkeepsie
— A Muslin Underwear Factory in New York, Brooklyn and Carlstadt
— A Silk Waist and Skirt Factory in New York City
— A Mattress Factory in New York City
— A Candy Factory in New York City
— A Baking Powder Factory in New York City
— A Harness Factory in New York City
— A Chemical Laboratory in New York City

where over fifty articles are manufactured of the purest *tested* ingredients under the cleanliest and safest hygienic and sanitary conditions.

Special Notice: Department of Deposit.

To facilitate purchases by customers who do not like to have goods sent C. O. D., we have opened a *Department of Deposit*. By placing money to your credit with this Department, your purchases can be referred to it for payment. Interest will be allowed on balance at the rate of four per cent. per annum, to be computed every three months, with the distinct understanding that the account is only for the payment of purchases in the house, and not for general banking purposes.

The Old Macy System at the New Macy Store.

We Continue Not to Give

Credit, Discounts or Commissions. All Others Do to a Greater or Lesser Extent.

Saving the expenses and losses of having charge accounts, and refusing to tax one class to compensate for the discounts and commissions allowed another, render it doubly easy for us to undersell competition. And we do—make comparisons for your own satisfaction. The result never fails to vindicate our claim.

Our Prices Will Always Be Lowest.

This clears the mist of speculation for all who have inferred that our change of location implies a change of policy. *It certainly does not.* The Macy prices will continue to be lowest.
Concentration minimizes expenses—reduces outlay of money, labor and time. The concentration—the combination and co-operation controlled by modern methods—enables us to take every step of merchandising, from sweeping the floors to delivering your parcel, on a smaller percentage of cost than when Macy's was at Fourteenth Street.

1858——Forty-four Years of Macy's——1902.

The history of the store reads like a chapter from the Arabian Nights. It was started forty-four years ago, in an humble way, by *Rowland H. Macy*. His first day's sales amounted to **$11.06.**
From that beginning the store has developed into *the largest and among the most perfectly organized business enterprises in the world.*
The active needs and exigencies of the business made the erection of a building of the huge dimensions of the new Macy's an imperative necessity. We had to push twenty blocks northward in order to secure adequate space and logical location. Sweeping away thirty-nine stores and residences, besides one of the largest theatres in America, was a mere incident that prepared the way for the immense structure that our methods and your appreciation have made possible.
When casting about to find the ideal modern department store—architect, artist, merchant, customer—all, we believe, must ultimately turn to Macy's as the highest exponent—the best type.
Completed, it epitomizes the results gained by studying, adapting, combining and, whenever possible, bettering every phase of merchandising. All the most practical ideas that have been applied to American and European retailing may be found here, modified or amplified, as required, to render them of largest value to you and to us.

Trustworthy Advertising.

You've been reading our advertising for nearly half a century. Have you ever been misled? Every statement that goes into the papers must be exact. What we say to-day does not have to be unsaid to-morrow. That's why this business has grown. Confidence in Macy's is a heritage that thousands of families have sustained through three generations. The children of to-day believe in us because their parents do, just as their parents were won to Macy's by the rugged steadfastness of *their* parents. We still follow the policy that has made our friends so adhesive all these years.

A Forward Look.

The old Macy's—a new store, another location, larger stocks, greater facilities, better conveniences—but the same principles, changed only by broader opportunities for higher development. Our Past means much to us and to you. It is inspiration for the Present —the hope of the Future. Nearly half a century of retailing! Mistakes have been made, of course. But the heart of the business has been sound. Errors were corrected as quickly as discovered. Perfection has not yet been attained. Human endeavor may never reach that point. But our past is our bond to our public. There is no shadow on it—no period of its growth that we would obscure or discount by excuses or apologies. Our best has always been done—and that is why improvement has followed improvement. We lift the standard of service higher each day. Every blunder has had its lesson—and we have never been unmindful of it.

Reliable Qualities and Exclusive Novelties.

Increased space enables us to offer our old customers, in far greater assortments, the class of merchandise they have always bought of us. And we have strengthened every department by the addition of higher grades, which our former limited quarters did not permit us to carry.
The same sterling principles that have held and will keep on holding our old standbys, should appeal to and, we hope, will attract many *new* thousands to the *new* Macy store.

We Sell Goods Cheaper Than Any Other Store---But for Cash Only.

The New Store Is Ready.

Every Department Beneath the Roof Is a Complete Store.

Fearful of getting ash on his shirt and vest or allowing his clothes to absorb offensive odors, the Edwardian gentleman donned a smoking jacket before lighting his cigar or pipe. Relatively short in length, this elegant garment featured a shawl collar and turned-up cuffs made of a contrasting fabric.

Before the twentieth century, most personal timepieces were pocket watches. But in the early 1900s, as the miniaturization of watch movements became less costly, the lady's "bracelet watch"—an ornamented bracelet holding a watch of small dimensions— became available for the modern woman who appreciated novelty.

A 1904 photo of R.H. Macy & Co., clearly showing the store's trademark red star.

In the middle of the nineteenth century, as the supply of ivory became insufficient to meet consumer demand, the first celluloid was created. By the beginning of the twentieth century, this easy-to-mold plastic was being used to manufacture everything from knife handles to ornamental hair combs.

In 1902, *The Tale of Peter Rabbit* was published in England by Frederick Warne & Company. Both written and illustrated by Beatrix Potter, this delightful book—the first in a series of children's books—was to become a bestseller, with more than 40 million copies purchased worldwide.

OPENING OF MACY'S NEW BIG STORE

New Locality for Trade at Broadway and Thirty-fourth Street.

Original and Extensive Arrangements for the Convenience and Safety of Shoppers and Employes.

R. H. Macy & Co. threw open to the public the *doors of* their new big store yesterday, and everything was in readiness for the crowd that swarmed through the building at Broadway, Thirty-fourth Street and Thirty-fifth Street. The thousands that had hurried in and out of the doors of the old store at Sixth Avenue and Fourteenth Street went early to the new place, eager for an inspection, but they did not overcrowd the store, as it has a floor space of twenty-four acres

Dealing with big figures, it is difficult to realize that the store's floor area, if reduced into small shops, each fifty feet in depth and twenty-five feet in width would make a frontage equal to the distance from Eighteenth Street to One Hundred and Twenty-fifth Street. If the floor planks were placed end to end they would extend from New York seventy-five miles beyond Detroit. The weight of the building is 2,000,000,000 pounds. In the building are 2,150,000 pounds of ornamental metal, bronze and iron, and it has eighteen miles of brass tubing, forty-six miles of beams, thirty-three hydraulic elevators, four escalators, with a carrying capacity of 40,000 persons an hour; six iron and marble stairways, eleven water-tube boilers of 3,500 horse power, eighty electric motors, and thirty parcel conveyors.

The system of heating and ventilation has been planned carefully, so that the vitiated air is to be collected by ducts that are to be exhausted at the rate of 2,000 feet a minute. There is a novel system of cleaning by means of piping, with 180 one-inch outlets for hose connections. By means of an air pump dust from floors, shelving, and carpets is taken through the hose connected with the piping and sent through the pipes to a receiver located near the crematory in the boiler room. No dust flies, as it is sucked in the cleaning machine. The apparatus does the work of at least 1,000 scrubwomen. Sweepings, garbage, trash, packing boxes, and the many combustible things in the waste of a big building are burned. The matter consumed will heat one of the boilers.

Everything is done for the healthfulness of the building, and included in this is the comfort of the employes. They have their luncheon and recreation rooms, and sick-rooms to which they can go for medical attention. These would occupy less space if combined, but, as 4,000 persons are employed, and as they go to work at the same hour and leave at the same time, there would be a congestion that could not be endured. Figuring on four elevators carrying forty persons each, one elevator would have to make twenty-five trips. This would take an hour and forty minutes. Each person must be moved four times a day. For these reasons the employes had to be accommodated with very valuable space in each story.

The delivery department is original. There is an arrangement of moving belts from all of the wrapping counters of the main floor for carrying parcels to the main delivery department. The goods are sorted from a circular table on which they are deposited by the belts. The parcels start on another belt journey to the delivery wagons. The element of careless handling is eliminated.

There are two tube offices, or cash rooms, one in the basement and the other in the fourth story. The tube office in the basement is fitted with 130 double terminal stations and thirty single or office stations, also four three-inch dispatch tubes for small parcels.

In the fourth story there are ninety double terminal stations and fifteen office stations, making 270 in all. The total tube system is 93,000 feet in length. It and the terminals make eighteen miles of pipes and tubes. The entire system of tubes is used as an interchangeable dispatch medium for carrying messages.

In the building there are 1,400 inclosed arc and 15,000 incandescent lamps. The power is distributed by eighty electric motors, ranging from one-half to 100 horse power. The switchboard is ten feet in height and forty-two feet in length, made of Tennessee marble.

The restaurant is in the eighth story, and it has the advantages of light, air, and a fine outlook. It can accommodate 2,500 persons. There is a forty-ton absorption machine in the basement, which is used for refrigerating and cooling the drinking water to a temperature of about 40 degrees. By means of the thirty-three elevators and the four escalators, it is easy to move the shoppers from one story to another without overcrowding.

The management takes particular pride in its fire department. Although the building is of fire-proof construction, every precaution has been taken to avoid fire, and to control any blaze as soon as discovered. There is an organized fire department, with a superintendent, a chief engineer, the superintendent on each floor, and a chief of battalion. The last-named is the drill-master, and there are to be regular drills. There are three call stations in each story to be used in case of alarm. The central station is at the Superintendent's desk in the main story.

By means of electric switches the attendant, or whoever is nearest the desk, can answer an alarm and send any company or the entire department to the place threatened. There are six stand-pipes, each four inches in diameter. There are standard fire department outlets in each story with tested linen hose, stretched and ready for instant use. There is a strong water pressure from a tank on the roof, and an automatic fire-pump in the basement. There are three Siamese connections for the city Fire Department to stand-pipes outside of the building.

The *New York Times'* rave review of Macy's Herald Square store. This article appeared on November 9, 1902, one day after Macy's opened for business at its new location.

In 1902, Scottish-born American industrialist Andrew Carnegie established the Carnegie Institution in Washington, DC. Over the years, the institution would grow to support science in several areas, including developmental biology, plant biology, astronomy, and earth and planetary sciences.

By halting work in the anthracite coal fields of eastern Pennsylvania, the Coal Strike of 1902 threatened to shut down the winter fuel supply to all major American cities. Fortunately, President Theodore Roosevelt intervened, ultimately ending the strike and providing the miners with greater pay for fewer hours of work.

Jesse Straus (left), Percy Straus (right), and their uncle Oscar Straus (center) on Macy's 1902 opening day.

Macy's system of pneumatic brass tubes was widely advertised when the Herald Square store first opened its doors in 1902. The concept was simple. When a customer purchased an item, the sales clerk would place the sales check and the customer's money in the tubing, which used compressed air to transport the items to the change room. There, another clerk would examine the receipt, make the change due the customer, and send the change back to the first clerk— again, via tubing. Finally, the item and the change were given to the shopper.

Built into the Macy's structure was a vacuum cleaning system that included 180 one-inch outlets to which hoses could be connected. An air pump removed dust and dirt from the floors, shelves, and carpeting, and whisked the debris down to the boiler room for disposal. It was estimated that 1,000 scrubwomen would have been needed to manually perform the work of this innovative cleaning system.

New York's department stores had long been known to be close and stuffy during shopping hours, when the large, poorly ventilated buildings were crowded with patrons. The Strauses had overcome this problem by installing great fans, which pulled air down from the roof through ducts, heated or cooled it as necessary, and distributed it throughout the floors of the building.

On the eighth floor of the new Macy's building was a restaurant offering refreshments for Macy's customers. Unbelievably, the restaurant could seat 2,500 hungry shoppers. *The New York Times* noted that the dining room had "the advantages of light, air, and a fine outlook." Other amenities of the store included ample fitting rooms, accommodations desks, an information counter, and comfortable restrooms.

Recognizing that toys were a marketable item not only during the Christmas season, but all year long, Macy's and other early department stores established the first toy departments. Dolls, rocking horses, miniature railway systems, and games such as Tidley Winks flew off the shelves.

As the Edwardian man began to participate in sports, designers created casual outfits that allowed freer movement. The fashionable man enjoyed outdoor activities attired in suits made of tweed or flannel fabrics. Plus-fours and knickerbockers—loose breeches fastened below the knee— were a must for golf, cycling, and rowing.

Originally, the ninth floor of the building was not needed for selling space, but was used as a large exhibition hall. New Yorkers and visitors alike flocked to the midtown area to enjoy Macy's extravagant flower shows, poultry shows, and even one of the country's first automobile shows.

At the time of its opening, Macy's employed a total of 4,000 people. Not surprisingly, the Strauses had designed the store not just for the welfare of their customers, but also for that of the people who worked for them. Macy's declared that one of its goals was to promote the "healthfullness" of its employees, and it provided luncheon and recreation rooms, as well as "sick rooms" for workers who required medical attention.

The Straus family seems to have built the perfect store in the perfect area. In the years that followed, the city would see construction of the Pennsylvania Railroad, one of the world's greatest train stations, just a short walk from the Herald Square store. This would deliver literally hundreds of thousands of people to Macy's doorstep. Eventually, many other large department stores, such as B. Altman and Gimbel Brothers, would move to the area, as well. But Macy's was already there, and with room for expansion, it was poised to become the largest department store in the world.

Importers' Automobile Salon

Herald Square Exhibition Hall,
(Top Floor Macy Building.)

34th, 35th Sts. and B'way,

January 11th to 24th, 10 A. M. to 11 P. M. Daily.
Admission 50c.   Mondays $1.00.

Every important manufacturer of Foreign Automobiles represented.
1905 models direct from the Paris Exposition.

Mercedes	Decauville	Quinby	Martini	De Dietrich
Darracq	Renault	Panhard	Hotchkiss	Gabron-Brillie
Clement-Bayard	F. I. A. T.	Rochet-Schneider	Richard-Brasier	Delahaye
Napier	Mors	Pipe	Peugot	C. G. V.
Carre	La Minerve	Electromobile	Franklin	Leon-Bollee	Rothschild

And the latest imported novelties and accessories.

Decorations by eminent Foreign artists.
Music by the celebrated Italian Royal Marine Band.
Geisha Girls Serving Tea and Refreshments in the Japanese Gardens.

A 1905 ad for an automobile show held on Macy's ninth floor. The top floor of the building was not yet needed for selling space and was used for exhibitions instead.

In 1903, Michigan native Henry Ford proclaimed, "I will build a car for the great multitude." Only five years later, Ford realized his dream by introducing the Model T for under a thousand dollars. The mass-produced Tin Lizzy put America on wheels.

The stuffed animal known as the *Teddy bear* first appeared in 1903 as a response to a Clifford Berryman cartoon that pictured President Theodore Roosevelt on a hunting trip. Sales of the toy were so brisk that just a few years later, creator Morris Michtom was able to establish the Ideal Novelty and Toy Company.

CONTINUING THE TRADITION OF SERVICE

A 1905 photo taken at Isidor Straus's New Jersey summer home "Sunnyside." Back row, left to right: Vivian Straus (Isidor's daughter), Herbert Nathan Straus, Irma Nathan Straus (Jesse's wife), Jesse Isidor Straus, and Richard Weil (Minnie's husband). Front row, left to right: Edith Abraham Straus (Percy's wife), Percy Selden Straus, Ralph Isidor Straus (Percy's infant son), Dr. Alfred Fabian Hess (Sara Straus's husband, seated on grass), Sara Straus Hess (Isidor's daughter), Ida Straus, Jack Isidor Straus (Jesse's son), Beatrice Straus (Jesse's daughter), Isidor Straus, and Minnie Straus Weil (Isidor's daughter).

With the opening of the magnificent Herald Square store, the Strauses knew that they could offer their customers a greater selection of merchandise and a more convenient and comfortable shopping experience just by virtue of the building's generous dimensions. But the Straus family wanted to ensure that despite the new store's staggering size, Macy's customers would continue to receive the personal service they had come to expect.

All of Macy's employees were carefully selected to make sure they had the personality necessary to provide pleasant service, as well as the ability to master the store's many procedures and practices. Under the watchful eye of senior staff members and management, extensive staff training was provided both in classrooms and on the actual sales floors. Over the years, some of the mottoes used to inspire polite and courteous service included "A smile with every package" and "A thank-you as goodbye."

Although the modern shopper may be able to imagine the care that turn-of-the-century salesclerks took to help the customer—usually, a woman—find the items she desired, it is difficult today to conceive of some of the services

On December 31, 1904, Times Square hosted its first New Year's Eve celebration, with over 200,000 people filling the streets around Adolph Ochs' new Times Tower. Before this, city residents had greeted the New Year at Wall Street, where they could hear the chimes of Trinity Church.

The year 1905 is known as Albert Einstein's "Wonderful Year"—*Annus Mirabilis*—because it was then that he put forth ideas which were to change the world's view of space, time, and matter. Included in his *Annus Mirabilis Papers* was Einstein's special theory of relativity.

that Macy's routinely offered each and every patron. A shopper who needed items from several different departments didn't have to wait on line in each area to buy that department's goods, and then carry her purchases with her as she continued browsing. Instead, the price of the articles selected in the first department were marked in a small book given to the customer. These items were then sent to the wrapping room while the shopper—who now had to carry only a tiny book—made other purchases. Finally, the patron presented the book to the cashier at the main floor's transfer desk and paid the total amount. If she wished, the shopper was then presented with a neatly wrapped package containing all of her purchases. If she preferred not to carry bulky packages home, though, Macy's, at no cost, would send the items to the address of her choice.

A delivery pushcart—one of R.H. Macy's first means of delivering purchases to its customers.

In 1868, long before the store's move to midtown Manhattan, Rowland Macy had acquired the first horse-drawn delivery wagon for his growing business. By the time the Herald Square store opened in 1902, Macy's owned a hundred wagons for this purpose. Any package that the customer wished delivered was sent down a chute from the sales floor to the delivery department, where it was sorted according to its destination in Manhattan, Harlem, the Bronx, Brooklyn, New Jersey, or the "suburbs." Nearby neighborhoods received two deliveries a day, weather permitting. More far-flung areas such as Brooklyn and the Bronx received at least one delivery each day.

Polite service continued even after a customer left the store. The men who drove the Macy's delivery wagons were considered representatives of the company, and were trained to be just as friendly, efficient, and helpful as the salesclerks. Thus, loyal customers enjoyed a positive experi-

An R.H. Macy & Co. horse-drawn delivery wagon.

ence whether they were choosing a pair of gloves at a counter of the Herald Square store, or accepting a furniture delivery in their home. The Strauses knew that low prices, good quality, and great service would combine to make Macy's an irresistible shopping destination.

In 1907, waistlines were raised in a column-like empire line, and dresses became slimmer, especially for the younger, more fashionable woman. The long-line corset—which almost reached the knees, slenderizing the body along the way—provided the necessary foundation for this body-skimming style.

Published on July 29, 1907, *Ozma of Oz* by L. Frank Baum was the third book in the Oz series, and immediately became a favorite with children everywhere. Macy's book department offered Baum's new tale—along with other works of juvenile fiction—for ninety-eight cents, "cheaper than any other store."

Macy's and the Supreme Court

From the time of the store's founding in 1858, R.H. Macy & Co. had advertised good-quality items sold at the lowest prices in town. While the store's many loyal customers were thrilled by this policy, not everyone shared their enthusiasm. In fact, Macy's practice of selling merchandise at a discount price led to a court battle that lasted for more than a decade.

In 1901, the American Publishers Association asked dealers to sign an agreement to maintain the fixed prices set by each individual publisher. Macy's refused to sign the contract, insisting that the store had a right to set its own prices. In response, the publishers—who referred to department stores as "book butchers"—cut off the retailer's supply of books.

At that time, the head of Macy's book department was Lillian Kinnear. Through use of a special checking account, Kinnear purchased books wherever she could—from wholesalers, from retailers who had overstocked, and even from authors—and had the items secretly shipped to Macy's. Buying books from sources as far away as Havana, Cuba, Kinnear kept the store stocked throughout the time it was blacklisted by the publishers.

In 1902, Macy's department store, under the Sherman Antitrust Act of 1890, filed suit against both the American Publishers Association and the American Booksellers Association. It was the store's contention that the book publishers constituted an illegal trust and were imposing an unfair restraint of trade. Macy's further asserted that it was to the public's advantage that all restrictions be removed. In 1913, the United States Supreme Court decided in Macy's favor and awarded the company $140,000 in damages. The die had been cast, and department stores were free to sell merchandise, including books, at any price they wished to set.

A page from Macy's 1907 Christmas Catalogue showing "why all your books must reasonably come from Macy's."

MACY'S FIFTIETH ANNIVERSARY

The relocation to Macy's Herald Square proved to be a stunning success. Within a year, Macy's sales pushed to $11 million as crowds of smart shoppers made their way to the famous emporium.

Just six years after its move to spacious new quarters, Macy's celebrated its fiftieth anniversary. A February 2, 1908 newspaper noted that the "Father of Department Stores" was pulling out all the stops to make it a grand time for all with a full month of sales. "Five thousand employees of the biggest cash establishment in the world are busily engaged in handling the thousands of customers," the article proclaimed. "It promises to be a gala month and a record breaker."

There was no doubt that the store had grown by leaps and bounds. Rowland Macy, who had opened his New York establishment on October 28, 1858, had seen his staff expand to 1,000 by the time of his death in 1877. By 1908, it took 5,000 salespeople to make the store function, while another 5,000 were needed in the offices, on the cleaning staff, and in other nonsales positions. Approximately 250 employees worked in Macy's restaurant alone, while the delivery department employed 800 people—not to mention 400 horses, 175 of which were from Macy's own stables.

Macy's continued to sell for cash only; absolutely no purchases could be made on credit. But in 1902, Nathan Straus originated the idea of the Deposit Account. With this program, customers could make deposits of money with the store, and then charge purchases against them. Interest was paid upon the accounts on an annual basis so that the customer's money would not lie idle, and a yearly dividend was added, as well. Soon, thousands of Macy's shoppers became depositors, providing the Strauses with additional funds for investment in the company while enjoying a convenient new way of buying goods.

A good part of Macy's revenue came not from in-store purchases, but from orders that streamed in from around the country, and even other parts of the world. Since his first years in New York retailing, R.H. Macy had produced and distributed a store catalogue, which soon became popular with customers who were unable to make purchases in the Manhattan store or who simply liked the convenience of shopping by mail. By the time the Herald Square store opened, a large catalogue was issued twice a year, and a number of specialty catalogues—featuring groceries or holiday gift goods, for instance—were also available. Between 1902 and 1908, Macy's sent out 25,000,000 packages ranging from hairpins to pianos. Orders were shipped to locations as close as uptown Manhattan and as far away as India.

As Macy's grew, so did the benefits it offered to its employees. Since its formation in 1885, the company's Mutual Aid Society had helped workers

The Deposit Account was a unique arrangement that benefited both Macy's and its loyal customers. For shoppers, it meant enforced savings—with interest—and a convenient way to purchase items without going into debt. For Macy's, it meant a continual stream of cash that could be used to buy inventory and build the business.

As dresses developed a slimmer silhouette, hats were given lavish brims that swept around the face. Especially popular was the Merry Widow hat. Named for a hat featured in a 1907 operetta, the Merry Widow was gargantuan in proportions, with a brim that could be up to a foot in depth.

On January 21, 1908, a board of aldermen passed the Sullivan Ordinance, which barred the women of New York City from smoking in public. Although this ordinance was enforced the very next day with the arrest of Katie Mulcahey, Mayor Seth Low vetoed the law two weeks later.

The Timeless Art and Stylish Fashion

of the Macy's Catalogues

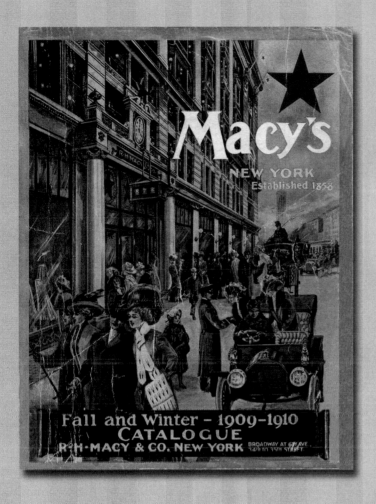

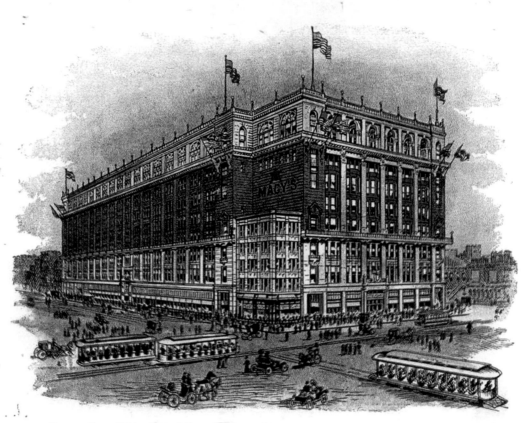

Imagine Having This Great Store in Your Home Town!

Of course, you couldn't move this mammoth 24-acre building, its $5,000,000 stock, and its army of over 5,000 employees—but YOU CAN HAVE THE SAME STORE SERVICE YOU'D HAVE IF YOU LIVED IN NEW YORK CITY.

Our Mail-Order Organization Makes Every Post Office a Doorway of the Macy Store

No matter where you live you can do your shopping here, enjoy the same ECONOMIES and select from the same vast stocks that appeal to New York City's millions.

The mainstays of our Mail Order organization are the

Big Catalogues Issued Twice a Year, and Sent Free Upon Request

In addition to these big books we issue a number of special catalogues—for example, a Grocery Catalogue, one of Holiday Gift Goods, one of Sporting Goods—and scores of smaller booklets and folders announcing important special sales.

There are over 80 departments in this great store, stocked with complete lines of BEST QUALITY MERCHANDISE. We sell everything from pins and needles to pianos and gasolene launches—everything from the latest foreign and domestic fashions to the choicest foreign and domestic foodstuffs.

Send for our catalogues—get your name on our mailing list, and you will receive the special announcements and samples of goods which are sent out frequently.

We want to prove to you that it will pay you to do your shopping at MACY'S—the largest retail store under one roof.

National Delivery Service

We prepay freight or express charges on all paid purchases, with the exception of bulky goods, such as furniture, pianos, etc., as follows:

$5— FREE delivery to any town in NEW YORK, NEW JERSEY, CONNECTICUT, DELAWARE, PENNSYLVANIA, MASSACHUSETTS, RHODE ISLAND, NEW HAMPSHIRE, MARYLAND, VERMONT and the DISTRICT OF COLUMBIA.

$10— FREE delivery to any town in MAINE, ILLINOIS, WEST VIRGINIA, INDIANA, KENTUCKY, MICHIGAN, OHIO and VIRGINIA.

$25— FREE to any town in ALABAMA, FLORIDA, GEORGIA, IOWA, NORTH CAROLINA, SOUTH CAROLINA, TENNESSEE, WISCONSIN.

$50— FREE to any town in LOUISIANA, KANSAS, ARKANSAS, NORTH DAKOTA, INDIAN TERRITORY, NEBRASKA, OKLAHOMA, MINNESOTA, SOUTH DAKOTA, TEXAS, MISSISSIPPI and MISSOURI.

$75— FREE to any town from the Atlantic to the Pacific.

R. H. MACY & CO., Broadway at Sixth Ave., 34th St. to 35th St., New York

A 1903 ad praising the "economies" of ordering Macy's merchandise by mail. Even at the turn of the century, Macy's shipped orders to locations around the world.

cover medical costs. Then in 1907, the store instituted a Mutual Aid loan fund, which enabled employees to withdraw money without providing collateral and without the accrual of interest.

In an effort to inspire thrift and economy on the part of the staff, Macy & Co. set up a savings bank within the store for the sole use of its workers. Amounts of a nickel or more could be deposited whenever an employee desired. Then, at the end of each business day, a messenger would transfer the funds to a New York savings bank that directly handled the accounts. Macy's even set aside a permanent fund as a loan reserve for its employees. Any man or woman who had been in the store's employ for three months or more could—if he or she had a satisfactory reason—secure an interest-free loan from this fund. Employees were limited to an amount that could be repaid in ten weekly installments.

In addition to offering practical help for its employees, Macy's encouraged the enjoyment of after-hours recreational activities. A circulating book library provided nearly a thousand volumes ranging from the classics to the latest novels, encyclopedias, and dictionaries in several languages. Macy's had begun holding company picnics long before its move to Herald Square, and this continued to be a popular annual event. Macy's employees even formed their own baseball team, the Macy's Red Stars, named after the signature star in the company's logo. The Red Stars played the teams of other department stores of

MACY'S DEPARTMENT STORE AND HERALD SQUARE NEW YORK

the time, including those of Wanamaker's, Bloomingdale's, Greenhut, Simpson Crawford, Siegel-Cooper, and Houghton & Dutton. Major matches, such as the August 28, 1909 game between the Red Stars and the Houghton & Dutton Nine, were known to draw crowds as large as 5,000 to 10,000 people.

The Macy's team won the August 1909 match, which the press described as an "exceptionally good example of the National game." In fact, both on the baseball field and in the ledger books, R.H. Macy & Co. was enjoying success. In 1910, the long-promised Pennsylvania Station opened on Eighth Avenue and Thirty-First Street, bringing throngs of shoppers to Macy's Thirty-Fourth Avenue store. Business was booming.

Soon after R.H. Macy & Co. moved to Herald Square, the great emporium became a popular tourist destination, and postcards were printed up so that visitors could send greetings to their friends back home. These souvenir cards were mailed out in 1906 and 1907, respectively.

On December 31, 1909, the Manhattan Bridge was opened to traffic. Connecting southeastern Manhattan to western Brooklyn, this was the last of three suspension bridges built across the East River; the first two being the Brooklyn Bridge (1883) and the Williamsburg Bridge (1903).

William Howard Taft was President from 1909 to 1913. Although generally regarded as a poor politician who lacked the energy and personal magnetism of his predecessor, Theodore Roosevelt, Taft had many accomplishments, including aggressive trust-busting, establishment of an improved postal system, and strengthening of the Interstate Commerce Commission.

At the time of the *Titanic* disaster, John A. Badenoch, Macy's grocery buyer, was on the *Carpathia*, bound for a buying trip in Europe. When the *Carpathia* received the *Titanic's* distress signal, the ship's captain, Arthur Henry Rostron, set a course for the foundering vessel's last position. Aware that the Strauses were aboard the *Titanic*, Badenoch wired the home office, informing them that he would give his stateroom to the Strauses when they were picked up. For hours, Badenoch watched the lifeboats as they arrived. But although the *Carpathia* was able to save 705 people, Ida and Isidor Straus were not among the rescued passengers.

THE *TITANIC*

In January of 1912, Isidor Straus and his wife, Ida, traveled to Europe on the steamship *Caronia*. On April 10, 1912, Isidor and Ida boarded the *Titanic* for the return trip to New York. Less than a week later, the *Titanic* sank, and 1,523 of its passengers and crew perished. Among them were Isidor and Ida Straus.

A great many people are aware of the bravery and mutual devotion shown by Isidor and Ida Straus during the sinking of the *Titanic*. Survivors of the disaster reported that after the ship's collision with an iceberg, the Strauses dressed and appeared on deck, where they calmly discussed the event. Both Isidor and the officer in charge urged Ida to board a lifeboat, but she refused to leave without her husband. At one point, thinking that Isidor was following, she did enter one of the boats, but when she realized that her husband intended to stay on the *Titanic*, she left the lifeboat to join him. When last seen, the Strauses were standing on the deck of the sinking ship, clasped in each other's arms as they watched the departing passengers.

On April 26, 1912, the Straus family was notified that Isidor's body had been recovered. Ida's body never was found. Funeral services, officiated by Rabbi Samuel Schulman of Temple Beth-El, were held for Isidor on May 8 at the family's New York home, with only members of the Straus family in attendance. To avoid a crowd of friends and admirers, news of the services was not released until the next day. *The New York Times* reported that the entire lower floor of the Strauses' home was banked with floral pieces sent by friends and business associates. Memorial services for Ida and Isidor Straus were held around the world.

The staff of R.H. Macy & Co. keenly felt the loss of Isidor Straus—whom they had addressed as "Mr. Isidor"—and wanted to provide a lasting memorial to him and his wife. On June 8, 1913, more than five thousand employees of R.H. Macy & Co. gathered in the store's restaurant and unveiled a bronze plaque featuring bas-relief figures of the couple. The tablet bore the inscription, "Their lives were benevolent, and their teachings glorious." Sylvester Byrnes, General Manager of Macy's, explained that the "gathering and simple ceremonies" were the suggestion of a young female employee of the store. After the presentation, the plaque was hung in the store's Thirty-Fourth Street arcade.

Isidor and Ida Straus, ca. 1910.

On March 25, 1911, one hundred forty-five people died in the notorious Triangle Shirtwaist Factory fire in New York City. This tragedy spurred the growth of the International Ladies' Garment Workers' Union, which once was one of the largest labor unions in the United States.

On May 6, 1912, thousands of women marched through the streets of Manhattan, demanding "Votes for Women." The marchers represented different classes, nationalities, and religions, and included hundreds of men who strongly believed in giving women the vote. National women's suffrage, however, did not exist until 1920.

IN WAKE OF THE *TITANIC*

The RMS *Titanic* in Southampton, England, before departing on her ill-fated maiden voyage of April 10, 1912.

Following the death of Isidor Straus in 1912, his interest in the business tranferred to sons Jesse, Percy, and Herbert. Half of the store was now owned by Isidor's boys, and half was owned by Isidor's brother, Nathan.

Like Isidor, Nathan Straus had sons—Hugh Grant Straus and Nathan Straus, Jr. The boys worked at Macy's, although in positions far junior to those of their older cousins. When Hugh and Nathan, Jr. asked for more responsibility in the running of the store, Jesse, Percy, and Herbert felt that their cousins did not have sufficient experience for the higher positions they sought. Isidor's sons arranged for an appraisal to determine the monetary value of R.H. Macy & Co. The figure was placed at $15 million, and with this information in hand, the boys approached their Uncle Nathan to ask if he wanted to buy their interest in the store and become sole owner.

Devastated by the death of his beloved older brother and his sister-in-law, Nathan had fallen ill after the *Titanic* disaster. During his recovery, he decided to withdraw from business and devote the rest of his life to phil-

There is a myth that Nathan and Lina Straus traveled with Isidor and Ida on their last vacation, but that Nathan and his wife missed the sailing of the *Titanic* because of a side trip to Palestine. In reality, Nathan and Lina had visited Palestine earlier in the year, and never made reservations on the *Titanic*.

As motorcars like Ford's Model T became more common, both men and women adopted the duster. Originally worn by horsemen in the Old West, this long, loose, lightweight coat was equally suited to protecting clothes during drives along the nation's unpaved roads.

The bronze plaque dedicated to the memory of Ida and Isidor Straus was conceived of by the Macy's staff. At the time of the plaque's unveiling in 1913, Macy's General Manager, Sylvester Byrnes, described it as "a mute token of sorrow as well as appreciation and affection."

92

Macy's—The Store. The Star. The Story.

Cable Address "Edison, New York"

From the Laboratory
of
Thomas A. Edison,

Orange, N.J. April 19 1912

My Dear Mr Strauss

I want to express to you my sympathy in the awful calamity that has fallen upon you. Would that I could offer more comfort than cold pen and ink can convey.

Allow me to express the admiration we all feel for the devoted heroism of the wife who would not leave her husband in the face of certain death.

Sincerely Yours

Thomas A Edison

A letter of condolence sent to the Straus family by American inventor Thomas Alva Edison.
This is one of thousands of letters sent to the Strauses after Isidor's death.

Nathan Straus and the Holy Land

Throughout his adult life, Nathan Straus was involved in many humanitarian and philanthropic activities. While he valued all of them, none captured his heart more than his work for Palestine.

In the early 1900s, Palestine was not the tourist destination that it is today, but was ravaged by disease, famine, and poverty. In 1904, when touring the Mediterranean with wife Lina, Nathan stopped in Palestine, not expecting to stay long. He wrote, "On reaching Jerusalem, we changed our plans. All that we saw in the Holy Land made such a deep impression on us that we gave up the idea of going to other places. . . . From that time on we felt a strange and intense desire to return to the land."

Nathan and Lina both became devoted to the Zionist cause. Nathan built soup kitchens for the aged and blind, supported workrooms for the unemployed, and established a household school for the instruction of young women in domestic service. An annual amount was provided for the relief of poverty, and $250,000 was given for the founding of the Jerusalem Health Center, which brought about remarkable results in the reduction of malaria, trachoma, and other diseases. Under Nathan's guidance and with his funds, the Pasteur Anti-Hydrophobia Institute was established. Nathan even built a button-making factory with the goal of enabling more of the people of Palestine to be self-supporting. Those who received his aid began calling him "The Great Giver," and the seaside city of Netanya was named in his honor.

Nathan and Lina Straus made many more trips to Palestine. By the time of his death in 1931, Nathan had devoted two-thirds of his considerable fortune to the Holy Land, with his known gifts to Zion totaling more than $2 million. Lina's commitment was just as great, and she often toiled beside her husband. In 1918, Lina donated her jewelry, valued at more than $18,000, to Hadassah in Palestine. The couple's view on helping others—whether in the Holy Land or elsewhere—was perhaps best expressed by Nathan, who once wrote, "It is my ambition to die a poor man, for then I shall enrich in happiness and in good works."

---

anthropic causes. A *New York Times* article of November 22, 1913, stated that Nathan would "engage in a world-wide campaign for the improvement of social conditions."

Nathan declined his nephews' offer and made a different proposal. The Straus family owned *two* stores—Macy & Co. and Abraham & Straus—as well as the original family business of L. Straus & Sons. Nathan suggested that Jesse, Percy, and Herbert Straus buy out his interest in Macy's, and in return, cede their interest in Abraham & Straus and L. Straus & Sons to Nathan's family. All the parties involved felt that this would be a good course of action, and the deal was struck. Thus, Nathan's younger son, Hugh Grant Straus, assumed the running of Abraham & Straus, while Nathan Straus, Jr. took over at L. Straus & Sons. And in November 1913, Isidor's sons formally became sole senior partners at R.H. Macy & Co.

In 1893, the Strauses had bought a half interest in the Wechsler & Abraham department store, and had changed the name of the store to Abraham & Straus.

In February 1913, the International Exhibition of Modern Art opened in New York City. Now considered a cultural watershed, the show introduced Americans to modern artists such as Edgar Degas and Vincent Van Gogh. Soon, newspapers were filled with reviews accusing the artists of insanity, immorality, and even anarchy.

Designed as headquarters for F.W. Woolworth Company, the Woolworth Building opened in lower Manhattan on April 24, 1913. Fifty-seven stories high, the impressive neo-Gothic structure was the world's tallest building until 1930, when 40 Wall Street and the Chrysler Building were completed.

Left to right: Herbert, Jesse, and Percy Straus, ca. 1920.

5.
The Merchant Princes

Horace Greeley, founder of the *New York Tribune*, once remarked, "We cannot all live in cities, yet nearly all seem determined to do so." Certainly, at the turn of the century, no American metropolis experienced more growth than New York City. Between 1900 and 1910 alone, the population of the five boroughs—Manhattan, the Bronx, Brooklyn, Queens, and Richmond—increased from 3,437,000 to 4,767,000, giving the country its highest ten-year population surge yet. To help transport the citizens of New York from one place to another, the city had opened its first official subway system in 1904, and soon expanded service from Manhattan to the Bronx (1905), Brooklyn (1908), and Queens (1915). Supplementing the train lines was a system of gasoline-powered buses. Soon, everyone within the five boroughs would have access to Manhattan's bustling midtown area, the home of R.H. Macy & Co.

As New York grew by leaps and bounds, three merchant princes—Jesse, Percy, and Herbert Straus—became sole owners of the big store on Thirty-Fourth Street and Broadway. The brothers had already worked in the family company for many years, and seem possessed of both the instincts and skills needed to make their business thrive. In fact, within a few years of taking Macy's helm, they would not only guide the company through a period of unprecedented growth, but also see it through two of the nation's greatest social and economic crises.

Macy's Herald Square store in 1913. Note how the structure in the "notch" has expanded upwards since the store's 1902 opening.

Woodrow Wilson entered the White House in 1913, just as Jesse, Percy, and Herbert Straus assumed leadership of Macy's. Although Wilson initially tried to preserve United States neutrality in the Great War, he ultimately asked Congress to declare war on the Central Powers and saw the nation through to victory.

In the early 1910s, the term *hobble skirt* came into popular use. This long garment was widest at the hips, and narrowed so much below the knees that it made a normal stride impossible. Because the fashion was impractical, wider skirts came into vogue around 1914.

Jesse Isidor Straus.

Percy Selden Straus.

Herbert Nathan Straus.

ISIDOR'S SONS STEP UP TO THE PLATE

At the time of Isidor Straus's death on the *Titanic*, his sons Jesse, Percy, and Herbert had already been involved in the management of Macy's for quite a few years. Many say that Isidor had increasingly stepped back from his leadership role as his sons became more active in the company. So although Isidor's sons deeply mourned the loss of their father, they were not intimidated by the task of running the busy store, nor did they miss a step in their efforts to continuously improve store operations.

Over the years, the Strauses had formed several in-house committees for the purpose of reviewing and coordinating store policy. In 1908, they had formed both a Managers Association, comprised of the store's buyers, and a Board of Operations, comprised of the controller, the delivery department, and other departments not directly involved in sales. In 1914, they added the Advisory Council, made up of Jesse, Percy, and Herbert, as well as Macy's managers. One of the tasks these various groups undertook was to collect and analyze customer complaints so that Macy's could identify and eliminate unsatisfactory merchandise, poor service, and other problems. But even when an existing policy seemed to be working, Macy's considered ways to improve it. For instance, since the opening of the Herald Square store, Macy's had used pneumatic tubing to send a customer's cash to a clerk in another part of the building, where change could be made and transported back to the purchaser. Although the system worked well, in 1912, the Board of Operations began an experiment to see if customers would be happier if change was made directly at the point of purchase. As you might expect, shoppers found it more convenient to have the entire transaction handled by a clerk stationed on the sales floor.

The Strauses had long used comparison shoppers to check the prices of their competitors so that Macy's could keep its promise of offering the best for less. Although for years, this work had been performed on a somewhat informal basis, in 1915, the company created a formal Comparison Department, and in 1917, this department was given the authority to reduce an item's price whenever a competitor was found to be selling it for less. Macy's also bought items from competing stores so that the merchandise could be examined by the store's buyers.

The Strauses provided ample opportunities for the staff to improve job-related skills through in-house education programs run by their Department of Training. Five mornings a week, between 8:45 and 10:45 AM, younger employees were given a chance to brush up on the three R's—reading, 'righting, and 'rithmetic—as well as on local geography and personal hygiene. At the end of each term, a representative of the Board of Education awarded certificates to the students.

On February 2, 1913, New York City's Grand Central Terminal officially opened for business—even though construction was not entirely complete. Popularly called Grand Central Station, it serves commuters traveling to counties in New York State and Connecticut.

On March 27, 1914, Belgian doctor Albert Hustin performed the first non-direct blood transfusion using sodium citrate as an anticoagulant. This ultimately made possible the banking of civilian blood for use by wounded soldiers during the Great War.

Macy's also offered Junior Training Classes for employees who wanted to reach the level of Junior Sales Clerks. In the morning, these employees would spend time in the receiving department, marking the merchandise. After lunch, they moved to a sales floor to get practical experience working with customers.

Macy's senior employees were encouraged to take the store's Textile Class so that they would become more knowledgeable about clothing and other textile-related merchandise. This class was so popular that one issue of Macy's in-house newsletter reported, "It is becoming difficult to find sales clerks in departments handling textiles who are not equipped to pass along accurate information to customers concerning materials."

Under the leadership of Jesse, Percy, and Herbert Straus, R.H. Macy's was running like a finely tuned watch. The Strauses took every step possible to ensure that their store offered the best-quality merchandise for the lowest price, and that the staff provided customers with the excellent service they had come to expect. But clouds of war were gathering over Europe and very soon, the storm would extend over the United States as well. Only time would tell how this would affect the retailing giant.

The Changing of the Guard

After the death of Isidor Straus in 1912, the great emporium known as R.H. Macy & Co. was managed by several different people over the next six decades. What remained constant, however, was that they were all members of the remarkable Straus family.

Isidor Straus's death passed the store into the hands of his brother, Nathan, and his sons, Jesse, Percy, and Herbert. But Nathan sold his share of Macy's to his nephews, who quickly assumed command. Led by Jesse, who was voted president of the firm in 1919, the three heirs were soon referred to in the press as "The Triumvirate of Merchant Princes"— and for good reason. Under their skilled leadership, Macy's was updated, expanded, and eventually built into the world's largest store.

Like their father, who had served as a member of Congress from 1894 to 1895, Jesse, Percy, and Herbert Straus believed in public service. So in addition to heading Macy & Co., Jesse Straus served on New York State's Tax Revision Commission, and also headed a commission charged with providing relief to New York's many unemployed during the Great Depression. Then on March 13, 1933, President Roosevelt appointed Jesse United States Ambassador to France, and on April 5, the eldest son of Isidor Straus stepped down as president of R.H. Macy's. Taking his place was younger brother Percy.

When Percy assumed leadership of the growing Macy's firm, he was assisted in his task by younger brother Herbert N. Straus, who was now both vice president of Macy's and president of L. Bamberger & Co. But on April 6, 1933, Herbert passed away from a heart attack at the age of fifty-one. Three years later, tragedy again struck the Straus family when Jesse died at the age of sixty-four. Of the three brothers, only Percy was left to guide the store and carry on the tradition established by Isidor and Nathan Straus.

In 1939, Percy stepped down from his position of command, and Jack I. Straus, Jesse's son, became the third generation of Strauses to run Macy's. Jack was to hold sway over the store's Herald Square headquarters until his retirement on October 4, 1968, when—for the first time in eighty years— Macy's was without a Straus in command.

MACY'S GOES TO WAR

On June 28, 1914, Gavrilo Princip, a Bosnian Serb student, shot and killed the Archduke Francis Ferdinand, heir to the Austro-Hungarian throne. This set into motion a series of events that escalated into the Great War, later to be known as World War One. Initially, the United States pursued a policy of isolationism, but after German hostilities resulted in the sinking of seven US merchant ships, President Wilson called for Congress to take action. The United States declared war on Germany on April 6, 1917.

A November 1918 *Sparks* cover encouraging employees to "dig deep for our soldiers."

The United States had a small army at the time of its entry in the war, but on May 18, the Selective Service Act was passed—an act that, by the end of the war, would lead to the drafting of 4 million Americans. By the summer of 1918, the United States was sending 10,000 soldiers to France every day.

The war effort was expensive. In fact, the United States was to spend $33 billion on the Great War. To raise funds while instilling traditional values of patriotism and saving, the Treasury Department issued Liberty Bonds. Popular entertainers of the time—Mary Pickford, Charlie Chaplin, Al Jolson, and Douglas Fairbanks—appeared at rallies, urging Americans to support the troops through the purchase of bonds. But not everyone could afford a Liberty Bond, the smallest of which was fifty dollars. For them, the Treasury Department sold Thrift Stamps. These tiny stamps cost only twenty-five cents each, and once you had collected sixteen of them, you could exchange them for Savings Stamps, which bore interest. The stamps were popular among children, but were also purchased by immigrants who were still struggling to establish themselves in America, and wanted to support their new country in any way they could.

Led by Jesse, Percy, and Herbert Straus, the Macy's staff enthusiastically did its part for the war effort. The company's employee newsletter, *Sparks,* created at the start of the war, urged the staff to buy war stamps because "Every Thrift Stamp is another nail in the Kaiser's coffin." A competition took place between some 1,800 department and dry goods stores, with each store vying to sell the largest number of stamps. Macy's employees did what they could, both for the store and for the war, with one member of the staff selling $25,000 worth of Thrift Stamps.

At the suggestion of employee George A. Geraghty, Macy's threw a block party for the purpose of boosting Liberty Bond sales. The event was held on Thirty-Fifth Street between Broadway and Seventh Avenue, with admission

On November 3, 1914, Mary Phelps Jacob received a patent for the "backless brassiere"—an alternative to the more restrictive corset. But the bra did not become truly popular until World War One, when the War Industries Board requested that women stop buying corsets to free up metal for war production.

During World War One, women who left the home for the workplace often adopted short hairstyles for practical reasons. Eventually, the "bob cut"—which involved bangs and hair that curved inward between the ears and chin—was considered a sign of the liberated woman.

Letters from Our Boys in the Service

When you write abroad always write out "American E. F." because "A. E. F." means "Australian" as well as "American" Expeditionary Force.

DEAR ANNA:

I received the August number of SPARKS for which very many thanks. I hope you received my letter; I know Carrie did as I had a letter from Mr. McDonnell to which I replied yesterday. I had a nice little time myself down in Carrick - on - Lais at my sister's place, which is not far from the sea coast. I was surprised to see a John O'Day in the Roll of Honor—don't say it's the one and only. It's a pity I can't talk war and other things but when you hear the bands playing and pass Old Glory flying, think what it's all about, and think especially of the poor "small nationalities." I agree with Mr. Jessie and my old pal, Corporal Edward Nolan that SPARKS is a go and just to keep it on the go I would like to become a regular subscriber.

I would hate to miss a copy of it now, I am ever so thankful for the copies read. Its as good as a visit to the old spot to read through them, hence the brain wave below. Its hardly classy enough for SPARKS but after reading all the nice poetry in the last issue, I felt it coming over me and like a bird singing in response to its mates, I simply had to let it out—some bird! I have no news (drat the censor) only that I am getting on splendidly in the hospital. Tell Carrie to get busy and let me know where she spent all her winter's earnings this summer. My best regards to you both and kindly remember me to all old friends in the store. Thanking you again, I remain

E. LOUGHNAN.

September 24, 1918.

DEAR MISS SIDNEY:

I am grateful indeed for the dandy sweater and other articles which you so kindly gave me, and I am writing you this short note in appreciation of them. There surely could be nothing more generous or patriotic to help in this world struggle than the wonderful work which the ladies of the Red Cross Auxiliary of R. H. Macy & Co., are doing for us boys. I am sure, also, that if they realize the real comfort and enjoyment which we obtain from the articles which they made for us, they would feel freely repaid.

The 42nd U. S. Infantry of which I am proud to be a member is now a part of the new 12th division which was recently formed at Camp Devens. Major General McCain has been assigned by the War Department to this division as Commander and we are now doing very intensive training in preparation for overseas duty. There is a splendid spirit among the fellows in camp and this, I believe to be due most entirely to the fact that the time is rapidly drawing near when we shall be able to do something worth while toward adding to the honor of dear Old Glory. Gas masks and helmets have already been issued.

One of the boys has been sending me his copy of SPARKS and I have found it most interesting. Its contents is ever bringing to mind the many pleasant occasions which I so thoroughly enjoyed during the eight years I was connected with the house of R. H. Macy & Co. Again accept my most hearty thanks Miss Sidney and kindly remember me to Mr. Price and Mr. Woods, for whom I am wishing all good things.

Yours sincerely,
Pvt. Ed. O. Junginger,
Hdg's. Co., 42 Inf. U. S.
Camp Devens, Massachusetts.

We Think it is a Pretty Good Picture

"This is a picture of me, well anyway it's supposed to be me. It is the best they could make of me. I can't kick about the army, because we get good eats and a nice warm bed. It's only these fellows who are used to being waited on who kick," says E. Uhelfelder.
Co. A 4th Repl. Regt.
Camp Gordan, Ga.
August 5, 1918.
U. S. S. Carola, Franc

DEAR OLD FRIENDS:

A few weeks ago Perper sent me a copy of your store magazine SPARKS, and to put it mildly I was just tickled silly (always was silly) to read of the activities of the old crowd.

Just like Johnny Walker "still going strong," and I trust that you continue to do so as the Community Club was the means of my spending countless happy hours that I shall never forget.

Most of the old crowd is missing I suppose and therefore things may be a little dull, but when this cruel war is over, things will be bright and happy as before.

being the purchase of a Thrift Stamp. Macy's was decked with bunting and Allied flags, while bands played patriotic tunes and items were offered for auction. Jesse Straus himself bid $50,000 worth of Liberty Bonds, winning a "handsome silk American Flag." More than 30,000 people attended.

Macy's also set up its own Red Cross chapter, Auxilliary No. 81. The Strauses strongly supported this effort, saying, "We wish to impress upon every co-worker in the house that the Red Cross of RH Macy & Co is open to all our men and women. We feel that with the spirit that now exists, every-one should be willing and able to come at least once a month if not more." Come they did, meeting first in the employee dining room for an after-hours dinner, and then in the recreation room, where they knitted and sewed items for the troops. Some 2,000 garments—sweaters, scarves, and wristlets—were knitted by the Macy's Red Cross workers, with many of them being sent to Macy's employees who had gone off to war. Even staff members who didn't know how to knit were urged to join: "We'll show you how to knit if you don't know already, the firm provides the wool and needles, all you have to give is your time and patience." Classes were also set up in sewing, garment-cutting, and surgical dressings.

As Americans struggled to maintain contact with family members serving abroad, Macy's established an on-site Service Bureau designed to help employees reach their sons, brothers, and husbands. The employee newslet-ter, *Sparks,* also served as a bridge between Macy's and those at war. Included in each wartime issue was "Our Own Roll of Honor," which listed the hun-dreds of young men who had left the employ of Macy's "to swell the greater ranks in the struggle for world freedom." *Sparks* also printed stories of brav-ery and victory in battle, as well as the inevitable "In Memoriam" tributes to men who had fallen. But the newsletter did more than tell those at home about those abroad. Copies of *Sparks* were often sent to Macy's workers who served in Europe, giving the men a welcome taste of home. One serviceman, George Copely, wrote to Macy's: "I read a late edition of *Sparks* and certainly did enjoy reading it and seeing all the familiar faces again. I thank you or the sender very much." Another serviceman, Arthur Becan, wrote: "A few weeks ago Perper [another Macy's employee] sent me a copy of your *Sparks* and to put it mildly I was just tickled silly to read of the activities of the old crowd."

Interestingly, the period of the Great War was the first time that Macy's had to rely heavily on classified advertising to staff its store. For many years, the company had enjoyed a solid stream of job applicants, many of whom applied at the suggestion of friends who already worked at Macy's. But once the draft began to pull young men from the nation's labor force, the store had to be more aggressive in its search for workers. Fortunately, America's involvement in the Great War was relatively short, and soon, hopeful job can-didates again began to seek out one of New York's foremost employers.

In February 1919, after the end of the Great War, an issue of *Sparks* proclaimed, "RH Macy & Co. led the Department and Retail Dry Goods division in the sale of War Savings Stamps for 1918. Our total is more than $500,000!"

The plaque donated by Macy's Men's Club to express appreciation for co-workers fighting in the Great War. The inscription reads: "We honor those who do us honor. In this metal we inscribe our humble appreciation to those of our co-workers who have gone from our midst to defend a principle and bring peace to a stricken world."

In 1916, Jeannette Rankin of the State of Montana became the first woman elected to the United States House of Representatives. A lifelong pacifist, Rankin has the distinction of being the only person who voted against the nation's entry into both World War One and World War Two.

The first timed, pop-up toaster was invented in 1919 by Charles Strite, but it was not until 1925 that a redesigned version—the Toastmaster—was made available to the public. This labor-saving device was an instant success with homemakers everywhere.

Macy's, now bigger and better than ever, displays a new electric sign topped by the famous Macy's star (ca. 1925).

September 8 of that year, Macy's held the official opening of the newly expanded emporium.

R.H. Macy & Co. now offered one hundred and forty-eight departments. Old departments had been greatly expanded in size, presenting shoppers with more items than ever before, all beautifully displayed. The entire fourth floor—now called "Young Folks World"—was devoted to children's apparel. The phonograph department had a bank of seventy-five "talking machines," allowing customers to sample the music of the day before making a purchase. In the grocery department, a new 150-foot counter featured a conveyor belt that moved purchased goods from checkout into the customer's hands. And the furniture department now included seven completely furnished rooms so that customers could get decorating ideas as they examined merchandise. To help shoppers find exactly what they wanted, Macy's staff had grown to 7,500, and provisions were made to expand the staff to 10,000 when needed at Christmastime. Fifteen new elevators and two new escalators allowed customers to move where they desired with speed and ease.

When designing the new building, the Strauses had wanted to ensure that the many additional delivery trucks needing access to Macy's would not greatly disrupt the traffic outside the store. The result was the construction of a sub-basement and sub-sub-basement, and the installation of four freight elevators large and sturdy enough to accommodate the mammoth delivery vehicles. A truck would be driven into the elevator and then lowered to below-street levels, where the merchandise could be unloaded. The elevator would then lift the emptied truck up to street level again.

With the 1924 expansion complete, Macy's had over 1.5 million square feet of retail space. It was now literally the "World's Largest Store."

The fourth floor of the newly expanded Macy's building was used for more than selling children's clothing. It was also the scene of parties and performances. In September 1925, for instance, several thousand children attended a party that featured Betty Bronson, a much-loved actress best known for playing the title role in the 1924 silent film version of *Peter Pan.*

A Macy's furniture delivery truck in the 1920s.

Macy's models sport popular twenties styles—four versions of a "little black dress."

Macy's Reaches Beyond New York

Although Macy's has always been an American institution, as it grew in fame, an increasing number of people outside of the United States became aware of the store's success. Macy's international reputation was particularly apparent in 1926, when a delegation of forty buyers arrived from London's Selfridge & Co. A well-known department store, Selfridge & Co. was established in 1908 by Henry Gordon Selfridge—an American who had learned about retailing at Chicago's Marshall Field's, but chose to build his own business in England. The goal of these and other trips was to compare and learn from different retailing practices.

The Macy's flagship store was bigger and better than ever, but the Strauses wanted to expand the company through more than just enlargement of their famous Manhattan emporium. They sought to own department stores throughout the country.

In 1922, Jesse Straus laid the groundwork for future acquisitions by putting forth a plan to issue $10,000,000 in preferred stock, as well as 350,000 shares of common stock. Macy's went public on August 16, 1922 to great excitement. Everyone wanted to own a piece of the store. By ten o'clock that morning, the offering was closed because of overwhelming demand for both classes of stock.

Using the income generated through stock sales, the Strauses began to make acquisitions outside of the New York City region. In 1924, Macy's acquired a controlling interest in LaSalle and Koch, the largest department store in Toledo, Ohio. In 1925, Macy's purchased Davison-Paxon-Stokes, a department store in Atlanta, Georgia. In 1929, Macy's acquired one of its most successful competitors in the business—the Newark-based Bamberger's, with locations in New Jersey, Delaware, Maryland, New York, and Pennsylvania. Included in this sale was WOR, the radio station established by Bamberger Broadcasting Service in 1922 in an effort to sell more radios.

The 1920s was just the beginning of Macy's acquisition of other stores. This trend would continue throughout the Strauses' ownership of Macy's and beyond. Although some of these retail establishments would eventually take the Macy's name, for the time being, they maintained their original names so that long-time customers would find the stores familiar and friendly places to shop. The Strauses, however, made sure that the stores met Macy's standards, and added to the store's inventory with goods supplied by what Jesse Straus referred to as "our American and Foreign buying organizations."

Fully Stocked and Ready to Sell

For decades, Macy's proudly offered a variety of high-quality items in its grocery department and delicatessen. Available

Titon the Taster—A Macy's Legend

Any large, long-lived store owes its success not only to its owners, but also to dedicated employees who work hard to make the store a "star." In the tale of Macy's, one of these people is William Titon.

William Titon was hired by Macy's in 1897. From the start, young Titon's drive and imagination made it clear that he was an asset to the grocery department in which he worked. Eventually, he became Macy's Wine and Food buyer, and traveled the world looking for top-quality wines, coffees, and other items suitable for sale. Thus, he became known as Titon the Taster.

According to Macy's lore, William Titon brought a number of innovative products to Macy's. The first of these was the Uneeda biscuit. In the early 1900s, crackers were sold loose out of grocery store barrels. Around this time, a man visited Macy's with a new soda cracker. Titon tasted it and asked that certain improvements be made, but even when the product met his high standards, Titon was not entirely satisfied. He wanted to make this cracker unique for more than its mouth-watering flavor. Titon suggested that the manufacturer place premeasured amounts of the crackers in packages, and sell this convenient new item to Macy's shoppers. The result was the first packaged cracker—the Uneeda Biscuit—produced by the National Biscuit Company and sold at R.H. Macy's.

When Titon began working for Macy's, there was no commercial mayonnaise available, so every delicatessen made its own version of the dressing and used it to prepare sandwiches and salads. In 1905, a man named Richard Hellmann opened a New York deli that featured his own special mayonnaise. The mayo was so delicious that Hellmann not only used it in the preparation of foods, but also sold it by the scoop to his eager customers. When Titon discovered Hellmann's product, he suggested that the deli owner package it in bottles for greater convenience. The result was Hellman's Blue Ribbon Mayonnaise, the first bottled mayo.

William Titon's daughter, Ethel Sheifer, proudly tells the story of another of her dad's ground-breaking ideas. For years, Macy's sold some of the finest teas in the world. Some time before World War One—the exact year has been lost over time—a gentleman offered loose tea for Titon's consideration. When the leaves accidentally spilled onto the tasting room floor, Titon gathered them into one of his linen handerchiefs and decided to brew the tea within the cloth rather than dumping it loose into the pot. Thus was born the tea bag, which Macy's proudly sold.

Finally, there is the legendary story of the Idaho potato. In 1926, William Titon was on an apple-buying trip in Idaho when he chanced upon something he had never seen before, an elongated potato with a white, starchy flesh. At the time, people back east used local potatoes for baking, choosing any type that was available—with mixed results. Titon realized that the special Midwestern spud had attributes that made it superior for baking, and soon, the Idaho potato was offered for sale at Macy's and served in its restaurant.

During the more than seventy years that William Titon presided over Macy's grocery department, no one thought to keep detailed records of the department's many innovations. Much of what is known has been enthusiastically passed down by staff members. But it is certain that for over half a century, Titon the Taster helped ensure that Macy's offered its customers not only the tried-and-true products on which they relied, but also an ever-changing array of original delights that would keep them coming back for more.

both in the store and through the Macy's catalogue, these were not items you'd find in a typical grocery store, but harder-to-find delicacies that were well worth the trip to Herald Square.

The Macy's Thanksgiving Day Parade

The Macy's Thanksgiving Day Parade began as a celebration of America and its special heritage. At the time, many Macy's employees were immigrants from Europe, and this first pageant gave them a means of expressing gratitude for their new country.

The story of R.H. Macy's is certainly one of a retail sales giant, but it is also one of great traditions. Nothing demonstrates this more than the history of the Macy's Thanksgiving Day Parade.

In 1924, what was then called the Macy's Christmas Parade was conceived of by Macy's employees. Many of the employees were European immigrants, and this event was rooted in the traditional festivals of their homelands. The Strauses enthusiastically supported the parade and wanted to make sure that it would attract the city's attention. So the day before the spectacle, Macy's took out newspaper ads promising "a surprise New York will never forget!"

On November 27, the parade commenced in Manhattan at Convent Avenue and One Hundred Forty-Fifth Street. Four hundred employees dressed in vibrant costumes marched to the store on Thirty-Fourth Street, accompanied by three horse-drawn floats, balloons, four professional bands, and live animals—camels, elephants, bears, and more—borrowed from the Central Park Zoo. At the parade's conclusion, Santa Claus was welcomed into Herald Square and enthroned on the balcony at the store's entrance. There he was crowned "King of the Kiddies." An estimated quarter million spectators eagerly watched the procession as it moved along its six-mile route, and Macy's, delighted by the city's response, announced that it would be an annual event.

For a few years, live animals continued to appear in what soon became known as the Macy's Thanksgiving Day Parade. But the animals were found to frighten some of the children, so in 1927, they were replaced by large animal-shaped balloons produced by the Goodyear Tire & Rubber Company of Akron, Ohio. That year, the Felix the Cat balloon made its first appearance. Felix was filled with air in 1927, but the next year, helium was used.

At the finish of the 1928 Thanksgiving Day Parade, the colorful balloons were released into the sky, where they surprised parade organizers by bursting. The following year, they were redesigned with safety valves that allowed them to float for several days. Address labels sewn into the back of each balloon directed the person who found it to mail it back to Macy's, which would reward the lucky individual with a cash gift.

No one at the time could have foreseen the ways in which the Macy's Thanksgiving Day Parade would grow over the years. They could not have imagined the building-size helium-filled balloons that would someday float above the crowds, nor would they have believed that the spectacle would eventually have over 50 million viewers worldwide. But as the 1920s drew to a close, one thing was certain: The parade created by the world's largest department store would return year after year, delighting children and adults alike.

Macy's first grand parade—then called the Macy's Christmas Parade—took place on November 27, 1924. Highlights of the early pageants included animals from the Central Park Zoo, a variety of beautiful floats, and towering balloons.

GREET SANTA CLAUS AS 'KING OF KIDDIES'

Crowds Cheer Him in Parade and Witness Coronation in Macy's New Store.

FLOATS IN THE PAGEANT

Visit to City on Thanksgiving Day Marks Unveiling of Big Christmas Window.

Santa Claus chose Thanksgiving Day this year to come to town. With a retinue of clowns, freaks, animals and floats, the bewhiskered man in red, in sight of thousands of persons, arrived at 9 o'clock yesterday morning, and three hours later was crowned "King of the Kiddies" on the marquee above the entrance to Macy's new store in Thirty-fourth Street near Seventh Avenue.

His expected arrival having been heralded several days in advance, a crowd estimated by the police at almost 10,000 gathered in Thirty-fourth Street between Sixth and Seventh Avenues to cheer his approach and his subsequent coronation. Children were in the majority, but a large part of the throng was made up of grown-up men and women.

Santa came in state. The float upon which he rode was in the form of a sled driven by reindeer over a mountain of ice. Preceding him were men dressed like the knights of old, their spears shining in the sunlight.

From the start of the parade, at Convent Avenue and 145th Street, to its conclusion men, women, and more especially children, lined the walks, sometimes four and five deep. Led by a police escort, the parade passed down Convent, Morningside and Manhattan Avenues to 110th Streets, where it turned west to Broadway, to Columbus Circle, Fortieth Street to and down Broadway to Thirty-fourth Street, where it was welcomed by such crowds that a large force of policemen had its hands full maintaining the police lines.

The majority of participants were employes of the stores. There were, however, many professional entertainers who kept the spectators amused as they passed by. Beautiful floats showed the Old Lady Who Lived in a Shoe, Little Miss Muffet and Red Riding Hood. There also were bears, elephants, donkeys and bands, making the procession resemble a circus parade.

When Santa seated himself on the throne he sounded his trumpet, which was the signal for the unveiling of the store's Christmas window, showing "The Fairy Frolics of Wondertown," designed and executed by Tony Sarg. The police lines gave way and with a rush the enormous crowd flocked to the windows to see Mother Goose characters as marionettes.

Quality Control

Although the Straus brothers were expanding R.H. Macy & Co. in many directions, they wanted to make sure that the quality of Macy's wares would not slip along the way. Quantity, they felt, would not make up for shoddy goods. So during the twenties, the Strauses took steps to guarantee that their merchandise would continue to satisfy loyal customers.

In the summer of 1927, Macy's established a new department called the Bureau of Standards and Testing Laboratory. Modeled after the National Bureau of Standards, this department tested the overall quality of items, compared similar items to decide which would be sold in the store, examined merchandise that had been returned by shoppers, and determined if Macy's wares lived up to claims made in store advertisements. Within a few months, thousands of items of clothing were tested for stability of dyes, washability, and waterproofing. Over the years, many more types of merchandise would be tested so that the Strauses could eliminate inferior products and feel confident that all claims reflected the true quality and performance of the store's wares.

Macy's Again Expands

The 1929 Macy's addition went up quickly, with the new structure being completed less than a year after demolition of the I. Blyn structure began. Accordingly, on September 4, 1929, Percy S. Straus congratulated the construction workers on the speed and skill with which they had erected the building, and awarded certificates of craftsmanship to twenty of the mechanics.

The 1924 expansion had made Macy's the largest store in the world, but it had not extended the structure as far as the Strauses desired. At the time, a shoe company called I. Blyn & Sons had occupied a building at 161 West Thirty-Fourth Street, limiting the growth of the store. But in 1927, the I. Blyn building went up for sale and the Strauses quickly acquired the property. They now had the room they wanted for expansion.

The new building would adjoin the structure erected in 1924, and, like the 1924 addition, would soar to nineteen stories in height. It would also be designed by Robert D. Kohn, the architect of the previous addition. But the Strauses were interested in making improvements beyond the addition of space. During the expansion, they would also substitute twelve electric elevators for eight hydraulic elevators. Moreover, on the ground and basement levels of Macy's, they would install the largest "air refrigeration system" of any retail store in the country. According to a *New York Times* article, the temperature on these floors would be lowered by ten degrees as compared with the street temperature—a substantial improvement at a time when the air conditioning industry was in its infancy.

Demolition of I. Blyn & Sons began in 1928, and less than a year later, construction was complete. By increasing the frontage by about two hundred feet on the Thirty-Fourth Street and Thirty-Fifth Street sides, the expansion moved Macy's farther westward, edging the department store closer to Seventh Avenue.

A loose-fitting, baggy style of trousers originally favored by members of Oxford University, *Oxford Bags* were popular with men throughout the 1920s and beyond. "Bags" could be paired with a jacket and tie, or even with a pullover sweater for a more casual look.

A bell-shaped, brimmed hat—generally made of felt to better conform to the head—the cloche was highly popular throughout the 1920s. In fact, many women adopted short, slicked-down hairstyles specifically to showcase the form-fitting cloche, which was worn low on the forehead.

May We Show You Around The World's Largest Department Store?

May We Show You Around The World's Largest Department Store?

114

Macy's—The Store. The Star. The Story.

The apron department.

The doll department.

The ground floor.

The Oriental rug department.

The china department.

The drug department.

The vase displays.

The wallpaper department.

The switchboard operators' room.

The men's club.

The perfume counters.

116

Macy's—The Store. The Star. The Story.

The *"Traveler"*—a distinctive feature
of our excellent service.

MENU

★

R. H. Macy & Co.
34th ST. & BROADWAY   *Inc.*   NEW YORK CITY

A la Carte

Assorted Sweet Pickles 19

Relishes

Plain Celery 21   Stuffed with Roquefort Cheese 34   Chow Chow 19   Gherkins 14
Smoked Salmon 39   Tomato Surprise 27   Caviar 69   Anchovies in Oil 29
Sardines in Oil 34   Sardines in Tomato Sauce 44   Queen Olives 13
Dill Pickles 14   Assorted Canapes 74   Assorted Hors d'Oeuvres (per person) 74

Sea Food

Crab Meat Cocktail 64   Lobster Cocktail 69   Fried Clams 44   Steamed Clams 39
Cherrystones 26   Little Neck Clams 27   Clam Stew 39   Clam Broth 21   Cocktail Sauce 6
Cape Cods 29   Blue Points 27   Oyster Stew 39   Fried Oysters, Tartar Sauce 44

Soups

*Clam chowder, Louisiana 18   *Vegetable soup 18
Cream of Tomatoes 18   Onion Soup au Gratin (15 min.) 34
Vegex Vitamine Consomme in Cup 16

Fish

*Paupiette of flounder, shrimp sauce 59   *Broiled mackerel, anchovy butter 59
*Boiled salmon, Hollandaise sauce 69

Eggs

Fried eggs or shirred eggs 31 with bacon or ham 54   Boiled 29
Scrambled 39   Plain omelette 42   Poached on toast 39

Entrees

*Minced beef, Deutsch, home fried potatoes 69   *Vegetable dinner plate 54
*Chicken fricassee, creamed corn 59   Breaded pork chops, stewed tomatoes 74
Cheese omelette 49

Roasts

*Roast loin pork, sage dressing, apple sauce and mashed potatoes 74
*Roast prime ribs of beef au jus, roast potatoes 74
*Roast chicken with dressing, French fried potatoes 89

*From
The Grill
(To Order)*

Small Sirloin Steak 98   Sirloin Steak (for 2) 196   Mixed Grill 98
Hamburger or Salisbury Steak 74   with Fried Egg 84   Lamb Chops (2) 89
Pork Chops (2) 74   Tenderloin Steak 1 24   English Mutton Chop, Bacon 98
Half Broiled Milk-fed Chicken with Bacon 98   Broiled Ham or Bacon 54
(French Fried or Mashed Potatoes Served with All Broiled Meats)

*Cold Joints,
Etc.*

Prime Ribs of Beef 79   Tongue 74   Ham 74   Lamb 79   Sliced Cold Chicken 98
Assorted Cold Cuts 89   with Chicken 98   Pickled Lamb's Tongue 54
Corned Beef 69   Home-made Head Cheese 59
(Choice of Salads Served with Cold Meats; Lettuce, Beet, Tomato or Potato)

Sandwiches

Ham 23   Tongue 23   Cold Roast Beef 42   Hot 49   Fried Egg 18
Corned Beef Sandwich 34   Cream Cheese 21 with Pimentos 24
Macy's Special Club 74   Chicken 44   on Toast 49   Swiss Cheese 23
Lettuce and Tomato, Mayonnaise 21   Sardine 27

Vegetables

Green Peas 18   String Beans 18   Colossal Asparagus, Hollandaise 34
Carrots with Cream 18   with Peas 18   Stuffed Green Pepper 21   Fried Egg Plant 19
Spaghetti au Gratin 21   Beets in Butter 18   Stewed Tomatoes 19
Spaghetti in Cream or Tomato Sauce 18   New Spinach 24
Boiled White Onions, Melted Butter or Cream Sauce 19   Asparagus Tips 31

Potatoes

Boiled or Mashed 12   Baked 12   French Fried 14   Lyonnaise 22
Saute 19   Parisienne 24   Hashed Browned 22   Julienne 22
Side Dish: Boiled, Mashed or French Fried Potatoes 09
Hashed in Cream 22   Au Gratin 24   Allumette 22
Sweet Potatoes Fried or Grilled 22   Southern Style 26

Salads

Lettuce 32   Tomato 32   Lettuce and Tomato 32   Romaine 32   Egg 32
Heart of Lettuce 37   Chiffonade 34   Asparagus Tips 32   Waldorf 34
Combination 34   Fruit 38   Chicken 98   Lobster 98   Tunafish 64
Fresh Shrimp 69   French or Mayonnaise Dressing Served with All Salads
Roquefort Cheese Dressing 19   Russian Dressing 12   Chili Dressing 14
Crab Meat Salad 79

*Desserts and
Pastry*

*Farina pudding with cream sauce 19
Charlotte Russe 16   Sand Cake 19   Fruit Jelly, Chantilly 14
Lemon Meringue Pie 17   Peach, Raisin, Apple or Lemon Pie 17
Cocoanut or Custard Pie 19   Cold Rice Pudding with Cream 16   French Pastry 14
Danish Pastry 09   Meringue Chantilly 19
Pineapple Pie 21   Fresh Huckleberry Pie with Cream 21

*Ice Creams,
Etc.*

*Biscuit Tortoni 32   *Frozen chocolate parfait 32   *Maple walnut ice cream 19
French Vanilla, Strawberry, Chocolate, Fresh Peach or Tutti Frutti
Mixed (2) Flavors 32   Peach or Pear Melba 39   (small) 26   (large) 37
American Vanilla, Chocolate or Strawberry (small) 16   (large) 22
Lemon or Orange Water Ice (small) 16   (large) 22   Mixed (2) Flavors 22

Breads, Etc.

Dry Toast 07   Buttered Toast 07   French Toast with Maple Syrup 24
Milk Toast 19   Cinnamon Toast 18   Cream Toast 24   Gluten Bread (2) Slices 09
Two Rolls or Two Slices of Bread with One Piece of Butter 05

Cheese

Pure Sweet Cream Cheese and Crackers 19   American or Swiss 19
Roquefort 26   Philadelphia Cream Cheese 19   Camembert 21
Philadelphia Cream Cheese with Individual Preserved Peach, Raspberry,
Strawberry or Red Currant Jelly 32
(Served with Toasties or Saltines)

*Coffee, Tea,
Etc.*

Coffee, Cup with Cream 12   Small Pot 17   Large 24
Kaffee-Hag, Per Cup 12   with Cream 17
Tea (small pot) with Milk 12   with Cream 17   Chocolate, Cup 11   Whipped Cream 16
Grade A Certified Milk (half pint bottle) 14   Milk, Per Glass (Grade A) 07
Buttermilk 07   Cream, Small Pitcher 06   Heavy Cream 11   Whipped Cream 06
Horlick's Malted Milk (plain) 10   with Milk 19   with Cream 23

Friday, September 18, 1925

All Dishes Marked * Ready To Serve   For Special Afternoon Tea, See Other Side of Menu

A 1925 menu from Macy's restaurant. The menu reflects the tastes
of the time as well as Macy's more-than-reasonable prices.

THE GREAT DEPRESSION

During the Roaring Twenties, spirits and fortunes had climbed as the economy was fueled by increased industrialization and new technology. But all was not as sunny as it seemed. Many ambitious investors had purchased stocks on margin, borrowing nine dollars worth of stock for every dollar invested. From 1921 to 1929, the Dow Jones Industrial Average rocketed from 60 to 400. Then on Thursday, October 24, 1929, panic selling took place as investors realized that the stock boom had been an inflated bubble. On October 28 and 29, the New York Stock Exchange crashed, with millionaire margin investors becoming bankrupt in what seemed like an instant. To make matters worse, banks had invested their deposits in the stock market, and once stocks were obliterated, savings institutions lost much of their depositors' money. When patrons tried to withdraw their savings all at once, banks failed, unable to provide adequate cash for their customers. During the Depression, 10,000 banks collapsed in all, and $140 billion of depositors' money disappeared. It has been estimated that 9 million bank customers lost all of their savings.

At first, many economists and leaders believed that the stock market crash was a mild bump in the nation's economy, a correction of the market. But as the Great Depression worsened—as personal income, tax revenues, prices, and profits all fell—it became clear that the country would take time to recover.

Just as Macy's had prospered during the economic boom of the twenties, it would be affected by the economic downturn of the thirties. Yet Macy's not only endured this devastating period of American history but was also able to grow, adapt to the changing times, and even extend a helping hand to fellow New Yorkers.

Between 1930 and 1931, some 11,000 teachers were laid off in New York City. During that same period, the street corners of Manhattan were crowded with apple sellers, with more than 6,000 unemployed individuals offering apples for five cents apiece.

Macy's Provides Additional Jobs

As the Depression continued throughout the 1930s, massive layoffs made unemployment an ever-present problem in the United States. In 1933, unemployment peaked at about 25 percent, with one out of every four people in the labor force unable to find a job. Despite new jobs being created, unemployment rates remained high until World War Two.

In the fall of 1930, New York City announced the beginning of an intensive drive to find jobs for the growing number of Manhattan's unemployed. R.H. Macy & Co. and a group of five other department stores were among the first to respond to the city's plea for large businesses to create additional jobs. In September, Macy's announced that the firm would add 1,000 men and women to the store's staff during that month alone.

Herbert Clark Hoover was President of the United States from 1929 to 1933. Elected during a period of national prosperity and optimism, Hoover was ineffective in his attempts to combat the Great Depression, and suffered a great defeat in the election of 1932.

As the Great Depression took hold of the nation, the lighthearted fashions of the twenties began to give way to a more conservative approach. By the end of 1930, skirts were longer and waistlines had risen from the hip to a more natural position. The playful look of the twenties was gone.

New York's Bank of the United States, located in the Bronx, collapsed in December 1931. The bank had over $200 million in deposits at the time, making this the largest single bank failure in the nation's history.

In 1933, with the country's unemployment reaching an all-time high, President Franklin Roosevelt's New Deal programs created the National Recovery Administration (NRA), which was intended to restore employment and regenerate the nation's industry. Headed by former General Hugh Samuel Johnson, the NRA called on every business establishment in the United States to accept a "blanket code"—a minimum wage between twenty and forty-five cents an hour, a maximum work week of thirty-five to forty-five hours, and the abolition of child labor. In August 1933, in accordance with the goals of the NRA, a group of executives representing the leading department stores in New York City—including Macy's—agreed to create a forty-hour work week. In order to provide service during business hours, they further decided that each store would divide its staff into two groups. One group would work from 9:30 AM to 4:55 PM, while the other would work from 10:30 AM to 5:55 PM, with each shift including a forty-five-minute break. To make this plan viable, the stores estimated that they would need to increase their staffs by about 10 percent. This would not only help remove more people from the unemployment rolls, but also give more families the means to buy goods, stimulating the flagging economy.

Join the NO-BILL-ity at Macy's

The thrifty folk who buy merchandise in Macy's Great June Sale will not get a bill for it on July 1st, or August 1st, either. What they buy they own outright, for Macy's sells exclusively for cash. This enables them always to face the first of the month without bill qualms, and it enables us to give them values of which we are truly proud. Indeed we believe there's nothing to compare with good liquid cash (plus volume and efficiency) for getting the most out of any market the wide world over. That's why we are constantly thanking our lucky stars, along with the thousands of thrifty customers who swear by our methods, that 75 years ago Captain Rowland H. Macy started the system which has enabled us to say ever since

No One is in Debt to MACY'S

Entire contents copyrighted by R. H. Macy & Co., Inc., 1935.

Macy's Reconsiders Its Cash-Only Policy

Since the founding of R. H. Macy & Co. in 1858, the store had maintained a strict cash-only policy. While other businesses were eager to sell on credit, Macy's accepted hard currency with no exceptions. During the 1930s, however, this policy was to be challenged a number of times, and ultimately, it was to change.

Between 1929 and 1933, the Great Depression included several runs on multiple banks. As a result, by March of 1933, many banks had failed, while others had been forced to place limits on the amount of money their depositors could withdraw. On March 5, 1933, only one day after Franklin Delano Roosevelt was inaugurated, the President mandated a four-day bank holiday. The Emergency Banking Act, passed on March 9, enabled the government to close down banks, and then re-open them only after federal inspectors had declared them to be financially secure. The act was designed to renew America's confidence in the banking system.

Over the years, R.H. Macy & Co.—always a smart and creative advertiser—used several different slogans to put a positive spin on its cash-only policy. The store's catch phrases included "It's Smart to Be Thrifty" and "No One Is in Debt to Macy's."

Leaders of the Retail Dry Goods Association of New York held an emergency meeting and decided that during the crisis caused by bank closures, they would extend credit to their cash-poor customers via charge accounts. On May 5, 1933, a group of twenty-three retailers printed a joint advertisement, informing shoppers that "the use of charge accounts is open to our customers in the present emergency." They further assured shoppers that a shortage of cash would not impair their credit status. Gimbels—Macy's chief com-

The only President to serve for more than two terms, Franklin Delano Roosevelt occupied the Oval Office from 1933 to 1945. Elected in the depth of the Depression, he is best known for spurring the nation's economic recovery and guiding it through the Second World War.

In the early part of the 1930s, men's suits were designed to make the torso look larger. Shoulders were squared with padding, lapels were long and broad, and sleeves were tapered to the wrist. Generously cut trousers completed the look. Most suits were conservative in color—charcoal gray, slate gray, or navy blue.

petitor—even printed a charge account application at the bottom of an ad, urging customers to "bring it to our Credit Department, 10th Floor, and let's get acquainted." While this certainly placed pressure on Macy's to change its policy, Percy S. Straus stated that the firm was "carrying on as usual," and would accept cash only throughout the bank holiday. Moreover, for the duration of the bank closures, Macy's would not provide cash refunds on returned merchandise. This was intended to prevent customers from using Macy's as a bank by returning merchandise for the money they needed.

Fortunately for consumers and retailers alike, the National Bank Holiday was short-lived, lasting for only a few days. Soon, retailers reported that sales volume had returned to near normal level. Again, Macy's had avoided changing its cash-only policy.

In 1937, as the nation's economy began to improve, Macy's introduced a new buying option to make shopping more convenient for its customers. Beginning on April 7, a representative of the Morris Plan Bank was stationed on the ninth floor, next to the furniture department. Customers were able to apply to the bank for a cash loan, and then use the cash to purchase merchandise in the store. The slogan coined to spread the word about this service was, "Buy Money on Time to Buy Merchandise for Cash." In this way, Macy's was able to offer its customers credit and a means of making large purchases through a series of payments, but did not have to assume any risk.

In June of 1939, Macy's cash-only policy was again in the news. Edwin I. Marks, a Macy's vice president, admitted to the press that for the past five years, management had been reviewing the possibility of offering installment plans to their customers. There were even thoughts of a two-price system in which cash purchasers would pay 6-percent less than those buying on credit. Macy's could certainly increase its profits with this strategy, as it was estimated that the store's sales revenue would soar from $8 million to $15 million a year if customers were offered charge accounts. But cash-only was still the rule.

On September 9, 1939, Jack I. Straus announced that Macy's was preparing to roll out another buying option. Christened "Cash-Time," the system would provide two alternatives to cash purchases. One option allowed the customer to open an account and receive a book of certificates that would be used as cash in the store. Each book was sold at $25, which included a service charge of $1.60. In other words, for each dollar purchased, the customer did not have a full dollar of buying power. The price of each book was to be paid at the rate of $5 a month. The other Cash-Time option permitted the account holder to buy goods on the installment plan, with the duration of the payments ranging from four to sixteen months, depending on the price of the item being purchased. Again, there was a small service charge.

The Cash-Time option was implemented on October 9, 1939, and enjoyed a positive response from Macy's customers. At the end of the first hour of

Three cards from Macy's 1939 postcard series. From the very start, Macy's Herald Square store was a popular shopping destination for New York's many visitors, and these cards made great souvenirs.

TWO BIGGEST . . . N. Y. Empire State Building, world's tallest, and R. H. Macy department store, world's largest.

MACY'S "LITTLE SHOP," N. Y. "fashion centre"

MACY'S THANKSGIVING PARADE . . . Annual mile-long pageant of giant helium-filled balloons escorts Santa Claus to the world's largest store at Broadway & 34th Street, N. Y.

On May 3, 1931, the Empire State Building opened in Manhattan. Because the skyscraper was completed during the Great Depression, much of its office space was unrented at first, prompting New Yorkers to call it the "Empty State Building." Fortunately for its owners, the observation deck alone generated $2 million in income during the first year of operation.

Opened to traffic on July 11, 1936, the Triborough Bridge connected New York's boroughs of Manhattan, the Bronx, and Queens. Actually a complex of three long bridges, as well as a number of smaller bridges and viaducts, the Triborough immediately gave New York residents greater access to the area's many resources.

business, more than a hundred Cash-Time accounts had been opened and more shoppers waited in line, eager to find a new way to buy goods at their favorite department store.

Macy's Weathers the Storms of the Depression

With unemployment high and money in short supply, the Depression was a dark time for the average Macy's customer. Yet Macy's more than survived. As one might expect, to an extent, its profits rose and fell along with the economy. In 1929, Macy's experienced a drop in revenue from the previous year, but in the first half of 1930, sales rose by 42 percent—only to fall again as the economy began its decline. Department store business improved in the mid-1930s and profits began rising, although they did not return to pre-Depression levels for some time.

Macy's third expansion underway in 1931.

Throughout the thirties, Macy's relied on advertising to let its customers know about the store's low prices. In 1931, Kenneth Collins, Macy's executive vice president, urged all retailers to put more money into advertising as an impetus to spending. Even at the depth of the economic slump, Collins took his own advice. In February 1933, Macy's kicked off a store-wide sales extravaganza by placing a sixteen-page section of advertising in local papers. The biggest sale to date in Macy's history, it offered an amazing 1,574 items at reduced prices during a three-week period.

Even after the stock market collapse of October 1929, Macy's continued to build and improve its Herald Square store. From 1929 through 1931, construction proceeded on Macy's final expansion. By August 1931, Macy's had finally replaced the store fronts on Seventh Avenue. The Largest Store in the World now virtually occupied an entire city block, stretching from Broadway to Seventh Avenue in one direction, and from Thirty-Fourth to Thirty-Fifth Street in the other.

An extensive renovation plan was also implemented during this period. When it was complete in September of 1938, Macy's had redesigned its Broadway entrance, ornamenting it with polished granite. Just as stunning were the six new plate-glass windows on the store's Broadway front. Described as "six little theaters," the windows featured lighting used in theatrical productions, and when first unveiled, showcased a group of thirty-six-inch dolls that entered the "theater," spun around, and danced out of sight. Indeed, Macy's Broadway windows would become world-famous, and over the years would exhibit everything from mechanized toys to exotic floral arrangements.

One plan to speed economic recovery was not successful. In 1935, a group of businessmen, including Percy Straus, conceived of an international

The 1930s presented women with a variety of shoe styles. Most women wore pumps with thick high heels, but ankle strap shoes with moderate heels were also available, as were lace-up fashions. Two-tone spectator shoes were most popular during the first part of the decade.

Although women's slacks had made their first appearance in the 1920s, it wasn't until the thirties that they were commonly worn for leisure activities such as skiing and sailing. Actress Katharine Hepburn, who was often photographed wearing men's-style trousers, helped make this fashion popular and acceptable.

exposition that would help lift both New York City and the country out of the Depression. Soon, plans were being made for the 1939 World's Fair. While the fair attracted millions of visitors, it failed to spur additional sales in the city's department stores. As a result of lower-than-anticipated revenue, Macy's gave nearly 12,000 of its employees an enforced one-week leave of absence between May and November of 1939. Fortunately, a profitable fall and Christmas season enabled the store to give its employees their lost salaries, and as the 1930s closed, R.H. Macy & Co. could look forward to better days.

Although for millions of New Yorkers, the 1939 World's Fair provided a welcome diversion from troubles at home, it also offered a window into problems overseas. In the first season of the fair, the pavilion hosted by Czechoslovakia—a country then occupied by enemy forces—sold sheets of souvenir stamps to support its exiled government. In the fair's second season, the Czech pavilion did not even open. France and England, America's allies, were already at war with Germany, and it was only a matter of time before the United States, too, became involved.

The 1939 New York World's Fair

The New York World's Fair of 1939 to 1940 was one of the largest fairs of all time. It was an international event, with many different countries participating. Its purpose, according to the official fair pamphlet, was to allow visitors to look at "the worlds of tomorrow." "Here are the materials, ideas, and forces at work in our world," stated the booklet. "These are the tools with which the World of Tomorrow must be made."

The New York World's Fair Corporation, which planned the event, was composed of some of the most powerful men of the time, including Grover Whalen, Winthrop Aldrich, Mortimer Buckner, Harvey Dow Gibson, Fiorello La Guardia, and Macy's Percy S. Straus. Robert Moses, New York City Parks Commissioner, removed a large ash dump in Queens and cleared the site for the exposition. At the same time, the fair was widely promoted by everyone from the Dodgers, Giants, and Yankees, who wore a World's Fair patch on the left sleeve of their jerseys, to Howard Hughes, who flew a special World's Fair flight in 1938.

In keeping with its mission to provide a glimpse into the future, the event had a number of technology-related exhibits. Inside the Perisphere, one of the fair's landmark buildings, was a

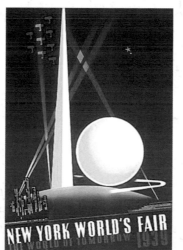

model city of tomorrow that visitors viewed from a moving walkway high above floor level. At the AT&T Pavilion, the Voder—a mechanized, synthetic voice—spoke to fairgoers. The IBM pavilion displayed electric typewriters and a new and extraordinary machine called the electric calculator, while another pavilion introduced the first television sets. But the fair was not strictly devoted to forecasting the future. Other exhibits invited fairgoers to view "Railroads on Parade," displayed priceless "Masterpieces of Art," or offered cuisine from countries around the world. And, of course, the Amusements Area offered a roller coaster and a number of carnival acts, as well as the Life Savers parachute jump.

Despite the fair's stated purpose, the businessmen who organized it were most focused on lifting the spirits of the American people and driving much-needed business to New York City. In this last objective, they did not succeed.

During the two seasons it was open—from April to October of 1939 and 1940—the exhibition attracted more than 45 million visitors, but generated only $48 million in revenue. Since the Fair Corporation had invested $67 million in the event, in addition to $100 million from other sources, the World's Fair of 1939 was considered an economic failure.

STORE Open Tonight TILL 9 P.M.

6.
War and Peace

Jack I. Straus.

On the morning of Sunday, December 7, 1941, the Japanese launched a surprise attack on the United States naval base in Pearl Harbor, Hawaii. When the assault was over, 2,388 people had been killed and another 1,178 people had been wounded.

Word of the attack reached President Franklin Delano Roosevelt as he lunched in the Oval Office on Sunday afternoon. Outraged, Roosevelt condemned the day of "infamy" and immediately urged Congress to declare war against Japan. When Germany declared war on the United States three days later, the European war—which had been raging for two years—became a world war.

Americans, once divided in their feelings on entering the conflict, were stunned by the Pearl Harbor attack, and soon united in a surge of patriotism. Over the next few years, the country would remain unified as both men and women went off to war, and those on the home front worked together to support the troops. Like people all over the country, the residents of New York City were issued ration books and began to limit their purchase of items ranging from sugar and coffee to gasoline and shoes. At the same time, they were urged to buy War Bonds and to effect a "dim out"—a dimming of lights meant to make the coast (and the American ships patroling it) less visible to German U-boats. New York City was mobilizing its people, and R.H. Macy & Co., a Manhattan icon, was ready to lend a helping hand.

On September 16, 1940, President Franklin D. Roosevelt signed into law the Selective Training and Service Act, creating the first peacetime draft in United States history. The act obligated all American males between twenty-one and thirty-five years of age to register for the draft.

During the Second World War, the rationing of fabric made it unpatriotic (and nearly impossible) to fashion long, extravagant wedding gowns out of silk. Most wartime brides chose a simple tailored suit instead, while grooms usually wore their service uniforms.

◀ The main floor of Macy's Herald Square store, ca. 1945.

MACY'S GOES TO WAR—AGAIN

During the Great War, Macy's, led by the Strauses, had organized its employees to knit garments for men in the service, sell War Bonds, and otherwise support the war effort. As World War Two began, Macy's again marshalled its "troops," appealing to both store employees and loyal customers to help the nation move toward victory.

Sparks Flies Again

Macy's employees often sent issues of *Sparks* to friends and relatives serving abroad—even when the recipients had never worked at Macy's. Because *Sparks* offered stories and photos of events in Manhattan, it was welcomed by everyone who called New York their home.

The Macy's employee newsletter *Sparks* had been created at the start of the Great War, and during that conflict, had both rallied the staff to patriotic action and served as a bridge to employees fighting overseas. As America became involved in the Second World War, *Sparks* again was pressed into service.

First and foremost, *Sparks* was used to make the staff aware of the many events that Macy's hosted to raise funds or boost the morale of United States fighting forces. On June 23, 1942, for instance, Macy's held a "barn dance" for soldiers, sailors, and Marines on the rooftop of the Herald Square building. Numbers attached to corncob pipes paired each serviceman with a staff volunteer, and the couples spent a memorable evening dancing and dining under the stars.

Sparks also became a great way for servicemen to keep in touch with friends in the States, and—for a few moments, at least—to enjoy a taste of home. Copies were sent to employees stationed abroad, and many of the men communicated to their Macy's "family" via the newsletter. In one issue, a Corporal Johnny Romano wrote:

> Dear Sparks, Just received the October issue of Sparks and it truly brought back a million memories, especially the picture of Herald Square. About 2 years ago my girl friend and I used to take walks about the Square during our lunch hour. She used to work in the Post Exchange and I worked in Dept 46 Men's Shoes. Sparks is really grand and makes a guy feel like he's back home again reading a copy while on a good old hectic subway ride.

It was not unusual for servicemen to request that *Sparks* be sent to them until they returned to New York. Far from home and friends, they were eager to read about the store and to hear news of the home front. On many occasions, the boys urged those at home to "keep pulling together," but Macy's workers were already devoted to the war effort and doing all they could to speed their friends' return.

The turban may have first been adopted to keep long hair from getting entangled in factory machinery, but it soon became a popular fashion that was worn away from the workplace as well. A tied Rosie-the-Riveter headscarf was less elegant, but served the same purpose on the job.

Letters from ▶ servicemen printed in the May 1944 issue of *Sparks*.

Somewhere in England

Dear Mr. McBride,

Cheer-i-o, pip-pip, what-hey, and blimey. As you can see, I've adopted the "bon-mots" (I had 3 years of French in school so I just want to show off) of our English cousins. I really sound like a Limey lately. . . . and from an Irishman . . . from Limerick yet. Sure 'en be golly me fadder would give me the back of his hand if he knew. How's everything with the Repair Dept. these days? I know, don't tell me . . . "I bought this watch here in Macy's fifty years ago and I've just discovered it never had a mainspring, you robbers you. I want my money back plus a new watch", or "Don't tell me it wasn't bought in Macy's, 'cause I know definitely it was. My aunt's sister's mother gave it to my brother's uncle's father and he gave it to me when I got married forty-nine years ago. So you see, I know definitely it's Macy merchandise." . . . Ah, yes, Mr. McBride, you do have your troubles, in fact, you ought to see Mr. Anthony.

So Mike and Freddy were home on furlough recently. I should live so long. And one's a Cpl. and the other a Sgt., again I should live so long, in fact I'm better off dead. However, I must remind you that since I'm now a PFC, there'll be no stopping me. (Gee, these Limey cigs are strong.) Things are just about the same in the ETO. I meet my brother each week-end (and we won't discuss the fact that he's a Sgt.) and we sure have a great time. My best friend is also here and I expect to see him very shortly. I haven't been to London recently; the reason should be quite obvious. I was in the city of Salisbury recently and made a tour of its very famous Cathedral, which was begun in 1220. (Lillie laid the corner stone). You might have seen it in the Newsreels lately . . . the American flag was presented to the Bishop. There are a lot of other places I'd like to tell you about, but the censor says No, No, and NO! By the way, Mr. McBride, would you see that someone gives my correct address to SPARKS. I get my copies months late. Believe it or not, my copy is forwarded to each camp that I've been in back in the States. I don't mind getting back copies, but the other day one arrived which had this recent item—"America might go to war." It was a little annoying. (Joke over).

My kid brother is quite the drape these days—second year in High School and all that. From what I hear he can do a mean Lindy and he's definitely hep to the jive. Gosh, only to have my youth back again.

He's wearing all my clothes and reports state that he's quite the sharp apple. I can't understand why he looks so sharp because I always dressed on the conservative side. (Will you please pick up Mr. Haller, he just fainted.) I know I promised you one of my suits, Mr. McBride, but after all! By the way, I've been doing some post-war planning in the event I return to Macy's after this mess is over with—first of all, my desk will have to be where you have yours, you can go in the back for awhile. See how you like it. Secondly, you and Mr. Haller will have to go out on the routes. I don't care who takes what route, you can decide that for yourselves, although I'll give you a little hint, Mr. McBride, grab the down-town one, don't be a chump! Every afternoon at one, Mr. Klein will bring in my lunch, while Mr. Baxter has my clothes pressed, and Mr. Haller is shining my shoes. Ah, what a wonderful dream, too bad I had to wake up. I better stop this nonsense before the censor goes completely mad,—and you go out of your mind and I end up with a Section 8 (not a bad idea).

Cheerio now, and regards to all in 100, 89, and 79 Depts.

JIMMY
(PFC James McNamara, formerly Balcony Repair)

Dear Miss Moore,

You may wonder who I am and why I am writing to you. My mother (who works in Macy's) always sends me copies of SPARKS, and even though I never worked at Macy's I almost feel like an ex-employee. Those shots of New York were great and SPARKS is passed around to a lot of New York boys. You can tell Bobby Voorhis her picture adorns the wall of my room. My friends agree she's some pin-up girl. Thanking you again for the many enjoyable hours I get reading your magazine.

PFC NORMAN KRAKOWER

Buddy Sarno, once a member of the IPE Force and now a fighting Seabee, smiles a "Hello" to his old friends. Buddy used to be one of our favorite "pin-up boys" . . . by which we mean that he used to put up the pictures on the SPARKLER Boards . . . and we might add that the title still holds good, in a different sense.

Dutch Guiana, South America

Dear Miss Moore,

Yesterday afternoon, after returning to my barracks from work, I found my monthly issue of SPARKS on my bunk. I was very pleased to receive it and I want to thank you and all fellow Macyites for making it possible for me to receive your magazine.

As I was reading "Letters From the Boys", which is my favorite page, I was very much surprised to find there a letter from Joseph Presto, whom I have been trying to locate for over a year. Joe and I both worked together in the Eighth Floor Packing unit, and became very good friends. We were separated by the war, when Joe enlisted in the Army Ordnance and I in the Air Force. I was just wondering if you couldn't send me his address, so that we could renew our friendship once more. I would be greatly indebted to you. The pictures of New York which are published in SPARKS are very good and bring home much closer to us. I want to say "Thanks" to you and all the other swell people in Macy's who are doing so much for us boys in the service.

Thank you very much for your help, and for your swell magazine, which helped me find a long lost buddy.

Sincerely,
PFC PETER CARROLL
(formerly Packing)

Jay Wolf's little son Richard received a letter from his Uncle Ray, which Mr. Wolf thought we might like to publish. We would, and here it is.

Dear Richard,

Uncle Ray just received your picture taken in the arms of your Daddy. I guess you're much too young to remember me, Rickie, but I hope the time is not too far distant when we will be able to renew our relationship. You see, Rickie, your Uncles Herbert, Jesse, and myself, along with millions of other American men and women, are presently engaged in making this world a suitable place for boys like you to live in and grow up in. I know right now that this doesn't mean a heck of a lot to you and I'm really glad that you have been spared the realization. But in years to come, when you are capable of thinking and reasoning for yourself, you and millions of kids like you will begin to understand what your uncles, daddies, and brothers were fighting for. My wish at present, Richard, is that in years to come you will be able to live in a world of freedom and peace, unsmirched by intolerance of any sort. I say this, for I hate to think that we today are sacrificing in vain. You see, Richard, later on you will also be able to understand people. We are a queer lot. Really Rickie, we forget things so easily, especially hardships, sacrifice, and bloodshed caused by eras such as we are now going through.

So I merely hope that out of all this will come a world for you, Rickie,—rich in peace, tolerance, and love of fellow man. It's an awful lot to hope for, I know. But you and kids like you are an awful lot to people like us and we think you deserve to live and thrive in such a world. So, God Bless You, Rickie, may the time come soon when we will all be rewarded and will enjoy the sweet everyday things in life.

Always,
UNCLE RAY
(The picture that inspired the above letter is on page 38.)

Here's our first letter from a Prisoner of War. Bob Rosenberg's parents were kind enough to let us have the letter for SPARKS. Lt. Rosenberg, formerly 123 Dept. Executive, is a Prisoner of War in Germany. See last month's issue of SPARKS for further details.

Dear Folks,

As yet I haven't received any mail from home, but with the logic that I am well, you must be too. What do I look like now? I suppose you are wondering. Well, to begin at the top, my hair is long, although trimmed around the neck-line—the fashion here where hats are few and weather cold. My upper lip now supports a mustache which I would remove without argument at anyone's suggestion. Overall, to continue, a little thinner, about 165 lbs., otherwise, the same as always. Still keep busy, mostly by reading and exercising, sleeping and eating. Maybe things will be different soon. Love to all,

BOB

Dear Sue,

I offer myself as a living refutation of the charge that the Army puts people in inappropriate jobs. Most of the time since I've been down here, I've been concerned in one way or another with Art and publishing for the Army. Of course, the job wasn't exactly comparable to the one Dorothy Reynolds used to take care of for me at dear old Macy's. The Army seems to be bigger. If each department in Macy's had a very large Art Dept. with a central one on the 13th Floor coordinating their efforts and seeing to it that they kept up to snuff, Fred Brauer, now a Captain, would be in charge of the latter. And I would be in charge of a small Art Dept. in Mr. Jack's office paying very little attention to Fred but existing mainly as a threat to the poor lad, and making special presentations to protect Mr. Jack against constant vicious attacks from the Mayor and Council!

That was close for the Army, but look what I'm doing now. I have almost exactly 50 clever lads and gals (there were 50 in the Art

4199

Dept. at Macy's) who operate three identical Army Service Force exhibits which travel from (guess what!) store to store around the country acquainting mammas and wives and sweethearts with the merits of the services which take care of their Johnnies physically, mentally, and spiritually. Minus Dorothy Reynolds, it's pretty hard work to keep track of them as they wander about the country. I've traveled about 7500 miles in the last month. I left Hollywood in pretty good shape considering that I moved through there two weeks ago! I've formed one opinion since I've been down here; General Somervell is the greatest executive the world has ever seen.

Yours,
JERRY
(LT. COL. SANFORD E. GERARD)
(formerly Art Director)

Anzio Beachhead
Dear SPARKS,

This is my first letter to you, and I feel like a black sheep after reading the letters from the other boys. Regardless of how many beachheads I have been involved in, SPARKS has followed me up as fast as our rations. After making the landings in Sicily and Salerno, I never figured on having to be in on another one, but we took a trip up here. We were having a quiet spell, but just as I started this I had to stop on account of an air raid. Jerry doesn't seem to like our presence up here, as he raised all kinds of hell with us a week ago, but we put him in his place. We seem to be getting out of the rainy season as we have had the sun shining for two days now. We thought it was bad on the southern front in the mountains, but this swamp has it topped. If we try to dig a hole it fills up with water, but with Jerry throwing his stuff around, we get right in. I see that quite a few of the Warehouse drivers have been changed to the depots, but I am sure after this is over, we'll all be together again. I seem to be running out of space, so I will have to close. Best regards to the bunch in the Warehouse Delivery.

PFC RICHARD T. BARRY
(formerly Warehouse)

Last month the Misses Lillian Katchka and Mildred Chawes from the Fourth Floor conceived the idea of sending Easter gift packages to Fourth Floor men in the service and to Halloran Hospital for distribution among 150 wounded servicemen. They volunteered their time and money to fill boxes full of everything "but black nightgowns". The Fourth Floor gals have received many letters of thanks from our boys and gals, and from the Red Cross too. Printed below are two letters from former Fourth Floor Macyites.

Dear Youth Centre-ers,

To write and say "thank you" would definitely be insufficient in expressing my appreciation on receipt of such a very thoughtful gesture. I was quite delighted with the very useful articles the package contained, but my friends in the barracks are furious. I was delirious with the ocarina and unconsciously am inflicting untold tortures (so they say) in trying to master it. When they visit New York, to quote them, they will make the Youth Centre their first stop and track down the sender of the ocarina and have them listen to one of my solos, to quote them again, CENSORED.

Seriously kids, thanks loads, and in saying "cheerio", I want to be remembered to everyone of my friends on the floor, Dept. 146 (my first love, 141, 43, 51) . . . what I mean is, say "hello" to everyone.

Sincerely,
CPL. RAE FRIES, WAC
(formerly Dept. 146)
(See picture on Page 37)

Dear "Macy's Fourth Floor,"

From the very bottom of my "sailor's" heart I thank each and every one of you for your gift. Each item will be put to good use. You can count on that! As for the musical instrument, I'm slowly driving Betty, the landlady, and everyone else out of the house with my sweet (?) harmonies. Just a year ago the end of this month, I timidly set forth on the high seas of Lake Seneca to engage in the "Battle of Sampson". I'm still a "dry land sailor" from up north. We don't even see the smoke of battle, but, if our victories in the Pacific are due partly to good Selection Office work, then I guess "yours truly" has been of some use. Let's hope so.

Again, thanks a million times over, and keep a spot warm for me to come back to. Here's praying we win in '44.

FRANK QUIGLEY, SP.(C) 2/c
(formerly SMX on the Fourth)

My dear Mrs. Chadwick,

It is well over two years since last we've corresponded. On several occasions the many friends I have made and the wonderful times I had while employed at Macy's keep crossing my train of thought. Even in the Pacific, I doubt that I could forget Macy's. We get some New York papers with advertisements, see an occasional cartoon which mentions Macy's, and in the movies when a department store is referred to, it is either Stacy's, Macy's, or other similar name. I borrowed a fishing reel from the athletic locker of a certain outpost once which had Macy's name

on it. The hundreds of such reminders keep me aware of the fine people I have left behind.

My shipmates say I'm still the same, but friends whom I don't see very often say they notice a slight change. Perhaps it will seem even greater to you, for like hundreds of other Macyites who are partaking in this conflict I find myself doing things and seeing places I never dreamed of before entering the service. The two years of war have caused me to experience feelings far sooner and more often than one can expect. I felt like every other American when Pearl Harbor was attacked and my brother was one of the wounded. Then there was that feeling of ignorance when my ship went into commission and I saw what I had to learn and what was expected of me. I think my greatest hardship was not in work, but in gaining the confidence of my superiors, which is not easy when their lives depend upon your actions. I have felt excitement when my ship enters enemy waters, confidence in my captain to carry out the mission successfully, the unexplainable feeling when depth charges start getting close, the respect for American material and workmanship when our hull has to challenge those depth charges till our skipper maneuvers us to safety . . . the patriotic feeling as we proudly stood by and saw our Captain decorated, and last but not least that wonderful satisfaction of knowing I am doing my part to the best of my ability, that my hardships are not in vain, that my relatives and friends are depriving themselves for my benefit and are preserving the things I love most. With their prayers for a speedy end and my safe return I find nothing to be afraid of, for I understand what we are fighting for.

With kindest regards to my many friends and my sincere wish that this letter finds you and yours enjoying the best of health, I remain,

Yours truly,
CONSTANTINE GUINESS, Mo. M.M. 1/c
(formerly Long Island Warehouse)

Virgil Schiavone, former Delivery entry clerk, is now in the European Theatre of Operations. Lots of luck to him and all his buddies!

Somewhere in China
Dear Sir,

I am writing this letter to you in appreciation for the Christmas package I received from the company. I received the package at a time when a fellow really needs some cheering up. I'm in the hospital with malaria and jaundice. I was in bed when the nurse brought the gift to me. It sure made me feel good. It's the first package that I have received, and I'll say it again, it sure did make a sick soldier happy. I want to thank you from the bottom of my heart. I'm recovering now, thanks to the medical corps. It's swell to know that the people back home are thinking of the boys who are fighting all over the world. Well, I guess I'll "take off" now and say so-long for the 15th Air Force.

A former Macyite,
PFC LAWRENCE A. HERMAN
(formerly Warehouse)

Keep writing us, fellows, and keep on asking for those special pictures which you'd like to see dedicated to you in our "Pictures For the Boys" series. We aim to please, you know, and whether it's a Macy scene or a New York scene, if you ask for it, we'll try to make sure that you get it!

PICTURES FOR THE BOYS: NO. 5 . . . *This picture of Dept. 129 is dedicated to Louis J. Perotti, SF 3/c, who thinks longingly of his old gang.*
MOONEN

The Blood Drive

In January 1941, at the request of the Surgeon General of the US Army and Navy, the American Red Cross agreed to organize a civilian blood donor service to collect blood plasma for injured troops. The first center opened in New York City on February 4 of that year.

Through articles in *Sparks,* Macy's urged its staff to visit the Red Cross building on Fifth Avenue and Thirty-Seventh Street. "It's easy to make a blood donation," advised the newsletter. "In the last war, when a soldier needed a transfusion it had to be made from person to person. In this war, you can literally save a life by means of your blood, for preservation of blood plasma has made possible long distance blood transfusions."

So great was the response of Macy's staff that the company decided to call on the store's customers, as well. On January 25, 1943, Macy's officially opened a Red Cross information and registration booth in the store's first-floor drug department. The goal was to sign up shoppers for blood donations and to enlist volunteers for the Red Cross. Although New Yorkers needed little urging to do their part for the war, Macy's made it easier for thousands upon thousands of busy Manhattanites to give much-needed blood—as well as their own time—to the national effort.

War Bonds

During the Great War, the United States Government had issued Liberty Bonds to raise money for the war effort, and the same strategy was adopted during the second global conflict. Shortly before World War Two began, Defense Bonds were issued. Once the United States had officially entered the war, the government also referred to the certificates as War Bonds, War Loans, and Victory Bonds. Bond coupons were offered for $10, $25, $50, $75, $100, $200, $500, $1,000, $10,000, and $100,000. For children, as well as adults on a tighter budget, 25-cent Savings Stamps were issued. Purchasers earned 2.9 percent interest each year, and were allowed to cash in their bonds after ten years.

Just as in World War One, Macy's offered enthusiastic support of the government bond drives. On June 13, 1942, the store gathered some 6,000 employees on the main floor of the Broadway building. After Jean Dickenson of the Metropolitan Opera company sang the national anthem, actor Burgess Meredith urged the assembled workers to purchase bonds through the store's payroll deduction program. Eager to help the troops abroad, more than 75 percent of the staff enrolled in the program.

In addition to funding the war effort, War Bonds were intended to control inflation by reducing the amount of currency on the open market.

A War Bond rally for Macy's employees.

During World War Two, a six-story-high replica of the Statue of Liberty presided over New York's Times Square on the traffic island north of Forty-Third Street. A stage on Miss Liberty's pedestal provided a site for noontime shows, which promoted the sale of war bonds. Daily sales were later tabulated as averaging $60,000.

First featured in women's clothing during the 1930s, shoulder pads became more popular—as well as far larger—once the United States entered World War Two. Worn in jackets, coats, and even dresses, the pads created a broad-shouldered, no-nonsense military look.

In September 1943, after President Roosevelt announced that the next War Loan drive was intended to raise $15 billion, Macy's set its own goal: The company's employees were to sell $2 million worth of War Bonds—enough to pay for the manufacture of twenty-seven Douglas Dauntless dive-bombers. Using the slogan "Back the Attack with War Bonds," Macy's offered a Certificate of Merit from the Treasury Department to any "Macy's Bondadier" who sold $200 in bonds.

To help its employees reach their $2 million objective, Macy's promoted a September 11 event called "The Hollywood Cavalcade of Stars." The show, which was to be held in Madison Square Garden, would feature an astounding lineup of popular entertainers, including Fred Astaire, Lucille Ball, James Cagney, Olivia de Havilland, Betty Hutton, Judy Garland, and Kay Kyser and his orchestra. Admission was open to anyone who purchased a War Bond on the fourth floor of the Herald Square store.

In October 1943—with departments throughout Macy's displaying brilliant "Red Stars of Achievement," signifying that they had met their quota—Macy's announced that its Bondadiers had raised $3,427,975, far surpassing the company's original goal. Through their passionate efforts, Macy's employees had made it possible to build forty-five of the much-needed dive-bombers.

Proud of its company's success in the 1943 War Bond drive, Macy's hosted a "Garden Party" for its staff on June 13, 1944. Held at Madison Square Garden—possibly the only venue large enough to accommodate the "Macyites"—the event featured Harry James and his orchestra, along with singer Kitty Kallen. Over 10,000 Macy's employees attended the event, which was shared with America via Coca-Cola's Spotlight Band radio broadcast. Yet Macy's knew that the fund-raising was not yet over. In fact, it had already announced that its next War Bond drive would aim at collecting $3 million.

R.H. Macy & Co. had long used newspaper advertising to inform New York City's shoppers of its sales, and in the Second World War, it also employed its ads to inspire patriotic action, including the purchase of War Bonds and War Stamps. On Sunday April 12, 1942, the store debuted "The Home Front." Described as a "little newspaper within a newspaper," it told readers to "buy thriftily, thoughtfully, and well," with an eye to conserving the precious metals that were needed by the Allied war effort. Finally, it reminded "Home Front" readers that War Bonds could be purchased at Macy's Herald Square store.

The 1942 Macy's catalogue for children's clothing.

R.H. Macy & Co. was not the only Manhattan store to support the war. Macy's ads informed New Yorkers that over 1,000 retail stores in the city offered War Savings Stamps for sale.

With fabric in short supply throughout the war, *Vogue* introduced a "Make Do and Mend" campaign that encouraged women to re-make men's suits into women's suits and turn women's clothing into children's garments. All over America, people took out needle and thread to support the war effort.

A *Sparks* article on the ▶ June 13, 1944 party given for Macy's employees at New York's Madison Square Garden.

The FIFTH was the Finest!

MACY'S 10,000 BONDADIERS SMASH ALL RECORDS AS "E" BOND SALES SKYROCKET TO $4,005,825 BY JULY 5 IN 5th WAR LOAN DRIVE! SALE OF BONDS IN "F" AND "G" SERIES BOOSTS TOTAL TO $7,630,375 . . . PASSING OUR 4th WAR LOAN SALES OF $4,324,700 AND MAKING MOST SPECTACULAR BOND SALE FIGURE EVER ACHIEVED BY COUNTRY'S LARGEST BOND SELLING TEAM!

(1) Macy's over-quota Bondadiers occupied four sections of reserved seats at the Polo Grounds. (2) A thrilling doubles match between Alice Marble and Frank Hunter versus Mary Hardwick and Vincent Richards opened the Sports Carnival. Marble and partner took the one-set match. (3) A "Parade of Champions", some in uniform, produced such sport champs as Henry Armstrong, king of the welterweights. (4) From left: Pvt. John Payne, Lt. Bill Holden, and piano-less quiz giant Oscar Levant. (5) Dept. 92 was heavily represented: Bob Clarke, 6th Fl. Supt. and Men's Club Pres., sits behind "Uncle Milt". (6) Mr. Howard, Publicity Director, front row, and Mr. Marks, Vice Pres., second row, showed profound pride in Macy's record. (7) Alice Marble follows through on a blistering forehand drive. (8) Al Schacht, versatile comedian, offered a trumpet solo with the Guard Band. Later, "Baseball's Clown Prince" went in for hilarious spoofing of tennis and baseball. (9) Marius Russo, former Yankee pitcher, and Sam Nahem, former pitcher with the Cards, opposed each other in an all-service game between Fort Monmouth and Fort Totten. (10) Service All-Stars and LIU Service Stars played a fast basketball game won by latter team. (11) Mr. Chinlund, Corporate Controller (straw hat), saw the Sports Carnival with his wife.

As anyone who knows can tell you, Macyites are "terrific" by definition—but this time we've stumped even the experts! We started selling Bonds on June 1; we had until July 8 to shoot for our quota of $3,000,000 in "E" Bonds.

At the mammoth Macy Madison Square Garden party on June 13, the thrilling announcement came that Store Bondadiers had already sold $1,500,000 worth of "E" Bonds (8,000 individual Bonds) and another million dollars' worth of "F" and "G" Bonds! It was the second day of the official national drive (which began June 12), and we were already at the half-way mark! Even the broadcast of Coca-Cola's Spotlight Band Broadcast right from our Garden party could not draw attention away from our achievement. The spotlight was on *us*! We saluted our fellow Macyites-in-arms during a solemn moment in the evening's festivities—we promised Major Allen V. Martini, hero of 27 bombing missions over Germany in the Flying

(Continued next page)

COCA-COLA SALUTES MACY'S 10,000 BONDADIERS AT MADISON SQUARE GARDEN

Fortress *Dry Martini*, who spoke to us that night, that we would back him to the limit! A Macyite's word is as good as his "bonds": by June 17, we had topped our $3,000,000 E Bond quota by $500,000!

Macy's gave us the party at Madison Square Garden to honor our achievements in previous War Loan drives . . . but we gave a party on June 17 at the Polo Grounds to all the people who bought Bonds from us! From eight until well past midnight, 30,000 people (including thousands of Macyites who saw the show free for having made their individual quotas of $300 by June 15) gathered to see one of the biggest galaxies of stars in the sports world put on a show. The evening's exciting events included basketball, baseball, soccer, tennis, golf, tug-of-war, and track competitions. Hollywood headliners who spoke were Lt. William Holden, Lt. Eddie Albert, Pvt. John Payne, Paul Whiteman, and Oscar Levant. Al Schacht and Mrs. Van Coutren (mother of twelve children, all in the service) were also on the program. From every luminary came unstinted praise for Macy's Bondadiers.

Final figures were not available to Sparks, which went to press before the Drive's end, but we know that it is characteristic of Macy people to start a job brilliantly and to finish it spectacularly. Congratulations of the highest order go to Macy's incomparable army-behind-the-army!

CDVO color guard and Mr. Howard, Publicity Director, stood at attention during one minute's silence while drums rolled.

Major Allen V. Martini, skipper of the Flying Fort "Dry Martini", told us that OUR medals in this war are the War Bonds we buy and sell.

Harry James and his orchestra (complete with singers Kitty Kallen and Buddy DeVito) appeared on Coca-Cola's Spotlight Band Broadcast from the Garden. Afterwards, Harry favored his fans by playing such James classics as "Two O'Clock Jump".

Morton Downey sang on the broadcast; returned later from his supper performance at the Waldorf to accompany himself in a selection of rollicking Irish tunes.

Harry Conover tells the crowd that judging the prettiest in this line-up has stumped him! He, his Conover Cover Girls, and others had ploughed through the crowded dance floor to select candidates for "Prettiest Girl at the Party". Upshot was—the audience voted on the beauties by applause.

Dorothy Bentley, guest of a Macyite, was the Prettiest Girl at the Party! Major Martini gave her a $50 War Bond and Harry Conover said, "Why don't you come up and see me some time?"

Six lovely Conover Girls came to the Garden party to find a competitor for their crown! The job was tough, first, because Macy's is notoriously a reservoir of beauty, and second, because the audience was so densely massed that if you pointed at one person, five responded to the summons.

Macy's Victory Barnyard

R.H. Macy & Co. always prided itself on being attuned to the ever-changing wants and needs of the public. At no time was this more apparent than in World War Two, when Macy's created a Victory Barnyard.

Introduced in February 1943, Macy's fifth floor Victory Barnyard—designed to answer the government's call for more food on the home front—offered "a great variety of baby chicks," as well as the feed and equipment necessary to raise them. "It's easier than you think to raise your own chickens and eggs," said *The Macy Gazette,* a sister publication of *Sparks.* "The Victory Barnyard will tell you how." Customers were permitted to buy twenty-five chicks or more, and were encouraged to get all the information and advice they needed from Macy's on-site Poultry Expert. The store stocked equipment ranging from tiny legbands to poultry houses, trapnests, incubators, and egg scales. A permanent display of thirty pedigreed breeds of hens, all in individual temperature-controlled cases, provided an additional attraction for the would-be poultryman, as well as anyone else who was interested in learning about eggs and chickens. Macy's handy "chick pullman" allowed customers to easily carry their livestock home. If preferred, the Victory Barnyard would deliver the chicks via parcel post or express.

What if a shopper wanted to raise something other than chickens? Macy's also had "a real live rabbit department," with quality-bred rabbits and all the equipment necessary for their care. Even kids were encouraged to

join in the country's victory food program through the store's branch of the 4-H Club. With Macy's help, everyone in the family could not only play an important role in the nation's fight, but also enjoy fresh and nutritious food throughout the war years.

Wartime Adjustments

For many years, R.H. Macy & Co. had cheerfully offered free delivery of merchandise to customers in much of the Greater New York area. But with the rationing of gas and tires, Macy's was forced to adopt a new stance. "Take It With You" was the slogan that urged shoppers to carry their goods along with them when they left the store. A newspaper ad spelled out the benefits of forgoing home delivery: "Here's How You Can Help Win the War—Carry Your Own Packages, Help Save Tires, Gas, and Heavy Wrapping Paper."

During World War Two, the US government encouraged civilians to plant victory gardens—plots of vegetables, fruits, and herbs that could be used to feed their families. In addition to reducing the pressure on the food supply, these gardens boosted morale by making people feel empowered by their contribution.

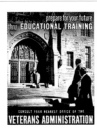

The GI Bill—officially called the Servicemen's Readjustment Act—was signed by President Roosevelt on June 22, 1944. Intended to prevent a postwar economic depression, it provided college tuition, unemployment compensation, and various types of loans for returning World War Two veterans.

Those Macy's patrons who did opt for home delivery were sometimes in for a surprise when the doorbell rang. With so many of the country's men off to war, the number of Macy's male employees had dwindled, and in 1943, the company hired several women to assist in package delivery. Each woman rode along with a driver and made light deliveries, leaving the handling of heavy packages to the driver. Because many of the women had to be home in the late afternoon to care for children, they were given an early shift of 7:00 AM to 3:30 PM.

Fashion on the Home Front

As the United States geared up for World War Two, Americans were introduced to the rationing of sugar, butter, coffee, gasoline, and other commodities. Quickly, people learned that everyday activities, from making dinner to driving to work, would have to be modified so that the nation would have the materials it needed to win the war. One of the many areas on which rationing had an impact was clothing.

In 1942, desperate to conserve cotton, wool, silk, and rayon, the government's War Production Board (WPB) set standards for clothing manufacturers. Simplification and standardization of design were viewed as the key to conserving both materials and effort. Patch pockets and pants cuffs—features that wasted material but were without function—were forbidden. Closures made of metal, which was needed by the military, were also not allowed. And only three and one half yards of fabric could be used in any one garment.

Women's fashion underwent the greatest change. To comply with wartime restrictions, designers shortened and narrowed women's suit skirts, topping them with big-shouldered, military-style jackets that were at most twenty-five inches in length. The concept of separates was introduced, allowing women to mix coordinating components—cardigans and trousers, for instance—so that several outfits could be created using only a few garments. Early in the war, silk stockings were replaced by "nylons," but when the WPB comman-

deered even nylon, stockings virtually disappeared, and were often replaced with ankle socks. To make sure that American women continued to feel feminine despite these deprivations, ruffles, lace, bows, and full sleeves were used to create flattering garments through minimal use of fabric. Yet the emphasis was still on simplicity, for during a time of shortage, it was considered tasteless to be ostentatious.

Men's clothing, too, was affected by rationing. Before the war, a man's suit was composed of pants, jacket, and vest. Once the war began and fabric was at a premium, the vest was eliminated, leaving men with two-piece outfits. Pants made during the war could have no cuffs, and in May 1942, the WPB also asked men to shear off the cuffs from existing trousers. These trimmings—along with the trimmings made from the bottoms of women's nightgowns—were used to manufacture blankets and other military necessities.

Rationing ended soon after the war, and in 1947, women's clothing designer Christian Dior introduced the "New Look," a style featuring longer, fuller skirts. Although women embraced the ultra-feminine silhouette, in many ways, fashion would always show the marks of the Second World War. Many women had moved into the labor force and continued to demand garments that would be practical in an office or other work setting. And casual separates, including pants, had forever become a part of women's clothing, paving the way for future trends.

Despite restrictions on fabric use, some men favored the zoot suit, a fashion that required many yards of material. Born in Harlem, New York in the 1930s, the zoot suit featured an oversized jacket with wide lapels, and baggy high-waisted trousers that dramatically tapered at the ankle.

The May 1942 issue of ▶ *Sparks* showing Macy's planned response to air raids.

MACY'S MEETS EMERGENCY

Last month we told you in detail the story of the complete precautionary set-up which has been arranged by our Maintenance Department to cope with the emergencies resulting from an air raid. This month, on Page 22, we continue our story of Macy's Own A.R.P. with an account of the elaborate first-aid arrangements which have been made to take care of emergencies resulting from an air raid. And herewith we present, as promised last month, a picture-story of what happens in the building when the air-raid alarm sounds—

* * *

AIR RAI-AI-AID! The alarm signal, a series of long and short rings, resounds throughout the building when the engineer in charge of the power plant presses this push button in the engine room. Immediately the efficient routine of the Macy A. R. P. organization is set in action.

Maintenance's Emergency Repair Crew swings into action; heads at once for the twelve locations which have been designated as chief emergency stations. These men must be on the lookout for any trouble which may arise, whether from air raid, mechanical failure, or accident. They must handle every contingency with quick and efficient action. John Coffin, Vince Perrotta, Paddy O'Keefe, and Jim Quinn give reassuring evidence of their training and competence.

Meanwhile the rest of the men in the engineering group, other than the members of the Emergency Repair Crew itself, go to designated posts where they will stand by for possible emergency duty if they are needed. "Engineers on the March" are Jack Phelan, Frank Homan, Ted Judd, Bill Lohrer, and Bill Murphy.

In order that the Emergency Repair Crew may have the necessary equipment with which to take effective action, seventeen emergency supply cabinets have been installed, each of which contains the following equipment: shovels, sand, water, stirrup pump, tarpaulins, power light, extension handled hoe, safety goggles, helmets, gas masks, asbestos gloves, reverse extinguishers, soda and acid extinguisher, 6 foot pike pole. In addition, a special cabinet contains fire hose, rope, and four asbestos suits. Three of the crew, looking like veritable men from Mars, demonstrate how completely they are equipped for fire-fighting and other disaster work.

Sparks 6

WITH COMPLETE Air Raid Precaution SET-UP

either for a drill or in grim actuality. It is true that these pictured events do not take place in sequence—but simultaneously, and it would take an all-seeing movie camera to record the instantaneous responses which, at the sounding of the alarm, are manifested from sub-basement to roof of the huge Macy building. We ask you to imagine, therefore, that the actions portrayed in our series of pictures are taking place all at once . . . for the drills have shown that within the astoundingly short time of six minutes the A. R. P. emergency set-up was completely accomplished.

* * *

In the conveyor shop near the engine room is the Emergency Control Room manned by the supervisor (in picture, Bob Melady). This is the heart of the building operations. It contains flashlights, keys for supply cabinets, and all data pertaining to emergency activity. The supervisor must phone all emergency stations and note if they are covered. He receives reports of trouble, sends help when it is needed, and works hand in hand with the engine room. He reports any damage or unusual condition to the Protection Department and may request it to send for outside help.

Meanwhile, on all floors throughout the building, air raid wardens and their chiefs man their posts. Floor Captains like Mr. Damerel on the Fourth maintain their places by the phones so that any unforeseen occurrence can be handled promptly. Each Captain (usually, the department head or supervisor), has his lieutenants; under them are the wardens.

Macy people proceed to their assigned safety zones in a quiet and orderly manner, fully aware of the seriousness of the situation. Here you see an air raid warden directing interior traffic during an alarm. A total of 1,100 people have been trained to protect customers and other employees by guiding them to safe areas and warding them away from danger zones.

May, 1942 7

At the top of the Air Raid Wardens organization is the Manager's Office, Mr. Mollos, Chief Air Raid Warden, gave us the complete story of the operations, plans for which are recorded in every detail in the thick book which lies before him on the desk. Included is a blueprint of every floor, carefully marked out as to safe and unsafe zones. Air raid wardens not only supervise the guiding of persons to safe areas but also are in charge of seeing that doors and windows are closed and that a fixed watch is maintained so that no one strays into a danger area.
Center:
During an air raid alarm the wardens are at their posts . . . so that we could not picture them both en masse and on duty, as it were. But this group of Fourth Floor wardens posed for us after one of their meetings. Remember that this is a group of wardens for a single floor and you will get an idea of how thoroughly Macy's has gone into the serious business of providing air raid protection.
Right:
Mr. Creeden, Chief Engineer, is responsible for seeing that the vital life blood of the building—light, heat, and power —keeps pulsing twenty-four hours a day, no matter what happens. The engine room of the Store, like that of a ship, is the factor most necessary to its safety; must function at all times.

* * * * *

Electricians shut off all outside Store lights as soon as the alarm sounds. Here Paddy O'Keefe puts his finger on the button which will produce the blackout.
Right:
Don't leave a blacked-out window open when you go home at night this fine spring weather! Here's how the kindly light will shine outside the Store to help lead the hostile bombers to their objective. This picture (staged by us, we are glad to say) is graphic evidence of the damage which may be caused by carelessness. Take the responsibility for closing all windows before you leave at night; it's a vitally important job for every one of us.

Sparks 8

On the Eighth Floor, the Emergency Hospital Unit is set up as soon as the alarm sounds. Drugs and hypodermics are rushed at once onto Car No. 55, which takes these special supplies directly from the 19th to the 8th Floor. Here Nurse Schrader carries her precious burden onto the waiting elevator, while operator Tony Piazetski keeps his hand on the controls of the car.

In the event of a daylight alarm, maintenance men swiftly close the blackout wings at all doors. These, in addition to shutting in all light, protect customers and employees from the danger of shattered glass. H. Anderson here closes the blackout wing at the 34th Street and Broadway door. These doors are put in place regularly every night, after the Store closes.

* * * * * *

Evelyn Christie, who might be called the "safe warden", puts all valuable records into the immense fireproof safe in the Controller's Office the moment the alarm sounds. There the records are securely locked away from all possible damage.

To protect the Store from incendiary bombs, metal containers of sand, plus shovels, hose, scoops, and other fire extinguishers have been distributed around the roof. Roof-spotters going into action are Jim Buttermark and Bill Hillmeyer.

ALL CLEAR!
The bell sounds again, this time with a welcome note. There has been no panic, no confusion, no let-up in the normal Macy business. All's clear—and all's well.

May, 1942

Macy's Balloons Join the Rubber Drive

In 1945, the current route of the Macy's Thanksgiving Day Parade was adopted, and—for the first time—the event was televised to much of New York.

The cost of fighting a world war had an impact on the lives of every American on the home front. Rubber was the first nonfood item to be regulated, for the national stock would have been depleted in less than a year without controls. Tires for cars and bicycles became virtually impossible to obtain, and President Roosevelt called on citizens to contribute scrap rubber in the form of old tires, old rubber raincoats, garden hoses, rubber shoes, and bathing caps.

Macy's rallied to the government's cry by contributing something far larger than a bathing cap or hose. On November 13, 1942, Jack I. Straus joined New York City Mayor Fiorello LaGuardia on the steps of City Hall, where Macy's donated the rubber balloons from its Thanksgiving Day Parade to the drive. The monster Dragon balloon had been inflated with air for the occasion, and the mayor ceremoniously deflated it with the thrust of a knife. The parade balloons would add 650 pounds of precious rubber to the war effort.

Jack Straus also announced that there would be no Thanksgiving Day Parade until the war had been won. He explained that as many as 3,000 police offers were needed each year to assist in the parade. With a war on, this would mean pulling the police from far more important tasks, such as the guarding of warehouses and docks. Moreover, the parade would utilize precious commodities such as gasoline and rubber tires—items that were sorely needed by the armed forces.

From 1942 to 1944, New York City celebrated the holiday season without the traditional Macy's parade. When the event resumed in 1945, the people of New York could feel proud that they had worked together to bring a return to peace.

Today, anyone who enters Macy's at 151 West Thirty-Fourth Street can see, next to the escalators, the Macy's World War Two Memorial Plaque. This plaque honors the 5,009 Macy's employees who fought in the war, including 80 staff members who made the ultimate sacrifice for their country.

Macy's plaque dedicated to the more than 5,000 employees who served their country during the Second World War.

During the war, many films were designed to lift the spirits of those on the home front. One such movie was the 1944 Academy Award-winning musical *Going My Way*, which tells the story of a young priest (Bing Crosby) who takes over a parish from an established veteran (Barry Fitzgerald).

On April 12, 1945, with the death of President Franklin D. Roosevelt, Harry S. Truman became President of the United States. Although Truman had not been informed about critical wartime issues during his stint as vice president, he was to see the country through to victory and guide its transition to a peacetime economy.

PEACETIME

For millions of New Yorkers, the Second World War ended at 7:03 PM on August 14, 1945, when the zipper sign in Times Square delivered the message, "Official—Truman announces Japanese surrender." By 10:00 PM, servicemen and civilians alike were dancing in the street amid 5,438 tons of falling confetti.

While Americans joyously welcomed the returning troops, many feared that the drop in military spending might bring back the difficult times of the Great Depression. These concerns proved to be unfounded. The wartime rationing of commodities had forced many Americans to bank their money. This—coupled with a strong desire for all the goods that had been unavailable during the war, and a relatively smooth transition from wartime to peacetime production—resulted in robust economic growth during the postwar period. With affordable mortgages being offered to returning members of the military, a housing boom added to the expansion, and a baby boom caused the number of consumers to swell.

Macy's had enjoyed solid sales throughout the war. In 1942, for instance, sales had totalled a record $168,326,055, and in 1944, sales rose even higher, to $197,414,000. Once the war was over, despite the retail industry's concerns that rising postwar prices would keep consumers away, New Yorkers flocked to the Herald Square store in greater numbers than ever before. On November 29, as Christmas shoppers streamed into midtown Manhattan, $1,472,000 worth of sales were made at Macy's—a record for a single day. On December 10, Macy's reported that for the first time in its history, it had enjoyed ten consecutive days of $1 million-plus sales. Of particular interest to postwar consumers were toys, radios, men's clothing, hosiery, toiletries, and liquor.

Jack Straus felt that continued expansion of R.H. Macy & Co. was important, as it would make possible the increased mass purchasing that would translate to lower prices for the consumer. Directly before the war, Macy's had opened two branches—one upstate, in Syracuse, New York; and one in Parkchester, a section of the Bronx. Although the Syracuse branch had failed, Macy's did well in Parkchester. World War Two had forced Macy's to temporarily shelve its plan to build additional Macy's branches, but on September 2, 1947, Macy's opened a new branch store in Jamaica, Queens. From the start, the store was a success, with 70,000 people entering the first day alone, and many taking advantage of the innovative rooftop parking facility.

Although the war ended in 1945, rationing did not come to an end until 1946. The consumption of meat, butter, and sugar inevitably rose.

The 1947 Macy's catalogue for children's clothing.

Catering to the fashion-conscious woman who had grown tired of World War Two's austere silhouette, Christian Dior presented the "New Look" in the spring of 1947. The Look's signature shape featured a full below-mid-calf-length skirt, a small waist, and a large bust. Ultra-feminine, the fashion lasted until Dior's death in 1957.

When the end of World War Two lifted the freeze on television manufacture, mass production caused the price of TV sets to drop, while national prosperity allowed many Americans to afford this new luxury item. By 1954, more than half of US families were able to gather around their own sets.

In the autumn of 1947, Macy's began constructing a fourth branch in White Plains, New York, north of New York City. Opening on March 21, 1949, the store had a floor space of 132,000 square feet—of which over 72,000 was selling space—making it the largest department store in all of Westchester County. Again, thousands of people enthusiastically welcomed the newest addition to the Macy's family.

A brief look at the White Plains store shows why Macy's experienced great success in its expansion into America's suburbs. The White Plains branch—although, of course, much smaller than Macy's flagship store—provided much of the merchandise selection available in the Manhattan emporium, as well as some added conveniences. Macy's White Plains had

Macy's store in White Plains, New York, ca. 1949.

In November 1948, Polaroid revolutionized photography by offering the first instant camera. Invented by Edwin Herbert Land, the one-step Land Camera enabled photographers to remove a developing print directly after the picture had been snapped. The print was ready for viewing after only a minute.

In the late 1940s, the men's Aloha shirt—also known as the Hawaiian shirt—first appeared on the United States mainland. Featuring short sleeves, a collar, and a brightly printed fabric, the Aloha shirt was even worn by President Harry S. Truman during his time in the White House.

When Johnny Came Marching Home

At the close of World War Two, thousands of soldiers returned to the United States eager to marry and settle down in a home of their own. Spurred in part by the GI Bill of Rights, which backed home loans for World War Two veterans, builders quickly began to fill the housing gap with new construction. Nearly everyone is familiar with Levittown—the planned community in Long Island, New York that in 1947, began providing low-cost mass-produced housing. But even before Abraham Levitt completed his first development in the Town of Hempstead, R.H. Macy & Co. made homes available to GIs.

In January 1946, in partnership with Precision-Built Homes, Macy's offered eight house models, ranging in size from three to six rooms, with prices as low as $5,000. A purchaser had to supply his own plot of land—wherever he wished to live—as well as a survey of the plot and information on local zoning laws. Precision-Built did the rest, beginning with excavation and ending with details such as painting and wallpapering.

Macy's offered their homes for only a short time before the rising costs of labor and building materials made their prices unrealistic. But for a brief period, Macy's—the largest store in the world—helped returning GIs find their own little piece of the American Dream.

a hundred departments offering an astounding 100,000 items. With very few exceptions, every department of the mammoth New York City store was represented at this convenient new location. Moreover, the branch store was designed with exceptionally broad aisles that provided a free flow of traffic to both the various departments and the counters. One feature of White Plains was especially innovative. Ketchum, Gina & Sharp—designers of the store's interior—had created "stock mezzanines" that, although invisible from the main aisles, made large quantities of merchandise quickly available to Macy's sales clerks. This unique feature translated into faster service and a more successful shopping experience for the store's busy customers.

As the 1940s came to a close and the nation continued to enjoy an economic boom, Macy's star continued to rise. Factory production was increasing, providing an ever-expanding volume and range of consumer goods, and Macy's missed not a step in its tradition of offering these goods for lower prices than those charged by its many competitors. Yet as a new decade dawned, the company—now, nearly a hundred years old—would once again face a strong challenge to one of its guiding principles.

Based on James Michener's Pulitzer-Prize winning book *Tales of the South Pacific*, the Richard Rodgers and Oscar Hammerstein musical *South Pacific* made its Broadway debut on April 7, 1949. The play was noteworthy not only for its brilliant score but also for its sensitive exploration of racial prejudice.

Invented by George Lerner and produced by Hasbro Toys in 1952, Mr. Potato Head was the first toy to be sold through national television advertising. Originally, the toy included separate plastic parts—accessories like eyeglasses and hats—that were to be stuck into a real potato. A plastic potato was added to the kit in 1964.

Miracle on 34th Street

The original *Miracle on 34th Street* poster.

In homes throughout America, the holiday season brings with it many dearly loved traditions, from the baking of festive cookies to the decorating of a Christmas tree. For many people, one of the most beloved traditions of all is watching *Miracle on 34th Street*—a 1947 movie that sets a tale of hope, love, and real-life miracles against the realistic backdrop of Christmastime at Macy's Herald Square store.

The idea for *Miracle on 34th Street* occurred to writer Valentine Davies in 1944, when a day spent shopping for holiday gifts awakened him to the growing commercialization of Christmas. Encouraged by friend and screenwriter George Seaton, Davies began to pen a tale about a kindly old gentleman who, claiming to be the "real" Santa Claus, takes a job playing Santa Claus at Macy's. Before the book was complete, Davies sold the story's film rights. With events moving at lightning speed, George Seaton wrote the screenplay, had it approved, and began directing the film for Twentieth Century-Fox in 1946.

Fans of *Miracle* know the story well. Doris Walker, played by Maureen O'Hara, is special events director at Macy's, where she hires a twinkly-eyed, white-bearded old man named Kris Kringle (Edmund Gwenn) to play Santa. Soon, customers begin to see that there is something very special about Kris. Could he really be Santa, as he claims? No-nonsense Doris and her young daughter, Susan (Natalie Wood), think this is impossible. But when Kris lands in Bellevue, considered insane for insisting he is Santa Claus, Doris's friend Fred Gaily (John Payne) offers to defend him in court. The events that follow not only free Kris, but also make Susan and Doris wholehearted believers in the magic of Christmas.

Because the story of the movie is so inextricably tied to Macy's Herald Square store, filming began in New York City early on Thanksgiving Day, with Edmund Gwenn taking Santa's place on Macy's

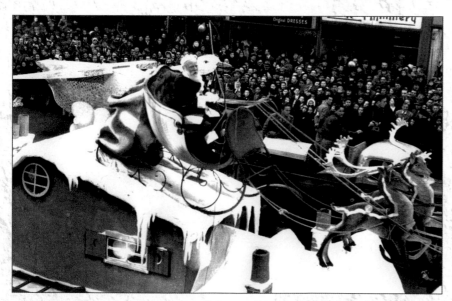

Actor Edmund Gwenn playing Santa in the actual 1946 Macy's parade.

most important parade float. Since the pageant was not nationally televised at that time, the movie would give people across America their first glimpse of the spectacular event. With the permission and blessings of Jack Straus, many of the scenes were shot in Macy's—particularly on the seventh, eighth, and thirteenth floors—giving the movie a wonderful feeling of believability. Bernard F. Gimbel, president of Macy's rival store, allowed the crew to film in his store as well. In fact, one of the movie's most famous scenes shows Mr. Gimbel (played by actor Herbert Heyes) and "Mr. Macy" (Harry Antrim) shaking hands in agreement.

In Maureen O'Hara's memoir, 'Tis Herself, she talks of the fun she had while filming in New York. Between takes, she and young Natalie Wood explored Macy's various departments and even tried on dresses. The entire cast enjoyed being in Manhattan at Christmastime, and Edmund Gwenn was especially fascinated by the elaborate holiday windows. Certainly, he was not the first adult to be enchanted by the displays that magically transform the city each year.

Fox was unsure how the film should be presented. Should it be touted as a Christmas film? As a romance? In the end, the studio covered all its bases by saying that it was a love story, a fantasy, and a Christmas treat. When the film debuted in June 1947, it was a hit with critics and moviegoers alike. Bosley Crowther, film critic for *The New York Times*, called it "the freshest little picture in a long time, and maybe even the best comedy of this year." While Crowther praised everyone in the cast, he was especially enthusiastic about Edmund Gwenn, who played Kris Kringle "with such natural and warm benevolence that, if ever the real Santa wants to step down, Mr. Gwenn is the man for the job."

In 1947, nobody dreamed that Fox's small summer release would be embraced by generations of movie lovers. Well over half a century after its debut, *Miracle on 34th Street* remains not only an American tradition, but also a wonderful reminder of the special relationship that exists between Macy's and the magic of the Christmas season.

A signed photo given to Jack Straus. Left to right: Edmund Gwenn, George Seaton (director), William Perlberg (producer), Maureen O'Hara, John Payne, and Artie Jacobson (assistant director).

CUSTOMERS SCHEME TO GET BEST BUYS

Families Deploy to the Various Counters, Shoppers Check Stores for Better Prices

Consumer combatants in the price war planned their strategy for storming the counters of Macy's and Gimbels as they advanced in waves yesterday upon the stores in the Thirty-fourth Street area.

"Bobby, you go to the Mixmasters," one mother ordered her son, while to her daughter she said: "Helen, you take the escalator to the Hopalong Cassidys and I'll get on the line to buy Papa a suit."

A guard inside the Broadway entrance of Macy's had little to do all day except say: "Downstairs to the toasters."

Fighting her way through the crowd around an information booth, a woman asked the clerk: "Which way is the price war?"

From an observation post near a fire exit, a man about to be married muttered: "I'll bet all our wedding guests are down here. Just think of all the duplicate pots and pans we'll have to return."

Rivalry is Pointed Up

In Macy's toy department, an angry customer finally agreed to buy a cowboy shirt for her son. She warned the salesgirl however: "I'll return it if I find it for less in Gimbels."

Traffic between the two stores was thick as men and women trudged back and forth comparing prices. By the time one weary man had returned to Gimbels, the last of the typewriters he wanted had been sold.

"You'd better go back to Macy's and get it," a salesgirl advised him. She did not try to sell him either of the two other brands hit by price-cutting.

The Woolworth store at Thirty-fifth Street and Broadway sprang a surprise on the harassed salesgirl at the souvenir counter. When she showed up for work in the morning, she found her wares hidden under an array of rayon panties, china figurines, Japanese glass pearls, washcloths, children's socks and leather belts for men.

Placards listed the "old price" for each item. The "new low prices" marked a few inches further down spurred business at her stand. A sign overhead read: "Big savings opportunity this week."

"Mr. Macy and Mr. Gimbel have a fight," the girl said, "and I get hit."

MACY'S FIGHTS A PRICE WAR

From 1902 to 1913, R.H. Macy & Co. had fought for the right to sell books at prices below those set by the publisher. Citing the Sherman Antitrust Act of 1890, Macy's said that by insisting on fixed prices, the publishers constituted an illegal trust and were imposing an unfair restraint of trade. Ultimately, the United States Supreme Court ruled in favor of the department store, awarding it $140,000 in damages and allowing it to charge any price it chose for the merchandise in its store. As a result, for many years, Macy's proudly stated, "We endeavor to save our customers at least 6 percent for cash."

Then in 1937, the Miller-Tydings Act was passed, amending the Sherman Antitrust Act. In an attempt to address concerns that big chains would push small retailers out of business, Miller-Tydings enabled manufacturers to fix prices on their branded goods. Because of this fair-trade law, Macy's was forced to state that it charged 6 percent less *"except on price-fixed goods."* But while Macy's signed fixed-price agreements with some manufacturers, it did not sign them with all of the firms from which it purchased products.

On March 29, 1950, General Electric (GE) asked for a temporary injunction to stop Macy's from selling electric blankets, fans, mixers, and clocks at less than fixed prices. GE stated that the firm intended to "enforce the maintenance of the minimum retail prices established under fair trade agreements." Macy's contention was that it had never signed an agreement with GE, and also that "77 percent of the stores below 96th Street" were cutting prices on price-fixed items. Macy's pointed out that the department stores were losing millions of dollars to discount businesses, which were all selling their products at below set prices.

When the Supreme Court ordered Macy's to stop selling GE products for less than price-fixed amounts, Macy's decided to proceed to trial. After a long court battle, in May 1951, the Supreme Court ruled that if a retailer did not voluntarily sign a price-fixing agreement, it would be exempt from the law.

On May 23, Macy's—thrilled with the Supreme Court ruling—not only trimmed 6 percent from nearly 6,000 fair-traded items, but also placed an ad proclaiming: "Now You Can Buy, 5,978 'Price-Fixed Items' At Less Than Fixed Prices at Macy's." Macy's spokesman, Richard Weil, Jr., stated that if the store's competitors matched the cuts, it would simply slash prices another 6 percent. Macy's didn't have long to wait. Since 1945, Gimbels had used the slogan, "Nobody, but nobody, undersells Gimbels." Quickly, Gimbels lowered its prices, and Abraham & Straus followed suit. Thus began the biggest price war in the history of New York retailing.

At first, other department stores did not enter the fray. But within a few days, Bloomingdale's, Saks, and dozens of smaller stores were lowering their prices, as well. All of Manhattan's major emporiums sent out comparative

---

A June 1, 1951 article describing "combatants" in New York City's price war.

shoppers whose mission was to note the prices charged by other businesses. It wasn't easy to keep track of falling prices, though. Shoppers lined up in front of charts on which price changes were scrawled and then erased, only to be changed again. In one week, James Jones' best-selling novel *From Here to Eternity* fell from $4.50 to $1.94, Palm Beach Suits were cut from $29.95 to $16.94, and Waterman fountain pens slid from $3.95 to $2.09.

A buying frenzy began. Shoppers turned out in record numbers, purchasing not only sale items but—using the money they felt they'd "saved"—full-price items as well. When customers tried to simultaneously push through the "In" and "Out" sides of Macy's revolving door, the door fell to the floor. Instead of selling their usual ten Sunbeam Mixmaster blenders per day, Macy's sold four hundred of the price-slashed items in forty-five minutes. Gimbels' customers purchased more Palm Beach suits in three days than they normally did in a month.

Eventually, the price wars settled down into a relative peace. But until 1975, when the fair trade laws were finally scrapped, R.H. Macy & Co. continued to make the case that fair trade laws were fair neither to stores nor to consumers.

At first, the 1951 price war had New Yorkers running from Macy's to Gimbels, comparing prices. But within a few days, other stores—such as Bloomingdale's, Saks, and Woolworth's—began offering savings, as well.

Does Macy's Tell Gimbels?

The Gimbel family opened its first stores in the Midwest, but in 1910, Gimbels came to New York City, setting up shop just a block away from R.H. Macy & Co. Gimbels prospered, becoming the chief competition of its Herald Square neighbor. While Macy's told consumers, "It's smart to be thrifty," Gimbels countered with "Select, don't settle." And despite the fact that Macy's made sure to offer the lowest prices in town, Gimbels insisted that, "Nobody, but nobody, undersells Gimbels."

Carefully cultivated by both camps, the "rivalry" between the two stores kept them in the public eye. The expression "Does Macy's Tell Gimbels?"—implying that one business would never tell its secrets to another—was put to good use by the stores, and became a catch phrase among New Yorkers. The public's view of the popular emporiums was also supported by the 1947 film *Miracle on 34th Street*, which cleverly wove the Macy's-Gimbels rivalry into the plot, and even showed Mr. Gimbel and Mr. Macy at last shaking

A Gimbels postcard, ca. 1949.

hands in cooperative agreement. This classic film also convinced generations of viewers that a "Mr. Macy" managed the famous Herald Square store.

In reality, Jack I. Straus and Bernard F. Gimbel were close friends and enjoyed their good-natured "feud." On December 8, 1955, when Bernard Gimbel visited Macy's, Gimbel's advertising agency told the press that he was entering "the enemy camp" to have a "man-to-man talk" with Jack Straus. Once in the store, Gimbel was heard to say that he might take the opportunity to get in some Christmas shopping, as "it's smart to be thrifty." The joke was continued outside the Macy's building, where signs proclaimed "This Way to Gimbels" and "When Macy's tells Gimbels, It Is the Miracle on 34th Street."

Gimbels closed in 1986, ending a seventy-year-plus relationship between the two stores. But the rivalry between Macy's and Gimbels will long be remembered as a colorful interlude in retailing history.

142

Macy's—The Store. The Star. The Story.

EXPANSION IN THE FIFTIES

Prior to World War Two, the United States population was centered in cities, with relatively little growth occurring in suburbs. During the 1950s, this settlement pattern began to change as residents—including veterans with affordable government mortgages—moved to the suburbs in search of less-expensive housing. Businesses, including department stores, followed.

As big retailers began building branch stores in the suburbs, there was mounting concern in the business community that Manhattan stores would suffer. But Jack Straus knew that the stores had to go where the people were, and that suburbanites living far from the city would not want to travel to the midtown area to make their purchases. Straus maintained that Thirty-Fourth Street was still a "fine shopping street," and would continue to serve city residents. He also recognized that New York City would maintain its lure as a tourist destination.

Macy's was among the stores that led the way in suburban branch expansion. In 1949, it had opened a highly successful branch in White Plains, New York. In 1952, Macy's announced that it would build another branch as part of the revolutionary Roosevelt Field shopping center in Garden City, New York.

The new mall was to be constructed at a cost of $35 million on the military airfield where pioneering aviator Charles Lindbergh had begun his historic trans-Atlantic flight. When the Roosevelt Field Mall opened in 1956, it was the largest establishment of its type in the country, with over a hundred stores and parking for 11,000 cars. One of the first to realize the modern "mall" as we know it, the shopping center had an art gallery, an ice skating rink, a 400-seat community theater, and a space for car and boat shows. Its two anchor stores were Macy's and long-time competitor Gimbels.

In August 29, 1956, Jack Straus attended the ribbon-cutting ceremony of Macy's-Roosevelt Field. The three-story glass and Belgian brick building boasted 343,000 square feet of selling space spread over 144 different departments, with a state-of-the-art air conditioning system that would make shopping pleasurable during even the hottest New York summers. Macy's described it as a "large, fully stocked downtown department store in every sense of the word"—transplanted to the suburbs. Yearly sales were predicted to be $60 million.

By 1956, R.H. Macy & Co. had grown to encompass thirty-two stores, including affiliates such as Davison-Paxon-Stokes, LaSalle and Koch, and Bamberger's. Due to both this expansion and a robust economy, Macy's reported that between 1919 and 1956, sales had risen from $36 million to a record $400 million. And Macy's was still growing.

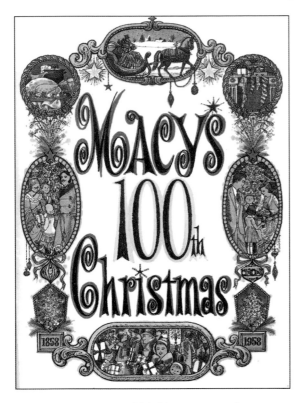

Macy's 1958 Christmas catalogue celebrating the store's hundred-year anniversary.

On June 15, 1952, *Anne Frank: The Diary of a Young Girl* was published in English. Interestingly, Anne's father, Otto Frank—who arranged for the publication of the diary—was a friend of Nathan Straus, Jr., and had actually worked at Macy's from about 1909 to 1911, during the brief time he lived in the United States.

"Peace and Prosperity" were the watchwords of Dwight D. Eisenhower, the thirty-fourth President of the United States. Beginning his first term in 1953—the year that Macy's Herald Square store had its first flower show—Eisenhower brought an end to the war in Korea, supported a balanced national budget, and expanded social security.

CHARGE IT!

Macy's was established in 1858 as a cash-only store, and long held to this business principle. Although the company did add its Deposit Account in 1902 and its Cash-Time plan in 1939, it continued to emphasize cash purchases. But Macy's was swimming against the tide. Charge accounts had been commonly offered by most department stores and other retail businesses since the early 1900s. During the Second World War, the use of credit was prohibited, but once peace was restored, it became even more accessible than before. Then in 1951, the Franklin National Bank in New York issued a card that allowed shoppers to charge items at a range of local retail establishments. Other banks, impressed by Franklin National's success, soon offered their own versions of the card. At about the same time, the Diners Club card premiered, providing account holders with credit in hundreds of restaurants nationwide. Americans everywhere were saying, "Charge it!"

On July 13, 1959, Macy's—breaking with over a century of tradition—announced the new Macy's Shopping D.A. Account. Loyal customers could now charge their purchases at Macy's, just as they did in other retail stores. Each day, the store would hand the bill to Macy's Bank, which had been formed in 1914. The bank would then send statements to the customers, who would have ten days to pay their bills without incurring a service charge. The new plan was an immediate success as shoppers hurried to Macy's to enjoy both low prices and a far more convenient way of making purchases.

Macy's Roosevelt Field store in Garden City, New York, ca. 1956.

Banks became interested in offering charge cards after the Second World War, when trends indicated that people who had these cards tended to spend more money. Since banks were already in the business of making loans, they recognized the profit potential behind attaching interest to charge accounts.

During the 1950s, the full and flaring circle skirt was in demand by women of all ages. Perhaps the most famous variation of this garment was that icon of the fifties, the poodle skirt—a felt circle skirt adorned with appliqués of poodles or other popular images of the time.

Blue jeans, which had originally been created as a practical garment for working men, became popular with young people during the fifties. Associated with film stars like James Dean—Hollywood's *Rebel Without a Cause*—these denim pants were long considered appropriate for only the most casual occasions.

And Delivery Is Free!

When the Straus family built its magnificent Herald Square store in 1902, they kept the welfare of their employees in mind. So in addition to building luncheon and recreation rooms, the Strauses also created sick rooms for workers who required medical attention. This area was referred to as the hospital.

Macy's hospital was staffed with doctors, nurses, dentists, and a chiropodist—a necessity for people who spent long hours working on their feet. It was designed as a place where employees could get swift medical attention whenever problems occurred, but it was also available to Macy's customers who became ill or injured while shopping. Over the years, the hospital was to treat many ailments, ranging from sore feet to cuts, scrapes, and even the flu. Amazingly, the hospital staff also delivered a number of babies!

During the years of the Great Depression, many New Yorkers were unable to pay the medical costs associated with the birth of a child. Some women, aware that Macy's had its own hospital, made their way to the store as soon as they went into labor. This enabled them to get excellent medical care free of any cost.

Once the Depression ended and New Yorkers became more prosperous, the average person did not require Macy's services when giving birth. But sometimes Mother Nature made it impossible for the mom-to-be to reach her own doctor in time. In the early 1950s, for instance, a pregnant shopper went into labor unexpectedly and was rushed to Macy's hospital. There, she gave birth to a baby girl. The delivery of Ann Macy Hertrich was so widely publicized that some women again decided that Macy's was a great place to have their children, leading to a string of in-store births. And Ann Macy Hertrich, who viewed Macy's as a second family, was always pleased to stop by the Herald Square store and visit her "godparents"—the staff that had helped bring her into the world.

SPROUTING BRANCHES IN THE SIXTIES

A 1960 display of women's coats in Macy's Herald Square store.

During the fifties, America and R.H. Macy & Co. had prospered together, with Macy's building branches outside the Manhattan area to serve growing postwar communities. As the 1960s began, Macy's continued reaching out to new areas.

In the early sixties, high-rise apartment developments made Elmhurst one of the fastest growing sections of Queens. When Macy's found a five-acre site on Queens Boulevard, at the intersection with the Long Island Expressway, the company knew that this was the perfect location for a new Macy's branch. There was, however, a problem: The property would not accommodate a conventional flat parking lot of adequate size. Fortunately, architects Skidmore, Owings and Merrill had a solution. Their plan involved a circular multi-level building that included, on its perimeter, a stack of six parking "rings" with room for 1,500 vehicles. The rings would be connected to ramps that spiraled around two helixes next to the main structure. It was estimated that a conventional lot would have to be seventeen acres in size to supply the same space! The store, which opened in 1965, was a huge success.

The 1960s also saw the construction of a Macy's branch in New Rochelle, New York, in the new Westchester Plaza Shopping Center. The store was to

John Fitzgerald Kennedy occupied the Oval Office from 1961 until his assassination in 1963. His inaugural address, which was one of the most famous speeches in United States history, called upon all Americans to fight tyranny, poverty, disease, and war: "Ask not what your country can do for you; ask what you can do for your country."

Founded by Sam Walton, Wal-Mart Stores, Inc. opened its first store in Bentonville, Arkansas on July 2, 1962. With the initial advertising slogan "Low prices, always," Wal-Mart appealed to customers whose incomes were below the national average, and who therefore were interested in buying goods at deep discounts.

be three stories tall and act as an anchor for the $27 million shopping center, which was to include bowling alleys, an ice skating rink, a 1,200-seat theater, fountains, art displays, restaurants, banks, and various retail outlets. The New Rochelle branch opened in 1967, and again, it seemed that Macy's had hit a home run.

It is interesting to realize that even though Macy's now had several large stores throughout the country, in 1964, Jack I. Straus stated that the New York division of R.H. Macy's regularly accounted for half the firm's revenue. During this time period, success of the Herald Square store was at least in part due to the highly popular New York World's Fair. Located in Queens' Flushing Meadows Corona Park, the fair—which was the third major exposition to be held in New York City—drew 52 million visitors during 1964 and 1965. Unlike the disappointing exposition of 1939, this event was a boon to businessmen throughout the New York area. Moreover, the fair left New York City with a much-improved park that would continue to draw visitors.

Macy's store in Elmhurst, Queens, ca. 1965.

The sixties began much as the fifties had ended, with women wearing bouffant hairstyles and men wearing conservative crew cuts. Women sported knee-length dresses, usually with high heels, while men, at their most casual, donned trousers and plaid button-down shirts.

Popularized by First Lady Jacqueline Kennedy in the early sixties, the pillbox hat—a small woman's hat with a flat crown and upright sides—was soon worn by women everywhere. The simple accessory paired perfectly with Jackie-style A-line dresses and suits topped with boxy jackets.

146

Macy's—The Store. The Star. The Story.

You'll Never Guess Who I Saw At Macy's!

President Dwight D. Eisenhower and
Vice President Richard M. Nixon.

Eleanor Roosevelt and entourage.

Jimmy Durante.

Bert Parks.

Bert Lahr.

Howdy Doody.

Hopalong Cassidy.

Jackie Gleason.

Imogene Coca and Sid Caesar.

Milton Berle.

148

Macy's—The Store. The Star. The Story.

Dale Evans and Roy Rogers.

Chuck Connors.

Soupy Sales.

Wayne Newton.

Michael Landon, Lorne Greene, and Dan Blocker.

MACY'S FLOWER SHOW

Virtually every New Yorker is aware of the Macy's Flower Show, which annually transforms the Herald Square store into a fragrant springtime celebration. But few know that this event had its beginnings in California.

In 1945, Macy's expanded westward by purchasing O'Connor, Moffat and Company in San Francisco. The reins of Macy's new acquisition were placed in the able hands of transplanted New Yorker Wheelock Bingham, who soon devised an imaginative way to make the public notice this "new kid on the block." In 1946, as part of a fragrance promotion, Bingham created a flower show in the cosmetics department. The show immediately captured the shoppers' attention and Wheelock was pleased to make it an annual event. For the first few years, the California flower show continued to have fragrance tie-ins, but beginning in 1949, each event revolved around a specific theme such as Paintings in Flowers (1952) and Gardens of the Dragon (2005).

Inspired by the success of its California store—and by its newly transplanted president, Wheelock Bingham—Macy's New York opened its first flower show on May 4, 1953. This debut event featured fresh floral bouquets created with blooms from East Coast nurseries, gardens, and greenhouses, as well as sources in California and Hawaii. Arches of daisies spanned the Thirty-Fourth and Thirty-Fifth Street entrances and the center aisle, while orchids, flowering dogwood trees, azaleas, and other plants decorated the Broadway windows and cascaded from the store's many ledges. The flower show lasted a week, with new blooms being added every day to keep the displays fresh and exciting.

When discussing Macy's first New York flower show, Wheelock Bingham—president of the Manhattan store—explained that he had two goals: to give pleasure and enjoyment to Macy's shoppers, and to contribute to the city by making it more attractive to visitors.

The 1947 flower show in Macy's San Francisco store.

It's one enormous, enchanted botanical garden

MACY'S FLOWER SHOW

Tomorrow and all this week on our street floor

Make a date with Mother
*Bring her to Macy's
to see the Flower Show*

SO FABULOUS
you'll be completely entranced by the beauty and fragrance of over 2,150,000 flowers . . . 178 different varieties

SO FRAGRANT
you'll think Spring itself has moved indoors

SO DRAMATIC
it's not just a Garden Page story —it's Page One news

SO MIRACULOUS
it just had to happen on 34th Street

SO COLORFUL
no artist's palette could hope to match it

SO IMPORTANT
a world-famous florist came to Macy's just to arrange it

SO BIG
it took six months to plan — years to grow—and occupies the whole Street Floor of our Broadway Building

SO MAGNIFICENT
it took over 100 flower arrangers to get the show ready for you

SO RARE
that (sorry) you can't buy any of these prize-winners

SO COMPLETE
we didn't stop at flowers — you'll see redwoods, bamboos, birch trees

SO SPECTACULAR
it took 90 trucks just to transport the flowers from the nurseries

SO UNIQUE
there's never been anything quite like it in all New York

does Gimbels tell Macy's?
no, Gimbels tells the World!

Gimbels isn't just telling Macy's (they know it already). Gimbels *is* telling the world (that remote corner of the world which hasn't heard) that the most glorious department store flower show in all the world is happening in miracle-crazy 34th Street at Macy's (just a block from Gimbels doors.) **Nobody but nobody** sold Gimbels these raves. When we first saw Macy's ads we raised heavy, competitive eyebrow over jaundiced competitive eye. At the stroke of 9:45 Monday, Gimbels big brass marched to Macy's with confident, competitive step. Have we seen Gimbels big wheels since? Not on your life. Our Mr. E. was last reported **up to his neck in anemones,** our Mr. M. was swooping low over a spray of lily-of-the-valley, our Miss F. was **languishing in the hydrangeas.** Even our great Mr. G. himself was **transfigured in the tuberous begonias.** Gimbels tells Macy's that Macy's flower show is the greatest miracle to hit 34th Street since 34th Street and miracles (and Gimbels and Macy's) were invented. **Gimbels tells New York** that the competitive spirit (for the moment) can go hang. **Gimbels tells the world** that it's just plain silly if it doesn't get to Macy's for the **greatest flower show 34th Street has ever known!**

Gimbels

Newspaper ads announcing the 1953 flower show at Macy's New York store. Even Gimbels was impressed.

Macy's New York flower show continued to be a yearly event through 1966, but due to the rising cost of maintaining cut flowers, it was then discontinued. The event was not to return until 1974, when it would take a new and different form.

ANOTHER FIXED-PRICE WAR

In the early fifties, Macy's had fought for the right to sell branded goods for prices lower than those set by manufacturers. Macy's had won that battle, and for several years, had continued to follow its policy of offering merchandise at 6 percent less. But in 1964, the company was once again faced with the prospect of losing the right to set its own prices.

After the repeal of Prohibition in 1933, Macy's had been issued the first liquor license in the country. Like other store merchandise, alcoholic beverages were sold at a discount in the great emporium. Then on December 21, 1964, two liquor distillers and an importer sought an injunction to prohibit Macy's from selling their products below the fair-trade prices. For a long time, the State Liquor Authority had been responsible for enforcing the distillers' minimum prices. But in November, individual distillers had become responsible for taking legal action on their own. The liquor concerns involved in the action accused Macy's of selling certain brands for as much as seventy cents less than the established minimum.

In July of 1967—after years of being bounced from court to court—the case was settled in Macy's favor. While New York's Court of Appeals believed that liquor prices could be maintained by the Fair Trade Law, it ruled that prices in New York could not be set higher than the lowest prices charged anywhere in the country. Macy's was once again free to set the price on any liquor sold in its store.

At the time of the 1964 lawsuit, Macy's sold a large volume of nationally advertised liquors as well as a wide variety of private label merchandise, which was generally offered at prices below those of national brands.

A 1939 postcard showing the laboratory in Macy's Bureau of Standards.

MACY'S FAMOUS BUREAU OF STANDARDS, N. Y. . . . where trained scientists have made 4 million tests to make sure the customer buys high quality for low cash prices.

THE TRADITION OF QUALITY AND SERVICE

In 1915 and 1927, respectively, the Straus family had created the Comparison Department and the Bureau of Standards—two in-house groups designed to ensure that Macy's wares were high in quality and were sold at prices lower than those charged by the store's competitors. Decades later, these departments were still going strong.

Well into the sixties, Macy's used the Comparison Department to make sure that every item in the store, from clothing to radios and tele-

Lyndon Baines Johnson succeeded to the presidency in 1963, after the death of John F. Kennedy. Johnson is well remembered for his vision of the "Great Society"—Medicare, Medicaid, civil rights, and the "War on Poverty." But his escalation of the Vietnam War eroded his popular standing, and in March 1968, he declined to run for re-election.

In 1964, the Beatles appeared on *The Ed Sullivan Show* and Beatlemania began. In addition to influencing the music world, the Fab Four introduced the hairstyle sometimes referred to as the *moptop*. A straight style that was collar-length in the back and sides, with a fringe of bangs in front, the moptop was soon being imitated worldwide.

CHRISTMAS
AT MACY'S
1961

How does the Christmas season begin in New York? With Macy's traditional Thanksgiving Day Parade . . . and this Macy gift catalogue glittering, like all of Macy's, with wonderful ideas to make your Christmas shopping merrier.

Macy's 1961 Christmas catalogue, celebrating the beginning of the holiday season.

vision sets, was offered for 6 percent less than competitor's prices. For many years, Hertha I. Hanssen was head of the Comparison Office, and the buyers of Macy's knew that Hanssen was determined to uphold Macy's policies and protect its reputation. Gerald Dun Levy, who joined Macy's in 1947 and eventually became the vice president of merchandise, said that when they bought, for instance, cashew turtles for sale at the store, Hanssen or one of her colleagues in the Comparison Department would buy samples of cashew turtles from other stores. They would then taste test all the candy to see if Macy's offering was comparable to that of the competition. After this determination was made, the Comparison Department—not the buyer—set the price. No advertising could be created for a product until this decision was made.

The purpose of the Bureau of Standards was to test any potential merchandise about which a claim was being made. When MacGregor approached Macy's in the late sixties and declared that its new golf ball, the XP270, would travel farther than any other golf ball made, Macy's didn't take the company's word for it. The head of the Bureau of Standards, Ben Chaucer, was a golfer, and he insisted on testing the XP270 against the best of the national brands. Astounded to find that MacGregor's product outperformed the rest, he approved an ad that stated, "We don't know exactly why, but this new golf ball drives 4 yds. to 12 yds. further . . . every time."

Macy's buyers were always looking for the next item that would capture the imagination of its shoppers, and it was the buyers who were chiefly responsible for making a profit for the store. But the Comparison Department and Bureau of Standards kept the store on the straight and narrow, making certain not only that customers got exactly what they expected, but also that they paid the lowest prices in town.

Since the earliest days of the Herald Square store, Macy's had worked to maintain high standards by providing extensive training for its employees. Always searching for the best and brightest to fill their executive positions, Macy's recruited graduates from colleges and business schools, and then sent them through six to nine months of instruction. During this period, recruits would get a complete picture of Macy's by working in different areas of the organization, both on the selling floor and behind the scenes. This training was mandatory even for those who had prior experience in retailing, and was actually responsible for drawing many potential executives to R.H. Macy's. Everyone knew that once you had completed Macy's training program and spent a year or so working in the company, you could get a job anywhere. But because Macy's inspired loyalty in its employees, it was not at all unusual for people to remain in the company throughout their retailing careers.

By the mid-sixties, British fashion designer Mary Quant was producing the miniskirt— a slim skirt that ended six or seven inches above the knee. Although this style had appeared earlier in the decade, it did not become popular until Quant presented it to young London girls, who eagerly embraced the "Chelsea Look."

Just when miniskirts made stockings impractical, tights and pantyhose appeared on the scene. Eliminating the need for girdles and suspender belts, tights—a must for the groomed young lady, who *never* went bare-legged—came in a variety of colors and patterns. For a brief time, fishnet tights were a fashion must-have.

Customer service was always emphasized, and even as executives moved through the Macy's hierarchy, they were encouraged to spend time on the selling floor. Only then would they know how the shoppers felt about the merchandise, be able to judge the level of service being provided by the sales clerks, and make knowledgeable decisions.

JACK STRAUS STEPS ASIDE

In 1939, Percy Straus had relinquished his command at Macy's to Jesse Isidor Straus's son, Jack Isidor Straus. Jack remained at Macy's helm for three decades. He became president of the company in 1940, and chairman in 1956. But on October 4, 1968, at the age of sixty-eight, Straus left Macy's top post. Replacing Straus was Donald B. Smiley, formerly Macy's vice chairman.

Jack Straus insisted that he was really not stepping down. "There will be no major changes," he said. Certainly, the event in no way marked the end of the Straus family's involvement in Macy's. Jack Straus was going to stay on as chairman of the executive committee; and his son Kenneth, who had joined the firm in 1947, was to rise to the posts of company director, chairman of corporate buying, and senior vice president for domestic and international corporate buying. Other family members, too— Gerald Dun Levy, John W. Straus, and Edward Straus—were to continue at Macy's in various capacities. But for the first time in three generations and eighty years, a member of the Straus family was not a chief executive of the company.

Under Jack I. Straus's direction, Macy's had grown to fifty-nine stores, although many, such as Bamberger's, had not adopted the Macy's name. Macy's had also become one of the few retailing organizations of the time that, on occasion, would do $1 million of business in a single day. In fact, during the Christmas shopping season, Macy's at Herald Square routinely enjoyed million-dollar days, while the chain-stores' yearly sales approached $800 million.

But far more had changed than the name of Macy's chairman. For decades, freestanding department stores had reigned, but now, some industry observers felt that these emporiums were becoming an endangered species. The relentless spread of enclosed malls—with each offering a galaxy of retailers under one roof—was transforming the way America shopped, while discount stores like Wal-Mart were specifically targeting the frugal consumer. In this evolving marketplace, would shoppers still agree that it was "smart to be thrifty" at R.H. Macy & Co.? Time would tell.

Donald B. Smiley.

The Apollo 11 spacecraft was launched on July 16, 1969, carrying Neil Alden Armstrong, Michael Collins, and Edwin Eugene "Buzz" Aldrin. On July 20, with half a billion people watching worldwide, Armstrong became the first human to walk on the moon, making the memorable statement, "That's one small step for [a] man, one giant leap for mankind."

From August 15 to August 18, 1969, the Woodstock Music and Art Fair—"Three Days of Peace, Music, and Love"—was held on Max Yasgur's dairy farm in Bethel, New York. Exemplifying the counterculture of the 1960s, the festival featured thirty-two of the best-known musicians of the day, including Richie Havens, Arlo Guthrie, Janis Joplin, The Who, and Jimi Hendrix.

7. Recreating an Icon

After the Second World War, an economic boom had enabled Americans to buy material goods that had been in short supply during the war—new clothes, modern appliances, cars, even new homes. It should have been no surprise, then, that R. H. Macy's, Manhattan's most famous department store, had thrived throughout the late forties, fifties, and much of the sixties. New Yorkers had long depended on Macy's Herald Square store for quality merchandise at reasonable prices, and with peacetime factories turning out exciting new products, residents flocked to their favorite store. Moreover, in wake of the war, Manhattan had become the leading metropolis of the world. Every year millions of tourists poured into the city, eager for all it had to offer, and many of these visitors viewed Macy's as an important shopping destination.

But as the 1970s began, even the most casual observer could see that Manhattan was going through troubled times. The economic stagnation plaguing the nation had hit New York City especially hard. In fact, the city neared bankruptcy during the administration of Mayor Abe Beam (1974 to 1977), and avoided that fate only with the aid of a federal loan. Large areas of the South Bronx, the Lower East Side, Harlem, and Bedford-Stuyvesant were marred by crumbling buildings, abandoned by their owners. Conditions in these areas gave rise to street gangs and other civil disorder, and the city became infamous for its high rates of crime. Times Square, the

The corner of Thirty-Fourth Street and Seventh Avenue, ca. 1970.

The thirty-seventh President of the United States, Richard M. Nixon served from 1969 to 1974. His term was marked by a negotiated ceasefire with North Vietnam that ended the Vietnam War, and the opening of diplomatic relations with China. Nevertheless, Nixon resigned in 1974 for his alleged cover-up of the Watergate scandal.

In 1970, the first New York City Marathon was held. Organized by the New York Road Runners Club, the twenty-six-mile route winds through all five boroughs of the city and is the largest marathon in the world. In 2008, approximately 39,000 people from all over the globe participated in the event.

◄ Macy's trademark Tree of Lights holiday display.

A number of elements contributed to the woes of Manhattan businesses during the late 1960s and early 1970s. Rising unemployment rates gave people less money to spend in area stores, while rising crime rates made people unwilling to shop at night. At the same time, new types of businesses, such as discount stores and specialty boutiques, pulled consumers away from traditional emporiums.

crossroads of the world, had become infested with sleazy shops and seedy characters. Many city dwellers had headed for the suburbs after World War Two, and with conditions in the city deteriorating, even more people were choosing to live outside Manhattan.

As the city became a less attractive place to live, work, and shop, Macy's sales suffered along with those of many other inner-city businesses. But the famous emporium was being affected by far more than an economic slump and urban decline, for the face of retailing itself had begun to change. Consumers no longer automatically visited their favorite department store to buy clothes, appliances, drugstore items, and other goods. Big box stores, discount drugstores, furniture warehouse showrooms, and specialty shops now offered stiff competition. Suburban malls, too, drew many shoppers away from stand-alone stores. If Macy's was to not only survive but also thrive, big changes would have to be made.

MACY'S PLOTS A NEW COURSE

In 1968, Jack I. Straus had stepped down from his post of chairman of R.H. Macy's. Taking his place was Donald B. Smiley, who had previously been president of R.H. Macy's. Ernest L. Malloy was Macy's new president and CEO. The New York division's sales gains and profits had actually begun to erode during the '60s, yet Straus and Smiley had made no major changes in the store, choosing to adhere to past buying and selling practices.

As Macy's problems grew, the company's top brass noticed that some department stores were flourishing despite the troubled economy. Bamberger's, the New Jersey-based chain acquired by Macy's in 1929, was doing very well. In fact, it was earning the best profits in the company. Bloomingdale's, which offered designer fashions to New York's young and affluent professionals, was enjoying record sales. It was clear that Macy's needed a new approach.

Help came in the form of Herbert L. Seegal. After being appointed president of Bamberger's in 1962, Seegal had carefully nurtured a team of younger executives, training them to follow his tenets. In 1972, when a series of personnel changes elevated Seegal to the role of Macy's corporate vice president, he was free to begin deploying some of the brightest members of his team to head up the company's divisions. Among these talented people was Edward S. Finkelstein, a man who was to change the course of Macy's history.

Ed Finkelstein was not new to the New York division. In 1948, he had been hired by Macy's directly after his graduation from Harvard Business School. Finkelstein worked at the Herald Square store for several years before becoming part of Bamberger's, where he helped boost the division's profits. Because of his success with the New Jersey-based chain, he was trans-

Herbert L. Seegal.

Edward S. Finkelstein.

On June 17, 1972, five men were apprehended inside the Democratic National Committee headquarters in the Watergate building. The burglary—one of many illegal activities authorized by President Richard Nixon's staff—led to the indictment of several of the President's advisors and to his own resignation in 1974.

The 1970s began with a continuation of the 1960s hippie look, complete with tie-dyed t-shirts and bell-bottom jeans. It became popular to modify the appearance of jeans through the use of bleach and tie-dye techniques, embroidery, and metal studs. It was also common to hasten the fraying of blue jean hems by cutting them off.

ferred to the presidency of Macy's San Francisco in 1969. There, he again improved sales, increasing them from $35 million to an amazing $200 million in five years' time.

In 1974, with the New York division in trouble, Finkelstein was shifted back to Herald Square. Now president and CEO of the New York division, he decided to apply the same methods and systems that had been so successful in New Jersey and California. One of his first changes was to introduce the concept of the Cellar.

Most New Yorkers are probably not aware that the Cellar had its roots in Macy's San Francisco store. While at the helm of the large California emporium, Finkelstein had noted the public's growing interest in cooking as a pastime for both men and women. Recognizing the success of stores like Williams-Sonoma and Pottery Barn, he decided that a gourmet kitchenware department would be appealing to Macy's shoppers. Since the housewares section was located on the basement level of the San Francisco store, Finkelstein called his modernized department the Cellar. Soon, business was booming.

Finkelstein wasn't absolutely convinced that sophisticated New Yorkers would respond to the Cellar with the enthusiasm shown by San Franciscans, so he first built the Cellar in the Macy's Roosevelt Field store, the largest suburban branch in New York. When it did well, a larger, grander Cellar was added to the Herald Square flagship store. Actually a tiled "street," the Cellar was

A 1970s ad for Macy's new Cellar.

lined with shops offering sparkling cutlery, gourmet food, stationery, pottery—complete with a potter at the wheel—and more. One end featured a replica of PJ Clarke's, a midtown Manhattan 1890s pub. Events such as cooking demonstrations drew crowds to Macy's exciting new space.

66 Working with Ed S. Finkelstein was amazing. I witnessed what it meant to change a company's culture. 99

—Rosemary Bravo, former Senior
Vice President of Apparel

The sales gains that Macy's began to enjoy in the mid-1970s were enhanced by the New York Court of Appeals' 1976 decision to strike down the state's blue-law bans, and allow stores to conduct business on Sundays. Macy's New York stores soon began opening their doors seven days a week, while many of the company's competitors—Bloomingdale's included—not only refused to open on Sundays, but fought to reinstitute the blue laws. For Macy's, Sunday hours translated into a 5-percent gain in sales.

Joseph B. Cicio.

Finkelstein did not believe that the creation of the Cellar alone would sufficiently boost sales at Macy's New York. Rather, this innovative department was part of a larger plan. The new president realized that it no longer made sense to emphasize the discount aspect of Macy's. The discount chain stores—which had not existed at the time that Macy's 6-percent-less policy was conceived—made Macy's smaller markdowns less impressive. At the same time, Macy's bargain-basement identity was preventing high-quality cosmetics and fashion firms from agreeing to sell their wares at the store. Out went the budget department, the bargain tables, and less-profitable lines such as pharmaceuticals and toiletries. Macy's was ready to court manufacturers of more exclusive products.

It took some time for Macy's to convince cosmetics and fashion manufacturers that its stores were a suitable market for their products, but gradually, it happened. Clinique was the first upscale cosmetic line to sign a contract with Macy's. Other cosmetic companies followed, along with high-fashion clothing concerns such as Evan Picone and Liz Claiborne. So-called "soft lines"—apparel, footwear, jewelry, linens, and towels—were emphasized. In a July 24, 1977 *New York Times* article, Macy's chairman, Donald B. Smiley, noted, "In the last five years, our soft lines' percentage of total sales has moved up from 55 percent to 63 percent. This is by and large the profitable part of the business."

Part of Macy's 1970s transformation involved a renovation spearheaded by Joe Cicio, whom Finkelstein had recruited from Lord & Taylor. Over the years, the Herald Square flagship store had become tired in appearance. Worse, years of repairs and décor changes had obliterated some of the most beautiful features of the original structure. The faceted columns on the main floor had been covered with vinyl wallpaper, and the capitals—the topmost structures of the columns—had been removed. The original exterior bronze light fixtures had been eliminated and stored in a subbasement. Aware of the store's heritage and of the splendor of the 1902 Beaux-Arts design, Cicio approached his work as a restoration rather than a renovation. The sixth floor—linens and domestics—was refurbished first, while restoration of the main floor was one of the last tasks accomplished. Columns were uncovered and original fixtures were restored to their rightful place. A fluted ceiling was added to the main floor to complement the stunning columns. Cicio also made a number of modifications with the annual Macy's flower show in mind. Sockets for additional lighting were inserted in the columns and water outlets were added to help keep floral displays fresh throughout each exhibition. Other changes included the creation of stylish boutiques selling fashionable lines of clothes.

66 The one consistency in retailing is change. If you don't change, you're going to be left in the dust. 99

–Gerald Dun Levy, former
Merchandise Vice President

EVERYTHING OLD IS NEW AGAIN

Although Ed Finkelstein was determined to make changes that would strengthen and build Macy's, he realized that the store and its customers would also benefit from the return of certain much-loved events that had been abandoned years earlier. These events included the flower show and the Fourth of July fireworks.

Although isolated flower shows were staged at Macy's Herald Square before the 1950s, the annual New York flower show had run from 1953 to 1966, when it was discontinued due to budget cuts. The store simply found it too expensive to maintain elaborate cut-flower displays during the week-long event. Ed Finkelstein knew that New Yorkers and visitors alike had loved the show, and that for many people, it had been a highly anticipated yearly event. So in 1975, the exhibition was begun anew. As before, it occupied the grand ground-floor space of Macy's flagship store. This time, though, cut flowers, which have to be replaced about every three days, were interspersed with less-fragile potted plants and trees. But none of the magic of the original floral exhibits was gone. Macy's was again transformed into a fragrant garden of delights, and although the newly invented flower show started on a relatively small scale, the public's enthusiastic reaction ensured that the event would both continue and grow.

Macy's summer fireworks shows had begun on July 1, 1958, when a display was staged by the Marutamaya Ogatsu Company of Japan. Set off over the Hudson River from barges located at Eighty-Fifth Street, the first show included fireworks in the shape of a whale as a tribute to Rowland H. Macy, who had served on a whaling ship as a young man. Annual pre-Fourth of July pyrotechnics continued until June 23, 1964, when the fireworks on one of the barges accidentally exploded, killing two workers and injuring four more. Stunned by the tragedy, Macy's discontinued its yearly show.

Shortly after Ed Finkelstein became president of Macy's New York in 1974, he pledged that Macy's Bicentennial gift to the people of Manhattan would be a spectacular fireworks display. "On July 4, 1976," Finkelstein said, "Macy's and fellow New Yorkers will join together with pride to celebrate

This and the following two pages present a selection of magnificent floral arrangements that have been featured in Macy's flower shows.

When the restoration of the main floor was complete, rave reviews appeared in the city's newspapers. *The New York Times* said, "The new main floor sets a splendid tone; it makes Macy's an architectural event for the first time in several generations, and it changes the experience of shopping there altogether."

Every Macy's flower show involves an army of people, from those who design and build the waterproof components of the displays, to those who artfully arrange the truckloads of flowers on the ground floor. Once the show has opened, a night shift of employees waters potted plants and trees, removes dead blooms, and replaces tired cut flowers with fresh growth.

America's birthday in grand style." The show would be perfectly safe, as well, as it was no longer necessary for workers to be present on fireworks-filled barges during the event. Now, the devices could be set off by push-button electronics.

R.H. Macy's more than kept its word. Working in conjunction with Walt Disney Productions, Macy's produced a magnificent display over the tip of Manhattan, with the ninety-year-old Statue of Liberty holding center stage as all of New York City celebrated the United States Bicentennial. The show commenced at 9:00 PM with a two-hundred-gun salute from warships at anchor. This was followed by an ever-intensifying barrage of fireworks that lit the sky over New York Harbor so brightly that the glow could be seen more than fifteen miles away. Hundreds of thousands of people packed the shoreline and riverfront to see the dazzling show firsthand, with many of them carrying radios so they could hear the synchronized patriotic music and commentary. Millions more watched at home as television networks broadcast the spectacle in color throughout the country. For those lucky enough to receive invitations, Bicentennial parties were held in harborside locations that afforded magnificent views of the event. Perhaps the most prestigious

The poster for Macy's Bicentennial fireworks display.

of these took place atop the World Trade Center, where guests Prince Rainier and Princess Grace of Monaco sipped champagne as they marveled at the sky-lighting extravaganza.

Since the fabulous Bicentennial event, Macy's has continued to provide the largest display of pyrotechnic creativity and firepower in the nation. Just as in 1976, Macy's Fourth of July fireworks are accompanied by a patriotic musical score and are telecast live to homes across the country.

On June 14, 1979, one of the most tragic events of Macy's history occurred when a fire broke out on the fifth and sixth floors of the New York flagship store in Herald Square. One fireman was killed and at least fourteen firefighters and shoppers were injured before the blaze was brought under control.

The following five pages begin with a ▶ dramatic view of the 1976 Bicentennial fireworks display, followed by colorful photos from more recent Fourth of July extravaganzas.

It has been estimated that each November, more than 60 million television viewers watch the Macy's Thanksgiving Day Parade as it proceeds along its two-and-a-half-mile route. More than eighty years old, the parade has been called the longest running show on Broadway.

Jean McFaddin.

Of course, no discussion of Macy's traditions would be complete without a look at that best-known event of all, the Macy's Thanksgiving Day Parade. Debuting in 1924, the parade continued until the Second World War, when it was suspended so that important resources such as gasoline would not be diverted from the war effort. The parade promptly resumed in 1945, however, and became a truly national event in 1952, when it was televised throughout the United States. At first, the telecasts were only an hour long, but in the 1960s, they expanded to two hours, and by the '70s, Americans across the country were able to view all three hours of the pageant. Since 1955, NBC has been the official broadcaster of the Thanksgiving Day Parade.

When Ed Finkelstein returned to New York in 1974, Macy's had been producing the parade without a hitch since 1945. But Finkelstein saw that several years of budget cuts had begun to dim the brightness of the event. Understanding the importance of the parade, he committed himself and his staff to re-invigorating this American tradition. In 1977, he hired Jean McFaddin to head Macy's special events, giving her the directive to make the parade bigger and better than ever. Under McFaddin, the department that designed the parade—as well as the fireworks and flower shows—worked year-round for the first time. Of course, McFaddin ensured that the parade would continue to feature spectacular floats and balloons, performances from the hottest Broadway shows, exciting celebrities, and spirited marching bands from across

Macy's Posters on Parade

1993

1999

the country—all the elements that people had come to expect. But the "Parade Lady," as she came to be called, also made a crucial decision. Realizing that the most famous features of the parade were the huge character balloons, she resolved to add to the balloon roster on a yearly basis, rather than every few years, and to emphasize well-known "stars" rather than generic images such as the Pilgrim and the Fish of earlier decades. In 1977, McFaddin's first year at the helm, Macy's introduced the Kermit the Frog balloon. Within the next few years, Macy's would roll out Yogi Bear, Garfield the cat, Spider-Man, Big Bird, the Pink Panther, Snoopy, Woodstock, Babe the pig, and many more favorites. Each year, children could look forward to new, exciting balloons of much-loved TV and film characters. But with all the newness that the parade had to offer, it still concluded with a familiar, treasured tradition as Santa Claus appeared, waving to the children and ushering in the holiday season.

In her expanding responsibilities as senior vice president of Macy's Public Relations, Media, and Events, Jean McFaddin remained producer/director of Macy's annual and special events until her retirement in 2000. In January 2001, Robin Hall, a long-time Macy's employee, took on the important job of directing and producing the Thanksgiving Day Parade, Fourth of July Fireworks, and other yearly displays and shows for which Macy's is so well known. Under his direction, Macy's special events would continue to delight New Yorkers and visitors alike.

The annual Thanksgiving Day Parade is such a vast undertaking that it requires the participation of over 10,000 people. Among the talented folks who make the parade a memorable event are Robin Hall, the parade's executive producer; Amy Kule, the parade's producer; and John Piper, the director of Macy's fabled Parade Studio.

Robin Hall.

2004

2005

The Rockettes sport vibrant holiday colors
in Macy's Thanksgiving Day Parade.

A Christmas Carol.

Macy's Thanksgiving Turkey.

Garfield.

Bart Simpson.

Clifford.

Bandleader Barney.

The Ship of States.

The Santa float.

Macy's Miracle Windows

In a city known for holiday displays so stunning that they attract visitors from around the world, the windows of Macy's flagship store have long been ranked among the best. And since 1938, when a renovation provided six huge plate-glass windows on the building's Broadway front, Macy's has had *two* spectacular sets of displays to create each holiday season—one on Broadway and the other on Thirty-Fourth Street.

For many years, Macy's featured seasonal merchandise in its holiday windows. This changed in 1999, when the store's visual director, Sam Joseph, discovered that exactly a century earlier, Macy's—then on Fourteenth Street—had presented the city with its first animated window displays. Why not also mark the end of the twentieth century with animation? The subject Joseph chose was the iconic movie *Miracle on 34th Street*. Six scenes from the film were chosen, and the Manhattan company Spaeth Design was given the job of creating animatronic characters. It took eleven months for every element to be finished, from the costumed figures to the ornamented dwarf Christmas trees. When the windows debuted in early November, the crowds were enchanted.

Since that year, Macy's has continued to present its one-of-a kind *Miracle on 34th Street* displays in—where else?—the windows on Thirty-Fourth Street. This leaves the Broadway windows free for a different spectacle each year. In 2004, for instance, the Broadway windows showcased scenes from the movie *Polar Express*. In 2005, animated books opened to reveal traditional Manhattan holiday scenes, such as the Radio City Christmas spectacular. Usually the windows are unveiled by mid-November, and they are always on view by Thanksgiving Day, when Macy's Santa inaugurates the holiday season.

A NEW DECADE, A NEW CHALLENGE

As Macy's Herald Square store continued to be restored and, to a large extent, reinvented, business analysts praised Ed Finkelstein and his team for brightening the faded New York icon. More important, Manhattan's shoppers noticed the change—and loved it. People who had not visited Macy's for many years began to rediscover the landmark store. As the Macy's Miracle gained momentum, annual sales soared not only in the New York store but throughout all the branches. In 1982, corporate sales gains of over 20 percent topped the industry.

Even as Macy's hit its stride, the economic climate was undergoing a marked change. Mergers and acquisitions abounded in a range of industries in the 1980s, and not all mergers were "friendly." Many companies began to fear hostile takeovers in which firms were acquired despite strong resistance from management. Sometimes the target company was kept intact by the firm that was aquiring it. Sometimes the company was dismantled and sold off in "pieces" for greater profit. In the consolidation process, long-time employees often lost their jobs as the purchaser merged old and new departments, or terminated entire divisions. Too often, the character of the original company was lost along with the dedicated individuals who had helped create it.

In 1985, Ed Finkelstein—now Macy's chairman and CEO—was well aware that R.H. Macy & Co. was a takeover target. He was therefore not surprised to learn that Canadian developer Robert Campeau of Campeau Corporation had visited Macy's real estate specialist, Jim York. It was already known that Campeau was looking for acquisitions that would add shopping mall real estate to his growing portfolio of assets. Moreover, a slowdown had hit the retailing industry in 1984, and although Macy's profit history was phenomenal, the retailing slump was causing analysts to question the company's future growth. With Wall Street wavering in its praise, it seemed possible that shareholders would welcome Campeau, thinking that a change in management would boost stock values. It might not matter to them that they were handing Macy's over to an investment firm rather than entrusting it to people who had years of experience in running the vast department-store chain.

Seeking to avoid a hostile takeover that would damage the recently revitalized company, Finkelstein and 350 other concerned executives made a bold move. In October 1985, they offered to buy the department store concern for almost $3.6 billion. Aside from protecting Macy's from hostile takeover, the purchase was designed to free the company's management from the pressures for short-term financial gain that are always imposed by a publicly owned company. Because management would own the company

As economic conditions changed in the 1980s and 1990s, mergers became prevalent in many industries—communications, transportation, retail, and more. Bell Atlantic acquired Nynex. AT&T absorbed Tele-Communications and MediaOne Group. Nabisco Brands and RJ Reynolds Tobacco Company merged and, in turn, were acquired by Kohlberg Kravis Roberts & Co. The list goes on and on.

 You have to have a belief, a strategy, a vision, and then it's all about surrounding yourself with the best and the brightest. **"**

—Janet Grove, CEO and Chairman of
Macy's Merchandising Group

In October 1985, when Macy's management offered to buy the company,
R.H. Macy's was comprised of ninety-
five outlets in fourteen states. This
included the twenty-three-store
Bamberger's chain.

and share in profits, the purchase would also motivate employees to remain at Macy's and strive for continued growth and success. Many Wall Street analysts agreed that as a private company, Macy's would be able to spend more freely to please its shoppers, and thereby gain an edge in the competitive retailing industry.

On June 19, 1986, R.H. Macy & Co. stockholders approved a $3.7 billion management buyout. The cash offer was for $68 a share. It was the biggest takeover in retailing history, and the first leveraged buyout of a major retail chain.

As 1987 began, Macy's celebrated its financial success. Sales had increased 16.4 percent in the last quarter of 1986, and just as important, many employees seemed to be responding to the change with a spirit of cooperation and increased passion. Despite the debt incurred to fund the 1986 buyout, R.H. Macy & Co. was doing so well that it could almost report a net profit in 1987.

With sales and optimism soaring, in 1988, Macy's purchased two West Coast department store chains—Bullock's and I. Magnin. The acquisition of these high-prestige stores was very much in line with Macy's plan to enter the Southern California market. Of course, the $1 billion price tag on the acquisition only added to Macy's debt, but Macy's was confident that by following its policy of keeping inventories high and promotions heavy, it would recoup the money.

All retailers—not Macy's only—rely on holiday sales to boost cash flow. This certainly was the case in 1989. But strong holiday sales depend on a strong economy, and towards the end of the eighties, the United States had begun its decline into a recession. With the economy showing the lowest growth rate since the Great Depression—with unemployment rising and purchasing power diminished—retail sales were more than disappointing. In 1989, Macy's saw holiday earnings drop 50 percent from the previous year. In 1990, sales were again below expectations.

Early in 1990, rumors began to circulate that Macy's was heading towards bankruptcy. Although Ed Finkelstein, Macy's chairman and chief executive, took out a full-page ad in *Women's Wear Daily* in an attempt to quell the rumors, industry analysts could see that the continuing recession had caused a poor retailing climate. In 1992, Macy's announced that there would be a delay in paying its suppliers. Finally, on January 27, 1993, Macy's declared bankruptcy.

Ed Finkelstein explained the company's decision: "We worked day and night to find a suitable solution and ultimately come to the conclusion that filing for Chapter 11 was best for Macy's future. I am convinced that beginning this rehabilitative process is the best way to protect our valuable franchise."

On July 29, 1981, Diana Spencer married Charles, Prince of Wales—the eldest son of Queen Elizabeth II and Prince Philip, Duke of Edinburgh. The event, which was billed as a "fairytale wedding," took place in Saint Paul's Cathedral and was viewed by a worldwide television audience of 750 million.

America's fortieth President, Ronald Wilson Reagan served from 1981 to 1989, guided by the desire to restore "the great, confident roar of American progress and growth and optimism." Through skillful dealings with Congress, Reagan obtained legislation designed to curb inflation, stimulate economic growth, increase employment, and strengthen the national defense.

MACY'S REORGANIZES

Macy's was in no way defeated. Under Chapter 11 law, the company had 120 days to formulate a plan that would get its business back into working order. At first, it seemed as if Macy's top managers would remain in place as the company decided how it would meet the financial requirements of bankruptcy and rebuild its financial footing. Then on April 27, 1992, Edward S. Finkelstein abruptly resigned his position at R.H. Macy & Co. Succeeding him was the two-man team of Myron E. Ullman, III and Mark S. Handler.

Ullman and Handler quickly devised a five-year plan for the ailing company. The strategy included a reduced advertising budget with more focused promotions, fewer private-label items, less one-day sales, improved customer service, and a new system of computerized inventory management. At the same time, Macy's would continue to expand by opening stores in promising locations, but would rid itself of unprofitable operations. In 1992, Macy's opened the company's first store in Minnesota; a new Bullock's in Burbank, California; and new I. Magnin stores in Phoenix, Arizona and San Diego, California. In 1993, the company closed eleven stores that had low growth potential.

In early 1993, Macy's showed its first profit since filing for bankruptcy. By June of that year, sales for the quarter were 5.8 percent higher than they had been during the same period the previous year. In spite of the nation's continuing economic difficulties, Macy's new strategy of cutting costs and increasing productivity was starting to pay off. But as Macy's began its long recovery, a question emerged: Should the company struggle under the burden of debt alone, or would it be stronger if it joined forces with another firm—a firm experienced in the management of department stores? This question would be answered within a year's time.

Myron E. Ullman, III.

FEDERATED DEPARTMENT STORES

Federated Department Stores was founded in 1929 as a means of providing separate chain stores with greater buying clout and protection from rival onslaught. With headquarters in Columbus, Ohio, Federated was originally comprised of John Shillito & Co. of Cincinnati, Ohio; F&R Lazarus & Company of Columbus, Ohio; Abraham & Straus of Brooklyn; and Filene's of Boston. Over the years, Federated continued to acquire new stores, such as Bloomingdale's, eventually becoming one of the largest retail firms in the United States.

Although Federated Department Stores was forced to file for bankruptcy in 1990, it soon recovered from its financial problems and resumed its role as a major player in American retail business. It should have come as no surprise, therefore, when in 1994, it was announced that Federated was merging with R.H. Macy &. Co.

Federated Department Stores was founded by Fred Lazarus, Jr. in 1929. A man with great financial and political clout, Lazarus is credited with convincing President Franklin D. Roosevelt to move Thanksgiving a week earlier in order to lengthen the holiday shopping period.

❝ What has made Macy's so successful for 150 years? The ability to present the broadest array of merchandise, more than any other retailer, consistently surprising and delighting customers.**❞**

–Ronald Klein, Chairman and CEO of Macy's East

The Parade Marches On

Early on the morning of September 11, 2001, Al-Qaeda terrorists intentionally crashed two commercial passenger airliners into the Twin Towers of Manhattan's World Trade Center. Over 2,500 people—mostly civilians—died when the towers burned and collapsed.

In the weeks that followed, New York reeled from the horrors of the attack. Yet even as residents mourned the loss of family and friends, they united with strength, resolve, and a strong spirit of patriotism. New York might be down, but it was far from out.

That November, a little more than two months after the tragedy of the Twin Towers, Macy's affirmed New York City's resilience by holding its yearly Thanksgiving Day Parade. Robin Hall, the director of the parade, explained Macy's decision to continue with this much-loved American tradition. "It has been a constant through good times and bad, enduring in times of both war and peace," said Hall. "The parade remains a symbol of continuity and stability. In light of recent events, this is an especially significant year for the parade because of the powerful and positive message it will send to the world."

The Twin Towers rising behind Lady Liberty.

The 2001 Thanksgiving Day Parade was recast as a confirmation of New York's spirit in the face of tragedy. The event included all of its traditional elements: floats, helium-filled balloons, clowns, dance and music groups, marching bands, and even the Radio City Rockettes. But at the front of the procession, Lady Liberty replaced Tom Turkey, and the candy canes in Santa's sleigh wore ribbons of red, white, and blue. Moreover, two fifty-four-foot American flags were borne by uniformed firefighters and policemen who had fought heroically on September 11.

New York's Mayor, Rudolph Giuliani, observed that the crowds seemed larger than usual. "After having gone through the worst and most horrible attack on this city in history," said Giuliani, "the city has emerged stronger, more unified, more determined than I've ever seen it."

The more than 4,000 volunteers who took part in the 2001 parade reported that they felt especially honored to be part of that year's spectacle. And those who watched—whether adult or child, Manhattanite or out-of-towner—gladly celebrated an all-American tradition while giving thanks that New York was alive and well.

William Jefferson "Bill" Clinton occupied the Oval Office from 1993 to 2001. Clinton presided over the longest period of peacetime economic expansion in American history, which included a balanced budget and federal surplus. Although impeached for obstruction of justice during the Monica Lewinsky scandal, Clinton left office with high approval ratings.

The forty-third President of the United States, George Walker Bush entered the Oval Office in 2001 and served for two terms. The eldest son of former President George H.W. Bush, George W. is perhaps best known for the policies he initiated after the terrorist attacks of September 11, 2001.

The merger of Federated Department Stores, Inc. and R.H. Macy & Co., Inc. created a true retailing giant by bringing together eleven department store chains with more than three hundred stores in twenty-six states. Now both parties would have opportunities for more efficient operations, as well as expanded buying powers. Federated would be able to benefit from Macy's knowledge of product development and its broad network of overseas contractors. Macy's would profit from Federated's access to capital, as well as its knowledge of the bankruptcy process. When the merger was approved by a Federal judge, Myron E. Ullman, III, chairman and chief executive officer of R.H. Macy & Co., Inc., said, "It is a very bright day indeed. Macy's has been restored to financial health and its franchise preserved." Allen Questrom—Federated's chairman and chief executive officer, whose retail expertise had been instrumental in bringing about Federated's resurgence—stated that the merger would create a "more effective provider of value to our customers in the years ahead."

Allen Questrom.

Like any merger, the marriage of Federated and Macy's resulted in a streamlining of operations. To eliminate intercompany competition, several smaller store chains were merged into the two large Macy's East and Macy's West divisions. On the East Coast, the Federated stores in the Abraham & Straus/Jordan Marsh divisions were converted into Macy's, Bloomingdale's, or Stern's. On the West Coast, the relatively unprofitable I. Magnin stores were discontinued, while all twenty-one Bullock's locations were changed to Macy's. To strengthen Macy's presence in the West, Federated also bought the eighty-two-store chain of Broadway Stores, Inc. In most cases, the newly acquired stores were renamed Macy's.

By the end of 1999, major renovations had been completed on Macy's East flagship store in Herald Square, as well as Macy's West flagship store in San Francisco. Macy's East now consisted of eighty-seven stores occupying a total of 23.8 million square feet. Macy's West comprised one hundred stores totaling 20.1 million square feet. Macy's was bigger and better than ever before.

During the merger process, New York Bankruptcy Judge Burton R. Lifland said he wanted it "etched in some form of stone" that Federated would not eliminate Macy's Thanksgiving Day Parade or Macy's Fourth of July Fireworks. When Federated's legal team promised to draft such a document, the merger was able to move toward finalization.

THE TWENTY-FIRST CENTURY

As the world rang in the new millennium, Macy's continued to show a strong and healthy bottom line. And the twenty-first century was to bring even greater growth to Macy's, for on February 28, 2005, Terry J. Lundgren, Federated Department Stores' CEO and chairman, announced the acquisition of May Department Stores for $11 billion. This amazing event transformed Federated—already the largest department store company in the nation—into a retailing giant with more than eight hundred stores and $30 billion in sales. Based on the success that Federated had experienced in converting its own regional brands to the Macy's name, it placed the Macy's nameplate on several hundred of May's department stores, as well.

Born Joseph Alois Ratzinger, Pope Benedict XVI was elected on April 19, 2005, only a few days after the death of Pope John Paul II. Benedict XVI is a theologically conservative pontiff who has emphasized the need to return to fundamental Christian values as a response to the growing secularism in developed countries.

On November 4, 2008, Democrat Barack Obama—a United States Senator from Illinois—became the first African-American to be elected President of the United States. In his election-night acceptance speech, Obama told cheering crowds, "Change has come to America," and called for "a new spirit of patriotism, of service and responsibility."

Yet another change was around the bend. On June 1, 2007, Federated Department Stores replaced its corporate name with *Macy's, Inc.* to more accurately reflect the firm's recent transformation. The company was no longer a federation of separate department stores but a business focused on Macy's and Bloomingdale's.

Today, Macy's is divided into four geographic divisions: Macy's East, Macy's North, Macy's Central, and Macy's South. With two national brands—Macy's and Bloomingdale's—the company seeks to provide a unique shopping experience with high-quality merchandise and excellent service.

Recently, Terry J. Lundgren—chairman, president, and CEO of Macy's, Inc.—reflected on Macy's success in a competitive marketplace and on its shining future. Lundgren feels that Macy's staying power can be attributed to its ability to evolve and meet the ever-changing needs of the consumer. "You have to keep reinventing yourself," said Lundgren. "You can't look at what happened ten years ago and say that didn't work ten years ago so it won't work now." Macy's has evolved by always staying aware of

Macy's spectacular celebration of its 150th anniversary.

the consumer's changing needs and meeting them. Once, it offered "bargain" goods. Now, it presents the most famous and sought-after brands in the world, from Estée Lauder to Lancôme, from Ralph Lauren to Tommy Hilfiger. Although it eliminated its toy department many years ago, it is now adding FAO Schwarz toys to over two hundred stores. And in many locations, Macy's is creating restaurants that satisfy the tastes of today's sophisticated shopper.

Lundgren is confident that the department store will continue to be important in American life. "I think the department store is really unique in the retail competitive landscape," says Lundgren. "It's still the place where you can satisfy most if not all the needs for yourself, your family, your children, your friends, your guests coming over for dinner, and your home."

Of course, the Macy's name now appears on hundreds of stores nationwide. Does that make Macy's Herald Square flagship store less important? No, says Lundgren. "It's the largest store in the world; it's two million square feet, a million square feet of selling space alone." It is also one of New York City's top tourist attractions after the Empire State Building and the Statue of Liberty. Most important, the beautiful Herald Square store is a lasting symbol of what Macy's has achieved in its one hundred-and-fifty-year relationship with the American people. Situated in the center of one of the most fashionable and exciting cities of the world, it is the red star that sets the standard for all of Macy's stores, lighting the way for future growth, innovation, and achievement.

Terry J. Lundgren.

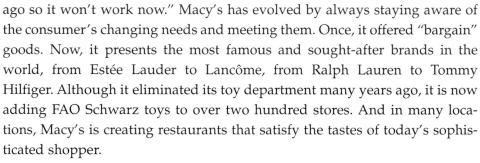

❝ You have to keep reinventing yourself. . . . You have to know what's relevant to the customer today. ❞

–Terry J. Lundgren, Chairman, President, and CEO of Macy's, Inc.

Conclusion

For over one hundred and fifty years, R.H. Macy & Co. has provided generations of shoppers with a wide array of merchandise and products offered at great prices. While other retailers have come and gone, Macy's has not only survived, but has become a true part of our American culture —from its spectacular Fourth of July fireworks displays to its fabulous Thanksgiving Day Parades and enchanting holiday windows. More than just the account of a successful department store, the story of Macy's encompasses the passion and drive of its founder, Rowland H. Macy, as well as the dynamic leadership of the Strauses. The tale also reflects the innovations and foresight of Macy's highly trained executives, managers, and buyers, both past and present. Macy's has created a culture of caring for its customers that continues to serve as a guide for all its employees.

I have wonderful childhood memories of sitting in front of our TV on Thanksgiving Day and watching the parade, as the aroma of Mom's roasting turkey filled the air. And I can tell you that from a young age, I was hooked. As a lifelong Macy's customer, I have enjoyed learning how the store was started and how it grew into America's most celebrated emporium. I wrote this book as a tribute to the people and events that shaped Macy's over the past century and a half. Through its words and images, I hope it has given you a vivid account of what it has taken to build this world-renowned American icon.

Today, the flagship store of the Macy's chain—a true historic treasure—is still there for you to experience and enjoy. While Macy's continues to reinvent itself to meet the evolving needs of those it serves, the physical beauty of the Herald Square emporium remains unchanged. I hope that this book has inspired you to pause for just a moment and feel the magic that is Macy's.

Whatever the future holds for R.H. Macy & Co., it is clear that this store has proven its ability to change, to adapt, and to rise like a star above its competitors. And for its many loyal customers, Macy's will continue to offer not only a stunning array of products, but also a rewarding shopping experience that will surprise, excite, and satisfy for many years to come.

Permissions

The maps on pages 4 and 5 and the photo on page 5 are reprinted courtesy of the Nantucket Historical Association.

The document on page 8 is the Crew List of the Emily Morgan; Collector of Customs, District of New Bedford Crew Lists, 1920–1915; Records of the US Customs Service, RG36; National Archives & Records Administration, Northeast Region, Boston. Reprinted with permission of the National Archives.

The images found within the text on pages 54, 55, 57, 58, 64, 70, 80, 82, 90, 92, 94, and 96 are reprinted courtesy of the Straus Historical Society, Inc.

The image at the bottom of page 74 is reprinted by permission of Corbis © Photo Collection Alexander Alland, Sr./CORBIS.

The article "Greet Santa Claus as 'King of the Kiddies,'" found on page 111, is from *The New York Times*, November 28, 1924. All rights reserved. Used by permission and protected by the Copyright Laws of the United States. The printing, copying, redistribution, or transmission of the Material without express written permission is prohibited.

The article "Customers Scheme to Get Best Buys," found on page 140, is from *The New York Times*, June,

1, 1951. All rights reserved. Used by permission and protected by the Copyright Laws of the United States. The printing, copying, redistribution, or transmission of the Material without express written permission is prohibited.

The photo of Herbert L. Seegal on page 156 is reprinted courtesy of Juanita C. Seegal. The photo of Edward S. Finkelstein on page 156 is reprinted courtesy of Edward S. Finkelstein. The photo on page 158 is reprinted courtesy of Joseph B. Cicio; the photo on page 168, courtesy of Jean McFaddin; the photo on 169, courtesy of Robin Hall; the photo on page 177, courtesy of Myron E. Ullman, III; the photo on page 179, courtesy of Allen Questrom; and the photo on page 180, courtesy of Terry J. Lundgren.

The photo on page 149 is reprinted courtesy of Betty McKenzie of Macy's West. The photo at the top of page 180 is reprinted courtesy of Macy's, Inc.— photographer, Carol Seitz. All remaining Macy's images found within the text appear courtesy of the archives of Macy's, Inc.

The publisher would like to offer his thanks both to Wikipedia and to Dr. George Lankevich, whose extensive historical library collection was the source of most of the images that appear along the bottom of the pages.

Index